# IFIP Advances in Information and Communication Technology 705

## Editor-in-Chief

*Kai Rannenberg, Goethe University Frankfurt, Germany*

# IFIP Advances in Information and Communication Technology

The IFIP AICT series publishes state-of-the-art results in the sciences and technologies of information and communication. The scope of the series includes: foundations of computer science; software theory and practice; education; computer applications in technology; communication systems; systems modeling and optimization; information systems; ICT and society; computer systems technology; security and protection in information processing systems; artificial intelligence; and human-computer interaction.

Edited volumes and proceedings of refereed international conferences in computer science and interdisciplinary fields are featured. These results often precede journal publication and represent the most current research.

The principal aim of the IFIP AICT series is to encourage education and the dissemination and exchange of information about all aspects of computing.

More information about this series at https://link.springer.com/bookseries/6102

Felix Bieker · Silvia De Conca ·
Jose M. Del Alamo · Yod Samuel Martín
Editors

# Privacy and Identity Management

## Generating Futures

19th IFIP WG 9.6/11.7 and IFIP WG 11.6
International Summer School, Privacy and Identity 2024
Madrid, Spain, September 10–13, 2024
Revised Selected Papers

 Springer

*Editors*
Felix Bieker
Unabhängiges Landeszentrum für
Datenschutz Schleswig-Holstein
Kiel, Schleswig-Holstein, Germany

Jose M. Del Alamo 🆔
Universidad Politécnica de Madrid
Madrid, Madrid, Spain

Silvia De Conca 🆔
Vrije Universiteit Amsterdam
Amsterdam, The Netherlands

Yod Samuel Martín 🆔
Universidad Politécnica de Madrid
Madrid, Madrid, Spain

ISSN 1868-4238        ISSN 1868-422X (electronic)
IFIP Advances in Information and Communication Technology
ISBN 978-3-031-91053-1        ISBN 978-3-031-91054-8 (eBook)
https://doi.org/10.1007/978-3-031-91054-8

This Springer imprint is published by the registered company Springer Nature Switzerland AG
The registered company address is: Gewerbestrasse 11, 6330 Cham, Switzerland

If disposing of this product, please recycle the paper.

# Preface

In this volume, we present the proceedings of the 19th IFIP Summer School on Privacy and Identity Management, which took place from 10 September to 13 September 2024 in Madrid, Spain. It focused on Generating Futures as a theme.

The 19th IFIP Summer School was a joint effort among IFIP Working Groups 9.2, 9.6/11.7, 11.6, and Special Interest Group 9.2.2, in co-operation with Universidad Politécnica de Madrid, and Plattform Privatheit (https://www.plattform-privatheit.de/). This IFIP Summer School brought together more than 35 junior and senior researchers and practitioners from different parts of the world and many disciplines, including many young entrants to the field. They met to share their ideas, build a network, gain experience in presenting their research, and have the opportunity to publish a paper through these proceedings. As in previous years, one of the goals of the IFIP Summer School was to encourage the publication of thorough research papers by students and emerging scholars. To this end, it had a three-phase review process for submitted papers. In the first phase, authors submitted short abstracts of their work. Abstracts within the scope of the call were selected for presentation at the school. After the school, authors submitted full papers of their work, which received two to three single-blind reviews by members of the Program Committee. They were then given time to revise and resubmit their papers for inclusion in these post-proceedings, and were offered in-depth shepherding where necessary.

In total, 31 abstracts were submitted, out of which 12 were presented at the summer school, and 9 were finally accepted for publication. At the summer school, Jose Such ("Human-centred AI Security, Ethics and Privacy"), Isabel Barberá ("GenAI and the Privacy, Agency and Identity Paradox: Redefining Concepts in the Digital Age"), Gloria González Fuster ("The future of data and future data laws"), Hanna Schraffenberger ("Digitalization of society: a value-driven design perspective"), Daniel Slamanig ("Privacy-Preserving Authentication: Theory vs. Practice"), Linnet Taylor ("The global politics of identification"), Teresa Martínez Sánchez ("The role of data protection authorities"), and Yod-Samuel Martín ("Standardizing privacy and data protection for GenAI") delivered insightful and engaging keynotes. Silvia De Conca held an academic career chat, discussing tips and tricks for junior academics. Furthermore, a total of four workshops on topics related to privacy and identity management complemented a diverse and educational program.

We are grateful to all who contributed to the success of this summer school and especially to the Programme Committee for reviewing the abstracts and papers as well as advising the authors on their revisions. We would also like to thank IFIP, Universidad

Politécnica de Madrid, and Plattform Privatheit, and the Steering Committee for their guidance and support, as well as all participants and presenters.

January 2025

Felix Bieker
Silvia De Conca
Jose M. Del Alamo
Yod Samuel Martín

# Organization

## General Chair

Jose M. Del Alamo            Universidad Politécnica de Madrid, Spain

## Program Committee Chairs

Felix Bieker            ULD Schleswig-Holstein, Germany
Silvia De Conca            Vrije Universiteit Amsterdam, Netherlands
Yod Samuel Martín            Universidad Politécnica de Madrid, Spain

## Program Committee

| | |
|---|---|
| Florian Adamsky | Hof University of Applied Sciences, Germany |
| Ala Sarah Alaqra | Karlstad University, Sweden |
| Claudio Ardagna | Universitá degli Studi di Milano, Italy |
| David Arroyo | Instituto de Física Aplicada, Spain |
| Vanessa Bracamonte | KDDI Research, Inc., Japan |
| Tanja Böhm | Ostfalia University of Applied Sciences, Germany |
| Sebastien Canard | Télécom Paris, France |
| Laura Drechsler | KU Leuven, Belgium |
| Prokopios Drogkaris | European Union Agency for Cybersecurity (ENISA), Greece |
| Michael Friedewald | Fraunhofer ISI, Germany |
| Lothar Fritsch | Oslo Metropolitan University, Norway |
| Nils Gruschka | University of Oslo, Norway |
| Marit Hansen | ULD, Germany |
| Meiko Jensen | Karlstad University, Sweden |
| Stefan Katzenbeisser | University of Passau, Germany |
| Os Keyes | University of Washington, USA |
| Agnieszka Kitkowska | Jönköping University, Sweden |
| Stephan Krenn | AIT Austrian Institute of Technology GmbH, Austria |
| Cedric Lauradoux | Inria, France |
| Konstantinos Limniotis | National and Kapodistrian University of Athens, Greece |

| | |
|---|---|
| Zoltan Mann | University of Amsterdam, Netherlands |
| Yannic Meier | University of Duisburg-Essen, Germany |
| Joachim Meyer | Tel Aviv University, Israel |
| Victor Morel | Chalmers University of Technology, Sweden |
| Frank Pallas | University of Salzburg, Austria |
| Sebastian Pape | Social Engineering Academy GmbH, Germany |
| Davy Preuveneers | imec-DistriNet, KU Leuven, Belgium |
| Arnold Roosendaal | Privacy Company, Netherlands |
| Ina Schiering | Ostfalia University of Applied Sciences, Germany |
| Stefan Schiffner | BHH Hamburg, Germany |
| Sandra Schmitz | Université du Luxembourg, Luxembourg |
| Yefim Shulman | Erasmus University Rotterdam, Netherlands |
| Christoph Sorge | Saarland University, Germany |
| Stefan Strauss | Austrian Academy of Sciences, ITA, Austria |

## Sponsoring Institutions

# Contents

x     Contents

# Keynote

Keynote

# Privacy-Preserving Authentication: Theory vs. Practice

Daniel Slamanig[(✉)] [iD]

Research Institute CODE, Universität der Bundeswehr München, München, Germany
`daniel.slamanig@unibw.de`

**Abstract.** With the increasing use of online services, the protection of the privacy of users becomes more and more important. This is particularly critical as authentication and authorization, as realized on the Internet nowadays, typically rely on centralized identity management solutions. Although those are very convenient from a user's perspective, they are quite intrusive from a privacy perspective and are currently far from implementing the concept of data minimization. Fortunately, cryptography offers exciting primitives such as zero-knowledge proofs and advanced signature schemes to realize various forms of so-called anonymous credentials. Such primitives enable online authentication and authorization with a high level of built-in privacy protection (what we call privacy-preserving authentication). Though these primitives have already been researched for various decades and are well understood in the research community, unfortunately, they lack widespread adoption. In this paper, we look at the problems, what cryptography can do, some deployment examples, and barriers to widespread adoption, which we discuss using the example of the EU Digital Identity Wallet (EUDIW) and the recent discussion and feedback from cryptography experts around this topic. We also briefly comment on the transition to post-quantum cryptography.

## 1 Introduction

Authentication and authorization are two closely coupled and important tasks that are frequently required when users want to access resources in the digital realm, e.g., services on the Internet. Loosely speaking, authentication is the task of confirming whether a user is really who they pretend to be, e.g., by demonstrating the knowledge of some secret such as a password or a secret signing key associated with the user. Today, one increasingly uses a combination of more than one factor (multi-factor authentication), like the knowledge of a password and the possession of Subscriber Identity Module (SIM) card. Authorization is the task of giving users permissions to access certain resources, i.e., deciding

---

This paper is based on a keynote with the same title given at the 19th IFIP Summer School on Privacy and Identity Management held between 10th and 13th September 2024 in Madrid, Spain.

© IFIP International Federation for Information Processing 2025
Published by Springer Nature Switzerland AG 2025
F. Bieker et al. (Eds.): Privacy and Identity 2024, IFIP AICT 705, pp. 3–28, 2025.
https://doi.org/10.1007/978-3-031-91054-8_1

whether a certain authenticated user has sufficient permissions to perform some action. Henceforth, we will just talk about authentication and note that typically authorization can be performed based on information associated with the identity after authentication and without any further interaction with the user. A typical example is the use of attributes associated with users, e.g., any user with attribute `role=Student` might be granted access to a certain service.

A convenient way to think about a digital identity is that of a set of attributes that describe a person. Now, in a typical scenario a person's identity comprises several not necessarily disjoint partial identities (cf. [56]), where each of them represents a person in a specific context or role and can be thought of as a certain subset of attributes. For instance, every person has a set of attributes related to health (e.g., health status, medical history), which they might not want to include in their partial identity for "work". The complete identity of a person is represented by the union of all the attributes of all the partial identities of this person. Since some of these partial identities include sensitive information, e.g., the health data mentioned above, from a privacy perspective it is desirable to have full control over which attributes are revealed in a certain context. This is particularly relevant in the digital realm where it is easy to collect such information, connect it to other information sources and use it to build up ever increasing profiles of individuals.

Limiting the amount of information that is provided as much as possible is known as data minimization. It is a concept of growing importance in a globally connected digitized world and a fundamental principle behind many data protection regulations such as the General Data Protection Regulation (GDPR) in the European Union or the Health Insurance Portability and Accountability Act (HIPAA) in the United States. This helps to preserve privacy and can help to ensure as much unlinkability as possible, making it harder to easily connect all the partial identities of a person. One issue that is important to stress is that for many services on the Internet, concretely identifying information such as `name` or `DateOfBirth` of a user might not be required in the process of authentication, e.g., it can be sufficient for an individual to demonstrate that they are old enough to consume a certain service. What, however, can be required in various cases such as governmental applications, is that actions of the same partial identity of a person can be linked over different sessions. This can be achieved via so-called pseudonyms, which represent identifiers other than the person's real name (or other uniquely identifying information) that are independent of the person and provide a sufficient degree of anonymity.[1]

After having introduced some basic concepts, our goal is to look into how authentication on the Internet typically looks today and how it could look when putting privacy as the main design goal. We will discuss issues with these existing mechanism and present a concept from the cryptographic literature called anonymous credentials. This is an important tool to realize privacy-preserving authentication first envisioned by Chaum [27] and later realized by Camenisch

---

[1] We stress that pseudonymity and anonymity are not used in the strict legal sense but rather in a technical sense relevant to the paper's context.

and Lysyanskaya [21] as well as Brands [15] in the early 2000s. After around 25 years, there is a large body of research on anonymous credentials and related primitives (cf. [26,42]). Unfortunately, although this concept is well known in the research community, and over the recent years increasingly attracting practitioners, it still lacks a widespread deployment. Besides providing a high-level discussion of the theory of anonymous credentials, this paper will also look at the practice of anonymous authentication and potential issues that are hindering a widespread adoption. As a supporting use case, we take the European Digital Identity Wallet (EUDIW), its architectural reference framework (ARF) and the recent feedback given by cryptographic experts [6], which highlights obstacles on the way to deploying such a "new" technology into an existing (legacy) infrastructure.

**Outline of this Paper.** In Sect. 2 we review traditional authentication on the Internet. Then, in Sect. 3 we introduce relevant privacy properties and discuss privacy of traditional authentication approaches. In Sect. 4 we introduce the concept of anonymous credentials from a conceptual (theoretical) perspective. Then, in Sect. 5 we discuss anonymous credentials from a practical perspective and in particular implementations, standardization efforts and real-world use cases. In Sect. 6 we take a look at the European Digital Identity Wallet (EUDIW), its planned realization and related privacy issues. Then in Sect. 7 we look at barriers and issues to be considered when aiming at deploying anonymous credentials such as integrating them into the EUDIW. Finally, in Sect. 8 we conclude this paper and give an outlook on future aspects related to deploying anonymous credentials.

## 2   Traditional Authentication and Identity-Management

The very traditional way of authenticating users on the Internet is that every service realizes its own authentication mechanism, meaning that a user establishes a partial identity with every single service (typically pseudonyms or more likely email addresses). These partial identities are though typically not distinct, as users tend to re-use their email addresses either as an explicit pseudonym or as an attribute given to the service provider. The latter is usually required for functionality reasons, i.e., account recovery.

### 2.1   Password-Based Authentication

The most common traditional authentication mechanism is via user-chosen passwords associated with user accounts. Since strong passwords are hard to remember, it is well known that users tend to choose too weak passwords [12] as well as reuse them among different services [67]. While there are password-management tools that help to overcome these issues, research shows that the use of such tools significantly lags behind [69] and due to various reasons does not see widespread use. Despite all these issues, due to its simplicity and easy deployment, it is still the most common authentication mechanism.

## 2.2   Signature-Based Authentication

From a security perspective, two-factor authentication that relies on strong cryptography is more desirable and has been increasingly promoted. A popular choice is the use of the FIDO2[2] de-facto standard from the Fast IDentity Online (FIDO) alliance. Here one either uses a dedicated hardware token or a pure software component (typically called Passkey[3]) as the second factor. The latter can be easily used with any device like a smartphone and thus enhances the usability.

The technical protocol details are out of the scope of this paper, but the relevant part is that it uses public-key cryptography and in particular digital signatures. We recall that in the context of a digital signature scheme every user can generate a pair $(\mathsf{sk}, \mathsf{pk})$ consisting of a secret (signing) key $\mathsf{sk}$ and a public (verification) key $\mathsf{pk}$, where $\mathsf{pk}$ is made public. A user knowing $\mathsf{sk}$ can produce a signature $\sigma \leftarrow \mathsf{Sign}(\mathsf{sk}, m)$ for any message $m$, and using $\mathsf{pk}$ and, given $(m, \sigma)$, anyone can check the validity of the signature using $\{0, 1\} \leftarrow \mathsf{Verify}(\mathsf{pk}, m, \sigma)$, where 1 indicates a valid signature. A valid signature gives the guarantees that $m$ has really been signed by the holder of the secret key corresponding to $\mathsf{pk}$ and has not been altered in any way. Security requires that a signature scheme is existentially unforgeable under a chosen message attack (i.e., provides EUF-CMA security). This means that when only having $\mathsf{pk}$ and access to signatures for arbitrarily and adaptively chosen messages, it is not possible to produce a valid signature $\sigma$ for some message $m'$ that has not been explicitly signed by the signer, i.e., for which no signature was requested.

In conventional web authentication, $\mathsf{pk}$ is typically just stored together with the identity and thereby establishing the binding between the individual and the key. More generally, this binding between $\mathsf{pk}$ and an identity is achieved via explicit certification. The most common way is to rely on a public-key infrastructure (PKI). This means that there is some trusted certification authority (CA) that signs $\mathsf{pk}$ together with a set of attributes of the user, resulting in a certificate that can be verified by anyone trusting the public key of the CA. This certificate is typically used for signature-based authentication when using an official governmental electronic identity (eID), as largely deployed within the European Union, where some governmental body acts as a CA.

## 2.3   Single Sign-On

A widespread concept used nowadays is that of single sign-on (SSO), a concept with a rich history and prominent schemes such as Microsoft Passport (cf. [55] for a comprehensive treatment of that topic). It makes account management simpler as it requires users to authenticate only at a single centralized entity (typically a large technology company such as Google, Microsoft, or Meta) acting as an identity-provider (IdP) for the user. Then one employs an authentication and

---

[2] https://fidoalliance.org/fido2/.
[3] https://fidoalliance.org/passkeys/.

authorization layer such as OpenID Connect (OIDC), which enables authentication at third-party services (so-called relying parties or RPs) via the IdP. We illustrate the process in Fig. 1.

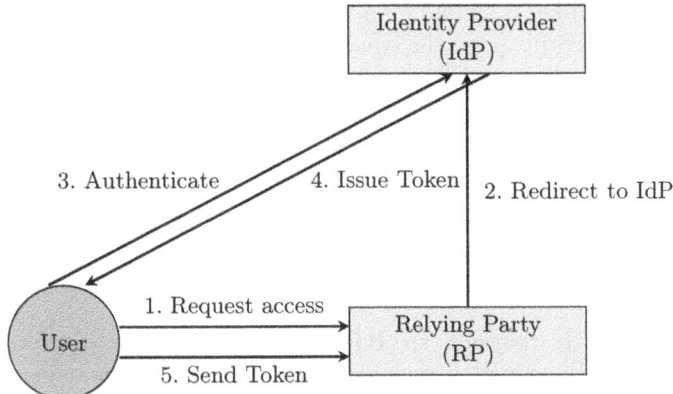

**Fig. 1.** Abstract concept of single sign-on.

Essentially, whenever a user wants to authenticate at an RP (1), the user is redirected to its IdP (2) where the user actually authenticates using e.g., password- or signature-based authentication (3). After a successful authentication, the IdP generates a token (an ID Token in case of OIDC), signed by the IdP (4), which the user can hand over to the RP (5) as a proof that the user has authenticated to the IdP.

## 3 Privacy Properties and Traditional Approaches

Now having discussed ways of authenticating users on the Internet, we want to discuss privacy properties that might be desirable in such mechanisms.

### 3.1 Privacy Properties

We will briefly summarize the privacy properties that are most important in the context of authentication at an intuitive level. We will not take into account other important security properties of authentication mechanisms which are not relevant to privacy, e.g., that it is hard to impersonate other users. Also in our further consideration we will not consider privacy on the network layer, i.e., identifiers such as IP addresses or other metadata on the network layer that might be used to identify users. There are overlay networks [30,63] and in particular Tor[4] to achieve anonymity. They can be used to hide such information

---

[4] https://www.torproject.org.

and obtain anonymity on the network layer in practice. For simplicity, we just assume that using such techniques, anonymity is realized in an ideal way. Yet we stress that in practice for such networks to be effective there are many issues that need to be considered [58]. Now we list the properties:

**Selective Disclosure.** It should be possible to let a user decide which information about their identity (e.g., the concrete attributes) will be revealed to a RP and thus adhere to the principle of data minimization.

**Unlinkability.** Technically, unlinkability means that different actions (or transactions) of a user cannot be linked together. We will use the terms IdP, even though it might be a certificate issuer only, and RPs as a generic term for service providers. Since in such a setting there are different parties involved, we have to consider unlinkability in settings where several of these parties collaborate in trying to break the unlinkability. Below, we will use the terminology in [6]:

**Unlinkability with respect to RPs:** If a user authenticates to different RPs, those RPs cannot determine whether these transactions correspond to the same or two distinct users. Thereby, RPs may have access to additional auxiliary information that might help to correlate the transaction data. Unlinkability should also hold for the same RP, i.e., when a user authenticates multiple times to the same RP-of course, unless the user has indeed established a unique pseudonym that would intentionally break unlinkability.

**Unlinkability with respect to IdP:** The IdP should not learn any information about which RPs a user authenticates to. So even if the IdP observes all actions at the RPs, it should not be able to learn such information. This property is sometimes called unobservability.

**Unlinkability with respect to IdP and RPs:** The above two flavors of unlinkability consider each party being malicious in isolation. A stronger and actually more realistic version of unlinkability considers a setting where the IdP and RPs can be malicious and collude, i.e., the IdP and the RPs can bring all their information together. Still it should not be possible to track and re-identity users. This property is sometimes called untraceability.

**What Does this Mean for Anonymity?** We stress that unlinkability is a technical term and needs to be rigorously formalized to capture the desired intuition. For instance, it is clear that unlinkability always needs to be considered along with the revealed attributes and it can only be guaranteed among a set of users with the same attributes, i.e., the set in which the identity of the respective user is hidden. The degree of anonymity provided in such a setting always depends on the size of this so called anonymity set, i.e., the set of users that could reveal the same attributes. Thus, a larger anonymity set implies stronger anonymity and the more unique the combination of revealed attributes, the smaller the degree of anonymity. Technically unlinkability can thus still be satisfied if there are at least two potential users, but for a small anonymity set the degree of anonymity will be low.

## 3.2   Discussion of Privacy in Traditional Approaches

Subsequently, we briefly discuss privacy in context of traditional approaches that are currently deployed in practice.

**Password-Based Authentication.** In the classical password-based authentication approach, every RP maintains its own system and simultaneously plays the role of the IdP (there is no external IdP). Consequently, there are no different flavors of unlinkability and different RPs can link any transactions of users when collaborating as long as there is sufficient information to link (e.g., common pseudonyms, email addresses, etc.). From a selective disclosure perspective, all the attributes that are revealed once to the RP (during registrations or actions) need to be considered as "always revealed". Data minimization thus can only be realized when the mandatory information required by the RP just represents the minimal information necessary.

**Signature-Based Authentication.** For a signature-based approach, just like in password-based authentication, the (required) user attributes are just stored with each RP. Besides, in this case, the certificate - which is required for authentication to check the authenticity of the public key - always reveals all attributes encoded within it.

**Single Sign-On.** For the single sign-on approach, as it is realized by OpenID Connect, we can observe the following. The IdP knows all the required attributes of the user, and when authenticating at an RP the IdP may only reveal attributes (via the ID token) that are required. But this is clearly outside the control of the user and so selective disclosure is not strictly enforced. When it comes to unlinkability, different RPs can typically track a user as the ID token contains some unique identifier of the user. The IdP clearly can link all interactions as it is the one issuing the ID token. Moreover, any collaboration between the IdP and RPs can trivially link actions of one user together.

**Beyond the Currently Deployed Approaches.** We want to mention that Kim Cameron with his Laws of Identity[5] and the design of Windows CardSpace (Infocard) in the early 2000s already advocated and pushed for integrating of user-controlled selective disclosure into SSO solutions. Moreover, while not (yet) practically deployed, we want to note that there are recent research works, e.g., by Lehmann et al. [45,46], that investigate how currently used approaches like OpenID Connect could work with an increased privacy protection. Also, Yeoh et al. [68] present an approach to increase privacy in the FIDO2 protocol. We will not further discuss these recent approaches here but note that they use techniques, in particular anonymous credentials, that we are going to discuss subsequently.

## 4   Anonymous Credentials: The Theory

We now first want to clarify what we mean by "privacy-preserving authentication". Essentially, this is a signature-based authentication approach that supports

---
[5] https://www.identityblog.com/stories/2005/05/13/TheLawsOfIdentity.pdf.

*i*) selective disclosure and *ii*) unlinkability in all the flavors that we have discussed. Consequently, even if IdP and RPs collude, it is not possible to track users. Note that this makes the user decide which information (e.g., attributes) are revealed and provide a strong unlinkability guarantee by default. As already mentioned in Sect. 1, there are different types of anonymous credentials with a set of different features as well as (closely) related primitives (cf. [26,42]). In the following we will consider a simple abstract concept and will then discuss different (basic) features in Sect. 4.3.

### 4.1   The Abstract Concept

Abstractly, anonymous credentials involve three types of entities: users, issuers (IdPs) and verifiers (RPs). For simplicity let us assume that we have only a single issuer in the system. The protocol flow is as follows (see Fig. 2): A user obtains a credential for an attribute set $A$ from an issuer via an interactive issuance protocol, e.g., a user might obtain a governmental ID containing name, date of birth, nationality, etc. At the end of this interaction, the user has a credential, which can be seen as a signature of the issuer on attributes $A$. Then, the user can perform a presentation protocol with verifiers, where in each interaction a subset $A_i \subseteq A$ of the attributes in the credential can be revealed. For simplicity, here we use a simple selective disclosure of attributes, but this could actually be a more complex predicate over a subset of attributes (as discussed in Sect. 4.3). For instance, a user might want to consume some content online where they need to demonstrate that they satisfy some age rating or that they are residents of some country. Note that in those cases revealing the full identity of the user is typically not necessary. If a verifier accepts such a presentation protocol, then it can be sure it interacts with a user who has a valid credential from the issuer for the subset of attributes that were revealed during the presentation protocol. Note that as long as none of the attributes presented are identifying, and there is more than one user who could potentially also reveal the same set of attributes, the user stays anonymous. Note that in Fig. 2 we can also have that both verifiers are the same entity.

**Security.** What we request from an anonymous credential scheme is that it is *unforgeable*, that is, it is not possible for a user to demonstrate some set of attributes for which they did not obtain a credential. Moreover, the scheme is *unlinkable*, which means that it is not possible to link together the presentations of the same user. We note that for any candidate scheme considered to be deployed in practice it is imperative to come with a rigorous proof of security in a realistic security model.

**Extensions to this Simple Model.** As briefly mentioned above, realistic scenarios often involve multiple issuers - a situation sometimes referred to as a multi-authority anonymous credential system. In such a setting, every issuer has an independent signing key to issue credentials, and a presentation might then involve more than one credential. Such an extension is typically straightforward,

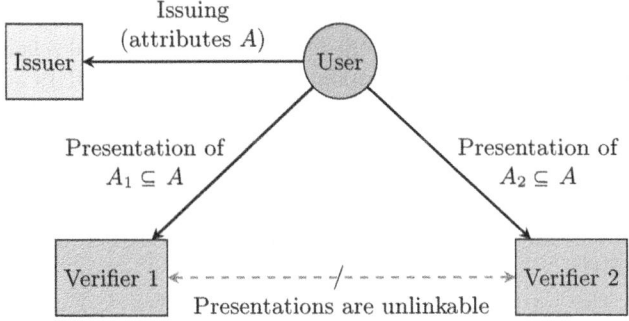

**Fig. 2.** Abstract concept of an anonymous credential system.

but if one targets at specific properties, e.g., constant-size credential presentations irrespective of the number of issuers, dedicated constructions exist [40,50].

Another flavor of having multiple issuers is that of threshold issuance anonymous credentials [31,62]. Here, rather than every issuer holding an independent signing key, all the credentials are issued under a single signing key. However, the key is shared among all the issuers using a $(k,n)$-threshold secret sharing technique. In such a setting, there are $n$ issuers each holding a share of the secret key and $k$ issuers need to collaborate to be able to issue a credential. Note that this is a means to distribute the trust in the issuers and adds security, as it is required that even leaking $t < k$ secret key shares does not allow one to learn the signing key. Moreover, it adds robustness as the availability of any $k$ out of the $n$ issuers is sufficient to issue credentials.

## 4.2 Anonymous Credentials and Distributed Ledger Technologies

We note that today there is a trend to move away from a centralized setting towards a decentralized identity. A popular concept in this decentralized identity space is that of self-sovereign identity (SSI), with Sovrin[6] being a prominent example that leverages distributed ledger technologies (DLTs) and concepts from this domain such as decentralized identifiers (DIDs).

When talking about the use of concepts from DLTs together with anonymous credentials, there are two different approaches that should not be confused. First, proposals such as decentralized anonymous credentials [37] or zk-creds [60], that crucially use DLTs to realize novel types of anonymous credentials. This is done with the goal of not requiring explicit credential issuers [37], or they are designed to solely rely on existing identity documents and thus do not require issuers to issue additional signature-based credentials [60].

Second, the practical implementation of existing anonymous credentials using technologies provided by DLTs such as DIDs. For instance, in the context of anonymous credentials, DIDs commonly provide a registry-based mechanism to

---

[6] https://sovrin.org.

"anchor" the identities of credential issuers, holders, and verifiers. Anonymous credential solutions might also leverage DLT to store credential schemas and registries for credential revocation. Consequently, even though DLTs and DIDs can function independently of anonymous credentials (and vice versa), they are often tightly intertwined in practice, and many standardization initiatives have evolved in parallel across both areas. Examples are Hyperledger AnonCreds developed alongside Hyperledger Indy, and the World Wide Web Consortium (W3C) Verifiable Credentials standards developed in tandem with DID standards (cf. Sect. 5 for more details).

Moreover, the European Union Digital Identity Wallet (EUDIW) later discussed in Sect. 6, although not related to DLTs and in contrast to Sovrin not yet related to anonymous credentials, can be viewed as an approach towards SSI. At a high level, users are collecting certified attributes, i.e., verifiable credentials, from different sources and then presenting (subsets of) verifiable credentials from this collection.

### 4.3   Features of Anonymous Credentials

In the following, we present some basic, distinguishing features of anonymous credentials, as well as a list of extended features. We try to be comprehensive in our presentation, but do not claim to be exhaustive. See also [18] for a discussion of features.

**Basic Features.** Some basic and distinguishing features of anonymous credentials are as follows:

**Single-use vs. multi-use credentials.** In the single-use case, if a credential is used more than once, different presentations become linkable. Multi-use credentials support an unlimited number of unlinkable presentations. When talking about anonymous credentials, one typically implicitly assumes multi-use ones.

**Support of attributes.** Typically it should be possible to encode attributes into an anonymous credential. However, over the recent years some use cases appeared in industry in which attributes are not really required. The latter concept is then typically called anonymous tokens, starting with Privacy Pass [29], which are built from blind signatures or related primitives such as oblivious pseudo-random functions (OPRFs).

**Non-transferability.** An issue with any digital credential is that it can easily be copied and thus illegally distributed. This gets particularly delicate in case of privacy-preserving authentication mechanisms where the identity will not be revealed. While there is no panacea, a typical approach is to bind it to hardware [14,39], as done within the related primitive of direct anonymous attestation (DAA) [16] built within every Trusted Platform Module (TPM), available in most modern computers nowadays. An alternative approach is to force users to share a valuable secret whenever they share their credentials [21], a concept which, however, seems rather hard to implement in practice. We stress that even when credentials are bound to hardware and thus a device, this does not yet prevent the sharing of the device, e.g., lending it to a family member or friend. There are recent approaches to involve biometrics to prevent this problem. Hesse et al. suggest to use a dedicated hardware token that displays a photo of the credential holder and which is bound to an anonymous credential [41]. Adams suggested to directly integrate a biometric template as attribute into the anonymous credential [1]. While this approach has recently been shown to be practical [59], it is best suited for physical access control (or requires additional trust assumptions).

**Expressiveness of attribute presentations.** Credentials may either only allow to reveal or withhold attributes (this can be thought of redacting the non-presented attributes) or be able to prove arbitrary statements about attributes encoded in the credential, e.g., attribute `country` represents any of the EU countries and attribute `birthdate` is so that the holder is above 18 years old. The latter requires the use of zero-knowledge proofs (cf. Sect. 4.4), while from a construction perspective former can be realized without them.

**Public vs. private verification.** Typically, credentials are publicly verifiable using the public key of the issuer. However, there are also constructions [24,53] and use cases, e.g., private groups in the Signal messenger [25], where the issuer is identical to the verifier and verification uses the secret of the issuer. This can allow for more efficient constructions that can avoid the use of bilinear groups and thus specific pairing-friendly elliptic curves (cf. Sect. 7.2 for a discussion).

**Extended Features.** Moreover, there are a number of additional features that can be highly relevant depending on the application.

**Revocation.** As in conventional public-key infrastructures (PKIs), one typically requires a means to invalidate already issued credentials before their expiration. However, when desiring unlinkability this cannot be a simple serial number that is always checked and consequently revocation in such a scenario is more complex and adds additional overhead. While this overhead is typically manageable from a computational perspective [47] it might introduce additional issues and needs to be thoroughly evaluated. Loosely speaking, it typically mirrors the concept of a credential revocation list, but in a privacy-preserving way. One trivial approach that avoids such mechanisms and is conceptually simple is frequent re-issuing of credentials to users. This, however, adds a significant overhead on the issuer and puts some online requirements on the user. Moreover, this can be dangerous from a privacy perspective, as a time-based correlation between issuing directly before using can drastically reduce the size of the anonymity set.

**Robustness.** Devices storing credentials can be lost or stolen. So it is important to make credentials recoverable or robust to device loss and unavailability respectively. One strategy is to back up credentials in a way so that they can be recovered when the device is not available anymore [5]. An alternative approach is to consider sharing the credential among more than one device (in a threshold way) and consider threshold presentation protocols for credentials [33], i.e., $t$ out of $n$ devices need to be available. To the best of our knowledge this issue is rarely discussed, but we believe that it is an important one that needs to be considered for practical deployment.

**Delegation.** A user might require to share access to resources and services with another person or among their different electronic devices. In practice, credentials are usually issued in a hierarchical manner, e.g., in a PKI there is a chain of certificates between the user certificate and a trusted root certification authority. In case this chain of issuers (or delegators) reveals sensitive information about the issuer's organizational structure or the credential holder, one can rely on delegatable anonymous credentials [7] (cf. [51] for a recent discussion on practically efficient schemes).

**Pseudonyms.** In some use cases it is required that while users are not identifiable, their action can still be linked together (even in case of multi-use credentials). Whenever this is required, it is possible to use context-specific pseudonyms. Here, from a unique value encoded in the credential (e.g., from its secret key) and a given context (string), a user always deterministically derives the same pseudorandom identifier that can be used as a pseudonym in this context. For instance, all actions of a user in the health domain are linkable, but are unlinkable to other domains.

**Issuer-hiding.** In a setting where a credential could have been obtained from multiple issuers, e.g., one country within the EU, it might be privacy critical to reveal the concrete issuer. The same holds when presenting multiple credentials from several issuers, where the combination of issuers might already leak a lot of information. Consequently, the issuer-hiding concept [10,28] allows to not reveal the issuer of a credential to the verifier during presentation. Rather than revealing the issuer, the user just demonstrates that an "issuer-policy", i.e., membership in a set of issuers, which is defined by the verifier, is satisfied.

**Blind issuing of attributes.** An issuer might be required not to learn certain attributes when issuing a credential. For instance, users typically need to include a secret key as an attribute into the credential, but the issuer is only allowed to get to know the public key. Moreover, it might be the case that the user wants to transfer a hidden attribute from one credential to another newly issued one without revealing anything about it (not even a function as in case of the secret and public key) to the issuer.

**Inspection.** Certain applications might require to make anonymity conditional and to escrow identifying information with the presentation of a credential (e.g., by encrypting it for a certain party). Consequently, this information can be opened by a third party when required and thus enables re-identification of the otherwise anonymous user.

## 4.4 Construction Principles

There are different ways to construct anonymous credentials on a technical level. At a high level, the user obtains a signature from the issuer on a set of attributes, which typically includes some secret of the user that is not revealed to the issuer.

For presentation, the user then demonstrates possession of such a valid signature from the issuer on a set of attributes that satisfies a certain relation. This can be just revealing a subset of the attributes or be some more complex relation. The important point is that the presentation does not reveal the original signature from the issuer directly and thus cannot be linked to the issuing. Also, what is revealed during the presentations is unlinkable.

**Zero-Knowledge Proofs.** If one wants to demonstrate a more complex relation, this typically requires the use of zero-knowledge proofs (ZKPs). We recall that ZKPs [38] allow one party (the prover) by interacting with another party (the verifier) to convince the latter that a statement (from some NP language) is true without revealing any additional information (the zero-knowledge property). At the same time, the prover is not able to make the verifier accept proofs about false statements (the soundness property). Often it is important to remove interaction in that the prover only needs to compute a single message (a proof), which can then be verified by everyone. These are so-called non-interactive zero-knowledge (NIZK) proofs [9]. It should be noted that deploying ZKPs or NIZKs introduces additional computational and implementation complexities and requires a certain level of cryptographic know-how.

**Dedicated Constructions.** Anonymous credentials with a focus on obtaining highly efficient instantiations can be constructed from specific types of signatures schemes. They can be based on signatures with efficient protocols like CL [23], BBS [11,64], BBS+ [4,17] or PS [57] signatures, which are specific signature schemes that are compatible with commitment schemes and efficient ZKPs. Alternatively, they can be based on signatures with specific randomization properties which allow to avoid ZKPs [36,66], or on specific redactable signatures that allow to redact signed messages [19,61].

As argued in the recent discussion in [6], BBS signatures are currently a popular choice for recent and ongoing projects. We will not take a closer look into how they or related schemes are constructed and for our purposes it suffices to consider all of them under the term *dedicated constructions*.

**Generic Constructions.** A second and more generic way is to construct them from *any* signature scheme, e.g., standardized and widely deployed ones like the Elliptic Curve Digital Signature Algorithm (ECDSA), and a NIZK proof system. While generically this does not yield concretely efficient (and actually rather theoretic) constructions, in the recent decade there has been enormous progress in the field of NIZK proofs and in particular on zero-knowledge succinct non-interactive arguments of knowledge (zk-SNARKs) (cf. [52,65]). zk-SNARKs are succinct NIZK proofs, where loosely speaking succinctness means that the proofs are short and the verification of proofs is efficient. Using recent advances in this directions makes the construction of such anonymous credential schemes relying on existing signatures such as ECDSA practically feasible. There are very recent works by Google [35] and Microsoft [54] leveraging zk-SNARKs to turn existing credentials (i.e., ECDSA and ECDSA or RSA signatures respectively) into anonymous credentials.

# 5  Anonymous Credentials: The Practice

It is fair to say that when considering industry adoption, anonymous credentials have not been a success story so far. Fortunately, the picture is changing
and we see increasing interest in deploying such technology. In this section we
want to look at the anonymous credential technology from an implementation,
standardization and deployment perspective.

## 5.1  Implementations

To the best of our knowledge, the first implementation of a multi-use anonymous credential system was the idemix system developed within IBM in the
early 2000's [20] (using strong RSA-based CL signatures [22]) and further developed and improved among others over a series of EU projects such as the EU
FP7 projects PrimeLife and ABC4Trust. Later, the idemix project has been
integrated into the Hyperledger project, now sponsored and managed by the
Linux Foundation[7], and is the basis for the Hyperledger AnonCreds[8] and related
projects (e.g., Aries Bifold or Hyperledger Aries), which plan to move to BBS
signatures in its version 2.0 [8]. Moreover, the first implementation of a single-use
anonymous credential system relying on the techniques in [15] was due to Brands
at Credentica in the early 2000's and was then acquired by and continued as the
U-Prove project at Microsoft[9].

We note that in the field of distributed ledger technology and verifiable credentials, there are meanwhile numerous open-source implementations of anonymous credentials based on BBS(+) signatures. We may mention here the Rust
bbs[10] or ursa crate[11], the docknetwork implementation[12] and the BBS implementation of Digital Bazaar[13], provided solely as some illustrative instances.
We also refer the interested reader to a recent work by Flamini et al. [34] for a
comparison and experimental evaluation.

The anonymous credentials zoo[14] provides an (somewhat outdated) overview
of some multi- as well as single-use anonymous credentials with some pointers to
implementations. Unfortunately, we are not aware of a place that compiles a list
of current open-source implementations, something that would be very helpful
and highly desirable.

---

[7] https://www.linuxfoundation.org.
[8] https://lf-hyperledger.atlassian.net/wiki/spaces/ANONCREDS/overview.
[9] https://www.microsoft.com/en-us/research/project/u-prove/.
[10] https://crates.io/crates/bbs.
[11] https://docs.rs/ursa/.
[12] https://github.com/docknetwork/crypto.
[13] https://github.com/digitalbazaar/bbs-signatures.
[14] https://tokenzoo.github.io.

## 5.2 Standardization Efforts

There are various ongoing efforts when it comes to the standardization of anonymous credentials and related technology. It is important to note that standardization is of utmost importance to guarantee interoperability of different implementations and thus the compatibility of services and products that rely on this technology.

First, we want to mention the Crypto Forum Research Group (CFRG) within the Internet Engineering Task Force (IETF), an open, global engineering community that publishes de facto standards called Requests For Comments (RFCs). There are ongoing standardization processes for BBS signatures [48], blind BBS signatures [44] as well as pseudonyms for BBS signatures [43]. Moreover, there are many (ongoing) standardization efforts for related primitives such as oblivious pseudo-random functions (OPRFs) or blind signatures.

In addition, there are non-profit organizations such as the aforementioned Linux Foundation or industry consortia such as the Decentralized Identity Foundation (DIF)[15], the World Wide Web Consortium (W3C)[16] or ZKProof[17] which are running working groups on anonymous credential technologies and the underlying technologies respectively.

Finally, there is the International Organization for Standardization (ISO) currently running a preliminary work item (ISO/IEC PWI 24843) on Privacy-Preserving Attribute-Based Credentials within the ISO/IEC JTC1/SC 27 WG 2 and on guidelines on privacy preservation based on zero-knowledge proofs (ISO/IEC CD 27565). Moreover, the European Telecommunications Standards Institute (ETSI) has several technical reports on related technology, such as ETSI TR 119 476[18] on selective disclosure and zero-knowledge proofs.

## 5.3 Real-World Deployments

The biggest real-world use cases related to anonymous credential technology and rolled out on billions of devices are the Direct Anonymous Attestation (DAA) scheme implemented in any Trusted Platform Module (TPM) or the Enhanced Privacy ID (EPID)[19] available in Intel's SGX. However, while somewhat close to multi-use anonymous credentials, those schemes were designed for specific use cases, do not consider attributes, and are thus not generally applicable.

When it comes to multi-use anonymous credentials in the conventional sense, we want to mention the Yivi App (previously known as IRMA) for smartphone use in the Netherlands[20], which is based upon idemix. Finally, privately verifiable

---

[15] https://identity.foundation.

[16] https://www.w3.org.

[17] https://zkproof.org.

[18] https://www.etsi.org/deliver/etsi_tr/119400_119499/119476/01.02.01_60/tr_119476v010201p.pdf.

[19] https://www.intel.com/content/www/us/en/developer/articles/technical/intel-enhanced-privacy-id-epid-security-technology.html.

[20] https://privacybydesign.foundation/irma-explanation/.

multi-use anonymous credentials have been used to implement the feature of private groups in the Signal messenger[21].

There are also various governmental use cases that rely on multi-use anonymous credentials, e.g., supporting sustainable economic development by the government of British Columbia (Canada) or digital travel credentials by the government of Aruba. We refer to [6] for more discussion on such use cases.

Apart from this, we want to mention the use of so-called anonymous tokens in various forms and use cases. Those represent single-use credentials, with or without attributes that are either privately or publicly available. This includes Privacy Pass [29] as used by Cloudflare[22], or the Anonymous Credential Service by Meta[23].

# 6   European Union Digital Identity Wallet (EUDIW)

With the EU Digital Identity Framework Regulation[24] (commonly known as eIDAS 2.0) entering into force in May 2024, the EU proposes the EU Digital Identity Wallet (EUDIW), which shall be a "fully mobile, secure and user-friendly" service, enabling users to identify themselves to public and private online services. Consequently, all member states are required to offer such an EUDIW to their citizens and residents by 2026. We refer to [6] for a more thorough discussion, and will only briefly discuss the initial design presented in the architectural reference framework (ARF) version 1.4.0 [2] and its shortcomings from a privacy perspective.

## 6.1   Signatures on Salted Hashes and Their Privacy Issues

The approach pursued in the ARF version 1.4.0 [2] is to follow the realization of selective attribute disclosure credentials from conventional digital signatures (e.g., ECDSA) as specified in the ISO/IEC 18013-5 (mobile driving license) standard. At a high level, the idea is that an issuer signs a list of "salted hashes" $(h_1, \ldots, h_n)$ instead of directly signing the attributes $(a_1, \ldots, a_n)$. Each salted hash $h_i = H(a_i \| r_i)$ is computed using a cryptographic hash function $H$ such as SHA-3 on input the attribute $a_i$ concatenated with a sufficiently long uniformly random string $r_i$. This can be viewed as a hash commitment, i.e., $h_i$ hides $a_i$ as long as $r_i$ is not known and hash value $h_i$ cannot be opened to a different $a_i' \neq a_i$, and thus is binding. Consequently, the commitment hides the attribute until the salt is revealed; even if the same attribute appears in different credentials, the added salt ensures that each hash is unique, thereby preventing straightforward linkage.

---

[21] https://signal.org/blog/signal-private-group-system/.

[22] https://blog.cloudflare.com/privacy-pass-standard/.

[23] https://engineering.fb.com/2022/12/12/security/anonymous-credential-service-acs-open-source/.

[24] https://oeil.secure.europarl.europa.eu/oeil/en/procedure-file?reference=2021/0136(COD).

The idea is now that when a user presents a signature for $(h_1, \ldots, h_n)$ to some RP for attributes it wants to present, it reveals $a_i$ along with $r_i$. For all attributes that are not disclosed, the user simply reveals $h_j$, which as discussed does not reveal anything about $a_j$ (as $r_j$ is not revealed).

**Privacy Discussion.** This represents the functionality of selective disclosure, i.e., the user can decide which attributes $a_i$ to reveal. However, when presenting the same signature multiple times, the signature as well as $(h_1, \ldots, h_n)$ are always revealed and thus can be trivially linked by any RP. This can be avoided by presenting every signature only once, i.e., viewing them as single-use credentials, which comes at the cost of requiring frequent re-issuance of new credentials and keeping track of already used signatures on the user side, and may reduce convenience. Moreover, the collusion of the IdP and any RP always completely breaks unlinkability as the IdP issues all signatures and thereby sees all attributes. We also refer the interested reader to [6] for a more thorough discussion of these aspects.

## 6.2  Privacy-Oriented and Desirable Solution

Now having discussed multi-use anonymous credentials in Sect. 4 and Sect. 5, it seems natural to consider this tool as a solution to the privacy problems raised above. Obviously, all the variants of unlinkability can be satisfactorily addressed by using anonymous credentials. And indeed, this is what a number of cryptographers suggested when invited by the EUDI Wallet Team of the European Commission to provide feedback concerning attestations and zero-knowledge proofs with respect to the ARF version 1.4.0 [2]. More precisely, the expert group suggested the use of anonymous credentials based on BBS signatures, which can be instantiated using pairing-friendly elliptic curves [6]. In the next section we will discuss why, although considered mature enough, such anonymous credentials cannot be readily deployed.

## 7  Barriers to Widespread Adoption

While there might be numerous reasons that slow down or prevent a widespread adoption of "new" technologies such as anonymous credentials, we will solely focus on technical aspects. And even here, we do not claim to be exhaustive and do not cover important aspects such as ensuring end-user usability or system interoperability. We will discuss two aspects which we consider really important (and non-trivial to solve) issues that complicate practical adoption. They have also shown up in a recent discussion about the EUDIW after providing the feedback in [6]. Moreover, at the end of this section, we will also briefly discuss challenges that are arising from the recently started transitions to post-quantum cryptography.

## 7.1  Dependency on Established Standards

If the decision of deploying anonymous credentials depends on the availability of standards for AC schemes, then this can result in significant delays. Having no standards available means that even if standardization is to be started immediately, depending on the standardization body, the time until a standard is finalized might take several years. This is especially true for large international standardization bodies like ISO or ETSI. For de-facto standards like the ones by the Internet Engineering Task Force (IETF) or the World Wide Web Consortium (W3C) this can be significantly shorter, but still typically requires several months to years. Nevertheless, in the latter case there are public versions available from the first draft, so that adoption can potentially start earlier.

Moreover, there might be standards that do not directly relate to the AC schemes and their technical details, that still can influence potential deployments of such schemes. One example is how credentials in such schemes are specified when it comes to the document structure. Here, the two currently dominating standards are verifiable credentials by the W3C[25] and the mdoc format specified in the ISO/IEC 18013 family of documents that specify the technical and operational requirements for physical and mobile driver's licenses (mDL). While in the design of the former the use of anonymous credentials has been considered, the latter does not do so. Actually, it is considered along with a dedicated solution to selective disclosure, which as we have discussed in Sect. 6.1 does not provide a sufficient degree of unlinkability. This might introduce overhead and the requirement for ad-hoc intermediate formats when using them along with anonymous credentials.

## 7.2  Hardware Support and Compatibility

While only requiring pure software implementations of new technologies such as anonymous credentials is a manageable task, the integration of new cryptographic approaches into existing ecosystems and infrastructure is a much more delicate task. In the former case it boils down to secure implementations of cryptography, which by itself is a non-trivial task and requires lots of expert knowledge. But it does not suffer from critical external dependencies. However, in the latter case it requires backward compatibility at many places. For instance, cryptographic keys and operations involving secret keys (such as signing) are typically handled by dedicated hardware such as hardware security modules (HSM), Trusted Platform Modules (TPMs), or other secure elements such as smart cards. Alternatively, they can be handled by Trusted Execution Environments (TEEs) such as ARM's TrustZone or Intel's SGX. Irrespective of the concrete realization, what is common to all those technologies is that the provided cryptographic functionality is limited to very few cryptographic primitives. When it comes to signature functionality, this typically either means RSA or ECDSA, and, in the latter case, specific standardized elliptic curves such as curve P-256 (also known as secp256r1 or prime256v1).

---

[25] https://www.w3.org/TR/vc-overview/.

However, anonymous credentials such as those based on BBS [11], as suggested in [6], require specific pairing-friendly elliptic curves such as BN-462 or BLS12-381[26] that are not readily available in the aforementioned technologies. Moreover, this requires other interfaces as those available for conventional signatures. Consequently, such a functionality is simply not available in currently deployed secure elements and TEEs. The only functionality that comes close is that of Direct Anonymous Attestation (DAA) in TPMs or EPID available in Intel's SGX. However, as already mentioned they were designed for the specific use cases and do not consider attributes in any way. While making anonymous credentials available in TEEs seems easier than when they are rooted in hardware, such changes might also require significant changes to software stacks, e.g., client platforms such as the Android system. Especially as such systems also require backward compatibility. A very informative recent talk on changing legacy cryptography and the associated problems[27] by abhi shelat is highly recommended at this place.

### 7.3   Transitioning to Post-quantum Cryptography

In response to the threats by scalable quantum computers to traditional public-key cryptography, the first standards for post-quantum cryptographic schemes are meanwhile available from the National Institute of Standards and Technology (NIST)[28]. Many governments are currently pushing towards post-quantum and are developing roadmaps for the transition from traditional to post-quantum cryptography. Clearly, this topic is also important for anonymous credential schemes. Consequently, it is strongly advisable to consider the post-quantum aspect in any current design so that a switch to a quantum safe replacement for the used anonymous credential scheme at some point does not require a partial or even complete re-design. In other words, it is important that a solution that is being deployed from now onward provides cryptographic agility.

It is important to mention though, that while we now see the first NIST standards for basic public-key cryptographic primitives (i.e., public-key encryption and signatures), we are still not close to having a clear picture of candidates for post-quantum anonymous credentials. There are recent constructions of lattice-based anonymous credentials [3,13,32] and first proof-of-concept implementations are available from IBM [49] or the EU QUBIP project[29]. While these constructions do not yet seem well-studied enough in terms of security and efficiency, it can, however, be expected that significant research will go into this topic in the upcoming years. Moreover, as discussed in more detail in [6], post-quantum security is less critical in authentication primitives than it is for encryption. Also it should be noted that if the privacy property of an anonymous credential system is unconditional (as it is the case for the BBS family mentioned in Sect. 4.4),

---

[26] https://members.loria.fr/AGuillevic/pairing-friendly-curves/.
[27] https://youtu.be/-YXCojP8IjE.
[28] https://www.nist.gov/pqcrypto.
[29] https://github.com/Cybersecurity-LINKS/pqzk-blns.

then even when instantiated from building blocks that could be broken by a hypothetical quantum computer, the privacy is not endangered and will hold forever (even when given unlimited computing power).

## 8    Conclusions and Outlook

It needs to be concluded that currently enrolled (and partly also planned) identity solutions typically provide rather weak privacy protection and are quite far from what could be considered the ideal case. Anonymous credentials are the right tool to achieve strong privacy protection and are well studied and well understood by the research community. However, although they have already been proposed back in the early 1980s by Chaum, and a large body of literature as well as practical use cases and open-source implementations exist, for a long time they did not see adoption in industry. Fortunately, in recent years we see a growing interest from the industry and governments to adopt such privacy-preserving technologies. However, deploying new technology comes with huge (financial) efforts, particularly when use cases require backward compatibility with existing hardware that only implements "legacy cryptography", which typically cannot be readily used with approaches and in particular modern anonymous credentials. Recent progress in cryptographic research and in particular in the field of zk-SNARKs, however, does now even enable solutions based on existing "legacy cryptography" and so even immediate large-scale deployments do not seem out of reach.

Nevertheless, when deploying solutions now, they are likely here to stay for quite some time. Thus, solid and forward-looking planning is essential. This particularly holds true for the governmental domain and large scale solutions like the EUDIW. For instance, when considering the rollout a new solution today, it is definitely advisable to consider quantum resistance (i.e., post-quantum security).

At the time of writing this paper, the technical implementation of the EUDIW is still under discussion.[30] At this point it cannot be determined with certainty how the final version of the ARF will look like and which technology will ultimately be adopted. We strongly hope that it will be a solution that considers strong privacy protection.

**Acknowledgments.** The author is very grateful to Yod Samuel Martín, René Mayrhofer, Omid Mir, Octavio Perez-Kempner and Mahdi Sedaghat for their helpful feedback on a draft of this paper.

## References

1. Adams, C.: Achieving non-transferability in credential systems using hidden biometrics. Secur. Commun. Networks **4**(2), 195–206 (2011). https://doi.org/10.1002/SEC.136

---

[30] https://github.com/eu-digital-identity-wallet/eudi-doc-architecture-and-reference-framework/discussions.

2. ARF: The european digital identity wallet architecture and reference frame-work version 1.4.0 (2024). https://eu-digital-identity-wallet.github.io/eudi-doc-architecture-and-reference-framework/1.4.0/arf/

3. Argo, S., Güneysu, T., Jeudy, C., Land, G., Roux-Langlois, A., Sanders, O.: Practical post-quantum signatures for privacy. In: Luo, B., Liao, X., Xu, J., Kirda, E., Lie, D. (eds.) Proceedings of the 2024 on ACM SIGSAC Conference on Computer and Communications Security, CCS 2024, Salt Lake City, UT, USA, October 14–18, 2024, pp. 1523–1537. ACM (2024). https://doi.org/10.1145/3658644.3670297

4. Au, M.H., Susilo, W., Mu, Y.: Constant-size dynamic $k$-TAA. In: Prisco, R.D., Yung, M. (eds.) Security and Cryptography for Networks, 5th International Conference, SCN 2006, Maiori, Italy, September 6–8, 2006, Proceedings. Lecture Notes in Computer Science, vol. 4116, pp. 111–125. Springer (2006). https://doi.org/10.1007/11832072_8,

5. Baldimtsi, F., Camenisch, J., Hanzlik, L., Krenn, S., Lehmann, A., Neven, G.: Recovering lost device-bound credentials. In: Malkin, T., Kolesnikov, V., Lewko, A.B., Polychronakis, M. (eds.) Applied Cryptography and Network Security - 13th International Conference, ACNS 2015, New York, NY, USA, June 2–5, 2015, Revised Selected Papers. Lecture Notes in Computer Science, vol. 9092, pp. 307–327. Springer (2015). https://doi.org/10.1007/978-3-319-28166-7_15,

6. Baum, C., et al.: Cryptographers' Feedback on the EU Digital Identity's ARF (2024). https://github.com/user-attachments/files/15904122/cryptographers-feedback.pdf

7. Belenkiy, M., Camenisch, J., Chase, M., Kohlweiss, M., Lysyanskaya, A., Shacham, H.: Randomizable proofs and delegatable anonymous credentials. In: Halevi, S. (ed.) Advances in Cryptology - CRYPTO 2009, 29th Annual International Cryptology Conference, Santa Barbara, CA, USA, August 16–20, 2009. Proceedings. Lecture Notes in Computer Science, vol. 5677, pp. 108–125. Springer (2009). https://doi.org/10.1007/978-3-642-03356-8_7

8. Bernstein, G., Kalos, V.: BBS+ applications, standardization, and a bit of theory (2023). https://csrc.nist.gov/csrc/media/Presentations/2023/crclub-2023-10-18/images-media/20231018-crypto-club--greg-and-vasilis--slides--BBS.pdf

9. Blum, M., Feldman, P., Micali, S.: Non-interactive zero-knowledge and its applications (extended abstract). In: Simon, J. (ed.) Proceedings of the 20th Annual ACM Symposium on Theory of Computing, May 2–4, 1988, Chicago, Illinois, USA, pp. 103–112. ACM (1988). https://doi.org/10.1145/62212.62222

10. Bobolz, J., Eidens, F., Krenn, S., Ramacher, S., Samelin, K.: Issuer-hiding attribute-based credentials. In: Conti, M., Stevens, M., Krenn, S. (eds.) Cryptology and Network Security - 20th International Conference, CANS 2021, Vienna, Austria, December 13–15, 2021, Proceedings. Lecture Notes in Computer Science, vol. 13099, pp. 158–178. Springer (2021). https://doi.org/10.1007/978-3-030-92548-2_9

11. Boneh, D., Boyen, X., Shacham, H.: Short group signatures. In: Franklin, M.K. (ed.) Advances in Cryptology - CRYPTO 2004, 24th Annual International CryptologyConference, Santa Barbara, California, USA, August 15–19, 2004, Proceedings. Lecture Notes in Computer Science, vol. 3152, pp. 41–55. Springer (2004). https://doi.org/10.1007/978-3-540-28628-8_3

12. Bonneau, J.: The science of guessing: Analyzing an anonymized corpus of 70 million passwords. In: IEEE Symposium on Security and Privacy, SP 2012, 21–23 May 2012, San Francisco, California, USA, pp. 538–552. IEEE Computer Society (2012). https://doi.org/10.1109/SP.2012.49

13. Bootle, J., Lyubashevsky, V., Nguyen, N.K., Sorniotti, A.: A framework for practical anonymous credentials from lattices. In: Handschuh, H., Lysyanskaya, A. (eds.) Advances in Cryptology - CRYPTO 2023 - 43rd Annual International Cryptology Conference, CRYPTO 2023, Santa Barbara, CA, USA, August 20–24, 2023, Proceedings, Part II. Lecture Notes in Computer Science, vol. 14082, pp. 384–417. Springer (2023). https://doi.org/10.1007/978-3-031-38545-2_13

14. Brands, S.: Untraceable off-line cash in wallets with observers (extended abstract). In: Stinson, D.R. (ed.) Advances in Cryptology - CRYPTO '93, 13th Annual International Cryptology Conference, Santa Barbara, California, USA, August 22-26, 1993, Proceedings. Lecture Notes in Computer Science, vol. 773, pp. 302–318. Springer (1993). https://doi.org/10.1007/3-540-48329-2_26

15. Brands, S.A.: Rethinking Public Key Infrastructures and Digital Certificates: Building in Privacy. MIT Press, Cambridge (2000)

16. Brickell, E.F., Camenisch, J., Chen, L.: Direct anonymous attestation. In: Atluri, V., Pfitzmann, B., McDaniel, P.D. (eds.) Proceedings of the 11th ACM Conference on Computer and Communications Security, CCS 2004, Washington, DC, USA, October 25–29, 2004, pp. 132–145. ACM (2004). https://doi.org/10.1145/1030083.1030103

17. Camenisch, J., Drijvers, M., Lehmann, A.: Anonymous attestation using the strong diffie hellman assumption revisited. In: Franz, M., Papadimitratos, P. (eds.) Trust and Trustworthy Computing - 9th International Conference, TRUST 2016, Vienna, Austria, August 29–30, 2016, Proceedings. Lecture Notes in Computer Science, vol. 9824, pp. 1–20. Springer (2016). https://doi.org/10.1007/978-3-319-45572-3_1

18. Camenisch, J., et al.: Concepts and languages for privacy-preserving attribute-based authentication. J. Inf. Secur. Appl. **19**(1), 25–44 (2014). https://doi.org/10.1016/J.JISA.2014.03.004

19. Camenisch, J., Dubovitskaya, M., Haralambiev, K., Kohlweiss, M.: Composable and modular anonymous credentials: definitions and practical constructions. In: Iwata, T., Cheon, J.H. (eds.) Advances in Cryptology - ASIACRYPT 2015 - 21st International Conference on the Theory and Application of Cryptology and Information Security, Auckland, New Zealand, November 29 - December 3, 2015, Proceedings, Part II. Lecture Notes in Computer Science, vol. 9453, pp. 262–288. Springer (2015). https://doi.org/10.1007/978-3-662-48800-3_11

20. Camenisch, J., Herreweghen, E.V.: Design and implementation of the *idemix* anonymous credential system. In: Atluri, V. (ed.) Proceedings of the 9th ACM Conference on Computer and Communications Security, CCS 2002, Washington, DC, USA, November 18–22, 2002. pp. 21–30. ACM (2002). https://doi.org/10.1145/586110.586114

21. Camenisch, J., Lysyanskaya, A.: An efficient system for non-transferable anonymous credentials with optional anonymity revocation. In: Pfitzmann, B. (ed.) Advances in Cryptology - EUROCRYPT 2001, International Conference on the Theory and Application of Cryptographic Techniques, Innsbruck, Austria, May 6–10, 2001, Proceeding. Lecture Notes in Computer Science, vol. 2045, pp. 93–118. Springer (2001). https://doi.org/10.1007/3-540-44987-6_7

22. Camenisch, J., Lysyanskaya, A.: A signature scheme with efficient protocols. In: Cimato, S., Galdi, C., Persiano, G. (eds.) Security in Communication Networks, Third International Conference, SCN 2002, Amalfi, Italy, September 11–13, 2002. Revised Papers. Lecture Notes in Computer Science, vol. 2576, pp. 268–289. Springer (2002). https://doi.org/10.1007/3-540-36413-7_20

23. Camenisch, J., Lysyanskaya, A.: Signature schemes and anonymous credentials from bilinear maps. In: Franklin, M.K. (ed.) Advances in Cryptology - CRYPTO 2004, 24th Annual International Cryptology Conference, Santa Barbara, California, USA, August 15–19, 2004, Proceedings. Lecture Notes in Computer Science, vol. 3152, pp. 56–72. Springer (2004). https://doi.org/10.1007/978-3-540-28628-8_4

24. Chase, M., Meiklejohn, S., Zaverucha, G.: Algebraic macs and keyed-verification anonymous credentials. In: Ahn, G., Yung, M., Li, N. (eds.) Proceedings of the 2014 ACM SIGSAC Conference on Computer and Communications Security, Scottsdale, AZ, USA, November 3–7, 2014, pp. 1205–1216. ACM (2014). https://doi.org/10.1145/2660267.2660328

25. Chase, M., Perrin, T., Zaverucha, G.: The signal private group system and anonymous credentials supporting efficient verifiable encryption. In: Ligatti, J., Ou, X., Katz, J., Vigna, G. (eds.) CCS '20: 2020 ACM SIGSAC Conference on Computer and Communications Security, Virtual Event, USA, November 9–13, 2020, pp. 1445–1459. ACM (2020). https://doi.org/10.1145/3372297.3417887

26. Chator, A., Green, M., Tiwari, P.R.: SoK: Privacy-preserving signatures. Cryptology ePrint Archive, Paper 2023/1039 (2023). https://eprint.iacr.org/2023/1039

27. Chaum, D.: Security without identification: transaction systems to make big brother obsolete. Commun. ACM **28**(10), 1030–1044 (1985). https://doi.org/10.1145/4372.4373

28. Connolly, A., Lafourcade, P., Perez-Kempner, O.: Improved constructions of anonymous credentials from structure-preserving signatures on equivalence classes. In: Hanaoka, G., Shikata, J., Watanabe, Y. (eds.) Public-Key Cryptography - PKC 2022 - 25th IACR International Conference on Practice and Theory of Public-Key Cryptography, Virtual Event, March 8–11, 2022, Proceedings, Part I. Lecture Notes in Computer Science, vol. 13177, pp. 409–438. Springer (2022). https://doi.org/10.1007/978-3-030-97121-2_15

29. Davidson, A., Goldberg, I., Sullivan, N., Tankersley, G., Valsorda, F.: Privacy pass: bypassing internet challenges anonymously. Proc. Priv. Enhancing Technol. **2018**(3), 164–180 (2018). https://doi.org/10.1515/POPETS-2018-0026

30. Dingledine, R., Mathewson, N., Syverson, P.F.: Tor: the second-generation onion router. In: Blaze, M. (ed.) Proceedings of the 13th USENIX Security Symposium, August 9–13, 2004, San Diego, CA, USA, pp. 303–320. USENIX (2004). http://www.usenix.org/publications/library/proceedings/sec04/tech/dingledine.html

31. Doerner, J., Kondi, Y., Lee, E., Shelat, A., Tyner, L.: Threshold BBS+ signatures for distributed anonymous credential issuance. In: 44th IEEE Symposium on Security and Privacy, SP 2023, San Francisco, CA, USA, May 21–25, 2023, pp. 773–789. IEEE (2023). https://doi.org/10.1109/SP46215.2023.10179470

32. Dubois, A., Klooß, M., Lai, R.W.F., Woo, I.K.Y.: Lattice-based proof-friendly signatures from vanishing short integer solutions. Cryptology ePrint Archive, Paper 2025/356 (2025). https://eprint.iacr.org/2025/356

33. Flamini, A., Lee, E., Lysyanskaya, A.: Multi-holder anonymous credentials from BBS signatures. Cryptology ePrint Archive, Paper 2024/1874 (2024). https://eprint.iacr.org/2024/1874

34. Flamini, A., Sciarretta, G., Scuro, M., Sharif, A., Tomasi, A., Ranise, S.: On cryptographic mechanisms for the selective disclosure of verifiable credentials. J. Inf. Secur. Appl. **83**, 103789 (2024). https://doi.org/10.1016/J.JISA.2024.103789

35. Frigo, M., abhi shelat: Anonymous credentials from ECDSA. Cryptology ePrint Archive, Paper 2024/2010 (2024). https://eprint.iacr.org/2024/2010

36. Fuchsbauer, G., Hanser, C., Slamanig, D.: Structure-preserving signatures on equivalence classes and constant-size anonymous credentials. J. Cryptol. **32**(2), 498–546 (2019). https://doi.org/10.1007/S00145-018-9281-4

37. Garman, C., Green, M., Miers, I.: Decentralized anonymous credentials. In: 21st Annual Network and Distributed System Security Symposium, NDSS 2014, San Diego, California, USA, February 23–26, 2014. The Internet Society (2014). https://www.ndss-symposium.org/ndss2014/decentralized-anonymous-credentials

38. Goldwasser, S., Micali, S., Rackoff, C.: The knowledge complexity of interactive proof systems. SIAM J. Comput. **18**(1), 186–208 (1989). https://doi.org/10.1137/0218012

39. Hanzlik, L., Slamanig, D.: With a little help from my friends: Constructing practical anonymous credentials. In: Kim, Y., Kim, J., Vigna, G., Shi, E. (eds.) CCS '21: 2021 ACM SIGSAC Conference on Computer and Communications Security, Virtual Event, Republic of Korea, November 15–19, 2021, pp. 2004–2023. ACM (2021). https://doi.org/10.1145/3460120.3484582

40. Hébant, C., Pointcheval, D.: Traceable constant-size multi-authority credentials. In: Galdi, C., Jarecki, S. (eds.) Security and Cryptography for Networks - 13th International Conference, SCN 2022, Amalfi, Italy, September 12-14, 2022, Proceedings. Lecture Notes in Computer Science, vol. 13409, pp. 411–434. Springer (2022). https://doi.org/10.1007/978-3-031-14791-3_18

41. Hesse, J., Singh, N., Sorniotti, A.: How to bind anonymous credentials to humans. In: Calandrino, J.A., Troncoso, C. (eds.) 32nd USENIX Security Symposium, USENIX Security 2023, Anaheim, CA, USA, August 9–11, 2023, pp. 3047–3064. USENIX Association (2023). https://www.usenix.org/conference/usenixsecurity23/presentation/hesse

42. Kakvi, S.A., Martin, K.M., Putman, C., Quaglia, E.A.: SOK: anonymous credentials. In: Günther, F., Hesse, J. (eds.) Security Standardisation Research - 8th International Conference, SSR 2023, Lyon, France, April 22-23, 2023, Proceedings. Lecture Notes in Computer Science, vol. 13895, pp. 129–151. Springer (2023). https://doi.org/10.1007/978-3-031-30731-7_6

43. Kalos, V., Bernstein, G.M.: BBS per verifier linkability. Internet-Draft draft-kalos-bbs-per-verifier-linkability-00, IETF Secretariat (2024)

44. Kalos, V., Bernstein, G.M.: Blind BBS signatures. Internet-Draft draft-kalos-bbs-blind-signatures-03, IETF Secretariat (2024)

45. Kroschewski, M., Lehmann, A.: Save the implicit flow? Enabling privacy-preserving RP authentication in openid connect. Proc. Priv. Enhancing Technol. **2023**(4), 96–116 (2023). https://doi.org/10.56553/POPETS-2023-0100

46. Kroschewski, M., Lehmann, A., Özbay, C.: OPPID: single sign-on with oblivious pairwise pseudonyms. Cryptology ePrint Archive, Paper 2024/1124 (2024). https://eprint.iacr.org/2024/1124

47. Lapon, J., Kohlweiss, M., Decker, B.D., Naessens, V.: Analysis of revocation strategies for anonymous idemix credentials. In: Decker, B.D., Lapon, J., Naessens, V., Uhl, A. (eds.) Communications and Multimedia Security, 12th IFIP TC 6 / TC 11 International Conference, CMS 2011, Ghent, Belgium, October 19–21,2011. Proceedings. Lecture Notes in Computer Science, vol. 7025, pp. 3–17. Springer (2011). https://doi.org/10.1007/978-3-642-24712-5_1

48. Looker, T., Kalos, V., Whitehead, A., Lodder, M.: The BBS signature scheme. Internet-Draft draft-irtf-cfrg-bbs-signatures-07, IETF Secretariat (2024)

49. Lyubashevsky, V., Seiler, G., Steuer, P.: The lazer library: lattice-based zero knowledge and succinct proofs for quantum-safe privacy. In: Luo, B., Liao, X., Xu, J., Kirda, E., Lie, D. (eds.) Proceedings of the 2024 on ACM SIGSAC Conference on Computer and Communications Security, CCS 2024, Salt Lake City, UT, USA, October 14–18, 2024, pp. 3125–3137. ACM (2024). https://doi.org/10.1145/3658644.3690330

50. Mir, O., Bauer, B., Griffy, S., Lysyanskaya, A., Slamanig, D.: Aggregate signatures with versatile randomization and issuer-hiding multi-authority anonymous credentials. In: Meng, W., Jensen, C.D., Cremers, C., Kirda, E. (eds.) Proceedings of the 2023 ACM SIGSAC Conference on Computer and Communications Security, CCS 2023, Copenhagen, Denmark, November 26–30, 2023, pp. 30–44. ACM (2023). https://doi.org/10.1145/3576915.3623203

51. Mir, O., Slamanig, D., Bauer, B., Mayrhofer, R.: Practical delegatable anonymous credentials from equivalence class signatures. Proc. Priv. Enhancing Technol. **2023**(3), 488–513 (2023). https://doi.org/10.56553/POPETS-2023-0093

52. Nitulescu, A.: ZK-snarks: a gentle introduction (2020). https://api.semanticscholar.org/CorpusID:211530704

53. Orrù, M.: Revisiting keyed-verification anonymous credentials. IACR Cryptol. ePrint Arch. p. 1552 (2024). https://eprint.iacr.org/2024/1552

54. Paquin, C., Policharla, G.V., Zaverucha, G.: Crescent: stronger privacy for existing credentials. Cryptology ePrint Archive, Paper 2024/2013 (2024). https://eprint.iacr.org/2024/2013

55. Pashalidis, A.: Interdomain User Authentication and Privacy. Ph.D. thesis, Royal Holloway, University of London (2006). https://web.archive.org/web/20060925104053/http://www.ma.rhul.ac.uk/techreports/2005/RHUL-MA-2005-13.pdf

56. Pfitzmann, A., Hansen, M.: Anonymity, unlinkability, unobservability, pseudonymity, and identity management - a consolidated proposal for terminology (2006). https://dud.inf.tu-dresden.de/literatur/Anon_Terminology_v0.28.pdf

57. Pointcheval, D., Sanders, O.: Short randomizable signatures. In: Sako, K. (ed.) Topics in Cryptology - CT-RSA 2016 - The Cryptographers' Track at the RSA Conference 2016, San Francisco, CA, USA, February 29 - March 4, 2016, Proceedings. Lecture Notes in Computer Science, vol. 9610, pp. 111–126. Springer (2016). https://doi.org/10.1007/978-3-319-29485-8_7

58. Raymond, J.: Traffic analysis: protocols, attacks, design issues, and open problems. In: Federrath, H. (ed.) Designing Privacy Enhancing Technologies, International Workshop on Design Issues in Anonymity and Unobservability, Berkeley, CA, USA, July 25-26, 2000, Proceedings. Lecture Notes in Computer Science, vol. 2009, pp. 10–29. Springer (2000). https://doi.org/10.1007/3-540-44702-4_2

59. Rodríguez, J.G., Krenn, S., Slamanig, D.: To pass or not to pass: privacy-preserving physical access control. Comput. Secur. **136**, 103566 (2024). https://doi.org/10.1016/J.COSE.2023.103566

60. Rosenberg, M., White, J.D., Garman, C., Miers, I.: zk-creds: flexible anonymous credentials from zksnarks and existing identity infrastructure. In: 44th IEEE Symposium on Security and Privacy, SP 2023, San Francisco, CA, USA, May 21–25, 2023. pp. 790–808. IEEE (2023). https://doi.org/10.1109/SP46215.2023.10179430

61. Sanders, O.: Efficient redactable signature and application to anonymous credentials. In: Kiayias, A., Kohlweiss, M., Wallden, P., Zikas, V. (eds.) Public-Key Cryptography - PKC 2020 - 23rd IACR International Conference on Practice and Theory of Public-Key Cryptography, Edinburgh, UK, May 4–7, 2020, Proceedings,

Part II. Lecture Notes in Computer Science, vol. 12111, pp. 628–656. Springer (2020). https://doi.org/10.1007/978-3-030-45388-6_22

62. Sonnino, A., Al-Bassam, M., Bano, S., Meiklejohn, S., Danezis, G.: Coconut: Threshold issuance selective disclosure credentials with applications to distributed ledgers. In: 26th Annual Network and Distributed System Security Symposium, NDSS 2019, San Diego, California, USA, February 24–27, 2019. The Internet Society (2019). https://www.ndss-symposium.org/ndss-paper/coconut-threshold-issuance-selective-disclosure-credentials-with-applications-to-distributed-ledgers/

63. Syverson, P.F., Goldschlag, D.M., Reed, M.G.: Anonymous connections and onion routing. In: 1997 IEEE Symposium on Security and Privacy, May 4–7, 1997, Oakland, CA, USA. pp. 44–54. IEEE Computer Society (1997). https://doi.org/10.1109/SECPRI.1997.601314

64. Tessaro, S., Zhu, C.: Revisiting BBS signatures. In: Hazay, C., Stam, M. (eds.) Advances in Cryptology - EUROCRYPT 2023 - 42nd Annual International Conference on the Theory and Applications of Cryptographic Techniques, Lyon, France, April 23–27, 2023, Proceedings, Part V. Lecture Notes in Computer Science, vol. 14008, pp. 691–721. Springer (2023). https://doi.org/10.1007/978-3-031-30589-4_24

65. Thaler, J.: Proofs, arguments, and zero-knowledge. Found. Trends® Privacy Secur. **4**(2-4), 117–660 (2022). https://doi.org/10.1561/3300000030

66. Verheul, E.R.: Self-blindable credential certificates from the Weil pairing. In: Boyd, C. (ed.) Advances in Cryptology - ASIACRYPT 2001, 7th International Conference on the Theory and Application of Cryptology and Information Security, Gold Coast, Australia, December 9–13, 2001, Proceedings. Lecture Notes in Computer Science, vol. 2248, pp. 533–551. Springer (2001). https://doi.org/10.1007/3-540-45682-1_31

67. Wash, R., Rader, E.J., Berman, R., Wellmer, Z.: Understanding password choices: how frequently entered passwords are re-used across websites. In: Twelfth Symposium on Usable Privacy and Security, SOUPS 2016, Denver, CO, USA, June 22–24, 2016, pp. 175–188. USENIX Association (2016). https://www.usenix.org/conference/soups2016/technical-sessions/presentation/wash

68. Yeoh, W., Kepkowski, M., Heide, G., Kaafar, D., Hanzlik, L.: Fast identity online with anonymous credentials (FIDO-AC). In: Calandrino, J.A., Troncoso, C. (eds.) 32nd USENIX Security Symposium, USENIX Security 2023, Anaheim, CA, USA, August 9–11, 2023, pp. 3029–3046. USENIX Association (2023). https://www.usenix.org/conference/usenixsecurity23/presentation/yeoh

69. Zhang, S., Pearman, S., Bauer, L., Christin, N.: Why people (don't) use password managers effectively. In: Lipford, H.R. (ed.) Fifteenth Symposium on Usable Privacy and Security, SOUPS 2019, Santa Clara, CA, USA, August 11–13, 2019. USENIX Association (2019). https://www.usenix.org/conference/soups2019/presentation/pearman

# Different Perspectives on Generative AI

# A Bottom-Up Movement to Develop Ethical Foundations for Generative AI in South Korea: Will It Simply Follow the West or Forge Its Own Path?

Saebyoul Yun[(✉)] [ORCID]

University of Edinburgh, Edinburgh, UK
saebyoul.yun@ed.ac.uk

**Abstract.** After the introduction of generative AI (GAI), numerous guidelines for the ethical use of GAI have been established. Although South Korea has not been a leading country in the development of ethical use of technology, not only government organisations, but also institutions and researchers have tried to establish GAI guidelines. In light of this, this study undertook a review of the GAI guidelines established by eleven universities in Korea, together with the announcements informing the established guidelines, and the relevant materials or opportunities provided. The eleven universities were classified into four groups according to their level of commitment to developing GAI guidelines. The eight main fields and 27 categories resulting from the guideline review were compared with the fields/categories of the GAI guidelines of Western universities. The aim of this study was to ascertain the rationale behind the establishment of GAI guidelines by Korean universities and to identify whether Korean guidelines demonstrate authenticity. The findings revealed that the bottom-up movement in Korea to develop GAI ethical guidelines could be described as a 'work in progress'. The establishment of the GAI guideline itself could be considered as a first step, and there have been attempts that deserve attention regarding improving the authenticity of GAI guidelines: unambiguous motivation to lead the development of GAI guidelines, reflecting institutions' core values or existing ethical codes, signed agreements and additional announcements for midterm/final exams to address current limitations related to the power of enforcement guidelines with, and ongoing efforts to identify the needs and difficulties of students and instructors.

**Keywords:** Generative AI · GAI Ethics · Ethical Guidelines · Emerging Movements · South Korean Universities · Asian Countries

## 1 Introduction

South Korea (hereinafter Korea) is a country well known for its IT infrastructure, including nationwide Wi-Fi networks and high levels of smartphone use, but it is not a leader in developing ethical standards or guidelines for the use of digital technology. For example,

F. Bieker et al. (Eds.): Privacy and Identity 2024, IFIP AICT 705, pp. 31–58, 2025.
https://doi.org/10.1007/978-3-031-91054-8_2

during COVID-19, Korea was one of the countries that used the highest level of digital surveillance systems to control COVID-19, such as electronic wristbands, facial recognition CCTV cameras, GPS-based tracking, and Vaccine Pass. It was possible because of the infrastructures the country has, but the problem was that the Korean government introduced a comprehensive digital surveillance system without prior social discussion or formulation of ethical considerations or guidelines.

As a result, various ethical problems arose, such as the digital divide, social discrimination and invasion of privacy, but none of these problems have been sufficiently discussed by society and clearly resolved [1]. The lack of ethical consideration and less awareness of socio-ethical problems such as privacy or digital discrimination have been identified as problems in Korea regardless of the field. The fields that have been most concerned with ethical issues in Korea are medicine and infectious diseases, as there has been at least some effort to identify other countries' trends or to develop ethical guidelines [2]. At the same time, many researchers and experts have criticised the practice of developing ethical guidelines for medical or infectious diseases in Korea, as most guidelines have simply followed those of Western countries and rarely reflected national contexts or culture [2, 3].

However, in the case of AI technology, Korea has tried in many ways to establish a government-led ethical foundation: developing ethical guidelines by the Ministry of Science and ICT (MOSI) in 2020 and establishing the National Trustworthy AI Strategy in 2021, as well as reports from government-funded research institutes. As a result of these efforts, the country received a high score in the Artificial Intelligence and Democratic Values 2021 and 2022 Reports [4]. Compared to the previous digital technology applied in the country, these new movements could be assessed positively. It is unfortunate that, despite the country's endeavours to cultivate AI ethics, AI-related incidents of a serious nature have occurred. One such incident involved an open-domain conversational AI called Lee Ruda. The chatbot was created by a startup named Skatter Lab, and the number of users increased dramatically after the service was launched in 2020. Problems soon arose as the chatbot used discriminatory and stigmatising words, gave out personal information such as home addresses or mobile phone numbers, and could be trained by answering questions based on sexual and violent language [5]. There was criticism because, although the general level of AI ethics and democracy in the country had been assessed and found to be high, the launch of the service in the country and the attitudes of the users did not seem to follow this level.

Other patterns have been observed. Following the emergence of generative AI (hereinafter GAI) such as Chat GPT, which generates natural-sounding text results based on hyper-scale data and deep learning algorithms [6], many educational institutions, including government education departments, universities and secondary schools, have developed their own ethical guidelines for teachers and students. Compared to other previous digital technologies that have caused ethical issues, and even AI technologies that have been used before, this pattern is clearly new, different and active in terms of ethical issues and foundations. In light of this, this research examines the guidelines established by higher education institutions (hereinafter HEI), focusing on the motivations, the reasons for developing the standards, the elements in the guidelines, and subsequent measures to promote the application of the principles. The research questions for this study are as follows:

- RQ1. What are the motivations of educational institutions to establish ethical guidelines for internal members using GAI?
- RQ2. Have they developed additional efforts to apply the guidelines in practice, such as establishing relevant training programmes?
- RQ3. Has the development of GAI guidelines demonstrated authenticity, reflecting institutional goals and particularities, or has it blindly followed Western trends?

In order to answer these questions, guidelines established in relation to GAI, the announcements associated with the guidelines, and subsequent actions to promote or to apply the guidelines in members' daily lives have been collected and analysed based on their motivation and focus. The examples of endeavours for building ethical GAI environments or lessons from this research would be applicable to the development of ethical use of GAI or other AI technologies, especially in contexts where there is a paucity of efforts to establish ethical guidelines or analogous initiatives. In particular, the findings of this research and implications would help Asian countries, including Korea, China, Hong Kong and Taiwan, which have proven to have sufficient infrastructure to deploy powerful technologies when needed, such as in the COVID-19 pandemic, but have not developed sufficient ethical foundations to minimise ethical problems in the use of digital technologies.

## 2 Literature Review

### 2.1 Generative AI and Efforts for Developing Ethical Guidelines in HEI

Following the launch of Open AI's ChatGPT, concerns and hesitations about its use have arisen. For example, in March 2023, an open letter called for a pause of "at least 6 months in the training of AI systems more powerful than GPT-4" [7]. In early April 2023, the use of ChatGPT was banned by the Italian data protection authority due to unlawful data collection and the lack of a feature to prevent underage users. About a month later, the country allowed access to ChatGPT after Open AI provided an age verification system, more information about personal data collection, and a new form to request the removal of personal data [8]. As of July 2024, Open AI supports 188 countries and regions to access the ChatGPT service [9], which means that many countries currently have little policy in place to ban GAI. Instead of trying to block GAI or its development, countermeasures, research, and ethical guidelines have been developed to prevent potential ethical issues and solve existing problems.

Concerns regarding AI technology, in terms of data privacy, biased or discriminatory data, and transparency already exist, and the ethical principles required to address these issues as well [10, 11]. Nevertheless, GAI has necessitated the implementation of novel countermeasures to ensure its ethical and optimal utilisation. In comparison to preceding AI systems, GAI exhibits a markedly elevated degree of performance threatening human control, a considerable risk of generating deceptive information that infringes upon intellectual property rights, as well as a high rate of dissemination to the general public [10]. In light of this, studies have explored concerns associated with using Chat-GPT, including the opacity of the model, misinformation, and potential influence on employment [12–14]. Wach et al. [15] identified seven main threats of ChatGPT, including "no regulation of AI market", "Social manipulation", and "AI technostress". Gupta et al. [16] investigated the malicious utilisation of GAI, encompassing cyber-attacks and automated hacking, and examined defensive strategies, including the malware detection and the formulation of ethical guidelines. The majority of studies on GAI have emphasised the significance of public comprehension regarding GAI itself, its ethical and security implications, and the necessity for social discourse and ethical guidelines. [10, 15, 16].

In particular, the introduction of GAI has prompted researchers to undertake further research into the responsible utilisation of GAI in educational contexts, and educational institutes to consider strategies for the mitigation of potential issues. This phenomenon is closely linked to the accelerated uptake of ChatGPT by students and the "problems of attribution of authorship" it has caused [17, 18]. Students may use GAI for their essay-based assignments, which could potentially lead to academic integrity issues pertaining to cheating, plagiarism, a decline in writing proficiency and critical thinking if they become overly reliant on GAI. [19–22]. Considering that, in April 2023, UNESCO IESALC[1] launched the 'ChatGPT and Artificial Intelligence in Higher Education Quick Start Guide'. They provided a guidance on the use of ChatGPT in HEIs and discussed the challenges and ethical implications in terms of "academic integrity", "lack of regulation", and "cognitive bias" [23]. Moorhouse et al. [19] conducted a review of the GAI guidelines for instructors created by the 23 top-ranked HEIs globally and identified three main areas: "academic integrity", "advice on assessment design", and "communicating with students". Other studies in the field of education have explored: the impact of GAI on HEIs and the obligation of the HEIs for students such as supporting them to prepare for industry and conducting research [24]; the educational and conversational interactions between humans and GAI as a social process [25]; a gap between the GAI policies of 102 high schools and those of HEIs, including the lack of ethical deployment or overlooked issues in some institutions [26]; and ways of supporting critical thinking, flexibility, and self-regulation to ensure the ethical use of GAI in education [27].

A review of these existing studies revealed the numerous organisations, institutes, and researchers in the field of education have established guidelines pertaining to the ethical and responsible use of GAI or at least, highlighted the importance of producing and maintaining updated GAI guides. In regard to the development of ethical guidelines or principles for AI technologies, several constraints have been identified: the guidelines or ethical codes have little impact on tech experts' behaviours [28]; economic considerations play a more significant role than ethical concerns in the utilisation of machine learning systems within business sectors [29]; discrepancies in the interpretation of ethical guidelines by different groups could impede their effective implementation [30]; and ethical guidelines lack the capacity for enforcement [29]. Despite the reservations expressed about the efficacy of the ethical guidelines, it is nonetheless evident that such measures are indispensable when utilising GAI as they serve to uncover "blind spots", promote "autonomy and freedom", and foster "self-responsibility" [29]. Furthermore,

---

[1] The UNESCO International Institute for Higher Education in Latin America and the Caribbean.

given the constraints of the AI/GAI guidelines, it would be advantageous to explore their efficacy in the field of education. This is because the objective of educational institutions is not solely focused on financial gain. Stakeholders within the same institution may also have a unified objective to develop an environment for the ethical use of GAI, thereby avoiding conflicts of interest. Furthermore, the institute may establish incentives or penalties contingent upon students' compliance with the guidelines. The following section will examine the development of GAI ethical guidelines within the Korean context.

## 2.2  Developing an Ethical Foundation for Generative AI in South Korea

Similar to other countries, there has been considerable interest at the national level in ChatGPT in Korea. This has led to the production of a substantial number of news articles, research papers, and reports by organisations, not only about GAI technologies but also about concerns, threats, and ethical issues related to it. In the Korean context, this response was noteworthy in light of the dearth of discourse on ethical matters pertaining to previous digital technologies. However, it is not particularly exceptional as the government, numerous organisations and researchers have been striving to develop an ethical foundation for the use of AI in Korea.

In December 2020, the MOSI announced the Standard of Ethics for AI, which placed the utmost value on "Humanity". The standard comprised three principles, "human dignity", "common good", and "appropriateness of technology", as well as ten core factors, including "protection of privacy", "solidarity", and "transparency" [31]. Subsequently, the government established a strategy for reliable AI including the establishment of a trust building mechanism, an AI impact assessment, and the reinforcement of education in AI ethics [32]. In February 2022, the International Association for Artificial Intelligence and Ethics (IAAE)[2] was inaugurated under the MOSI. The AI Ethics Charter was revealed to comprise ethical principles for experts and users, in addition to the Ethics Guidelines for Digital Humans. [33]. A substantial body of research on AI ethics and pertinent ethical issues has been conducted in the country: the formulation of ethical guidelines for using AI in specific domains or its development strategy [34–37]; the examination of research trends or challenges in AI ethics [38–41]; the critique of the development of AI ethics [42]; and the AI perception over ethical issues [43]. Despite the numerous endeavours and studies conducted in this field, the evaluation of AI ethical considerations revealed a tendency towards abstract, opaque, developer management-oriented, industry regulation-focused approaches, and a lack of reflection on the implications for diverse sociocultural backgrounds [10, 11].

With regard to GAI, it appeared to be a nascent trend to conduct studies on GAI and education-related subjects and to establish their own guidelines or ethical considerations for the ethical utilisation of GAI in HEIs. Kim and Min [44] reviewed 63 Korean studies on ChatGPT in education and found that "educational application" and "generation of contents" were the most prevalent interests in Korea. Park [11] concentrated on the

---

[2] The organisation was established in March 2019 under the name of Korea Artificial Intelligence Ethics Association (KAIEA) but they changed the name later.

issues of GAI hallucination and proposed themes for GAI ethics education for elementary school students. There have been numerous studies on the application of GAI in university classroom. These studies examine the experiences and perceptions of the students [45–48], students' ethical perceptions [49], their intentions of using GAI [50], and teaching strategies [51–54]. Han [55] devised a writing course utilising ChatGPT at his university and investigated students' experiences and perceptions. While the majority of students (91.2%) perceived ChatGPT to be beneficial in writing, they exhibited reservations regarding the dependability of the outcomes generated by ChatGPT. Furthermore, the research assessed four GAI guidelines established by universities in Korea. Jeon [56] conducted research at the university level on current issues and responses associated with ChatGPT and also identified traits of the five universities' AI/GAI guidelines. The establishment of manuals, guidelines, or instructions related to the use of ChatGPT was identified as one of the trends in Korea.

Although Korea is a relatively recent entrant to the field of AI and GAI ethics, it has nevertheless demonstrated a distinctive response compared to other digital technologies, evidenced by the considerable volume of research and the existence of established ethical guidelines. However, it remains unclear whether this phenomenon can be interpreted as an authentic grassroots movement for the development of GAI ethics in the country. This is due to a paucity of studies conducted to explore the features of the development of the GAI ethical guidelines in Korea. Accordingly, this paper examines the feature of the development of the ethical use of GAI in Korea, with a view to exploring whether it exhibits a revelation of authenticity. In the existing literature on GAI, the term "authenticity" was typically used to elucidate the originality of the assignments performed by students themselves [19]. While the definition of "authenticity" varies, this study accepted the explanation provided by the Authentic Personality Model to define the term. In this study, authenticity refers to a state of "acting in alignment with one's personal goals" with no mere adoption of "external influence" [57]. This study focuses on the ethical guidelines established by HEIs in Korea, as well as the motivations behind their production and subsequent efforts. It also identifies the alignment between the motivation and the element of guidelines and subsequent activities. In addition, it explores GAI guidelines in Western countries to examine any distinctive points of those in Korea.

## 3  Methodology

### 3.1  Data Collection

The objective of this review is to identify the rationale behind the establishment of guidelines for the utilisation of GAI in HEIs and the supplementary measures employed to implement the guidelines within their respective institutions. Through such a review and comparison with trends in the West, it seeks to examine the authenticity of the developments in HEIs GAI guidelines. In order to obtain data, this research employed a systematic approach to the selection of HEIs guidelines, taking into account the universities' programmes and locations, as well as the level of application of the guidelines: For the purposes of this review, universities were selected if they had established a department or programmes related to AI and were located in the Seoul metropolitan area, including Seoul, Incheon and Gyeonggi Province, where major universities are located. This seemed to demonstrate the development of an AI or GAI friendly environment in the university and the ability to generate GAI guidelines, including faculty members with expertise in GAI. As reported by the Ministry of Education in Korea, as of the 2023 academic year, 76 universities out of 190 had established AI-related programmes [58]. Of these, 36 universities in the Seoul metropolitan area were selected for review. While the selection criteria were limited in that they did not necessarily reflect the situation at all 190 universities in the country, the review was conducted in a systematic manner, thereby saving time.

At the outset of the review process, the official websites of 36 universities were accessed with the objective of locating the GAI guidelines or ethical codes. The keywords including "Generative AI", "Generative Artificial Intelligence", "Generative AI guidelines", "Generative AI guide", "ChatGPT", "ChatGPT ethical guidelines", and "ChatGPT guidelines" were used for search. A number of universities were excluded from the review process on the grounds that they had adopted the GAI guidelines established by other institutes or governmental organisations (such as Gyeonggi University). Only those universities that had created their own guidelines at the university level, rather than at the department level, were included in the review.

Following the completion of the inclusion process, 11 universities were identified as remaining for further consideration. The 11 universities had guidelines or ethical guidelines for the use of GAI (see Table 1). In order to conduct the analysis, the webpages of the guidelines themselves, any announcements regarding their establishment, and other webpages related to GAI were extracted. These included additional information on how to use GAI, examples of other students' use, and notes for relevant seminars. The aforementioned process for review, searching, and extraction was conducted between 1 July and 7 July 2024.[3] It is possible that some guidelines from a few universities may have been overlooked if they were only disseminated within an internal circle, as publicly accessible websites, webpages, and documents were solely included for the purposes of this research.

## 3.2 Conducting the Review

In order to differentiate between the methodologies employed in the analysis of the review guidelines themselves and those used to examine other pertinent data, such as official notifications of the launch of guidelines or educational programmes, two distinct levels of analysis were undertaken. These were the key components in the development of the ethical use of GAI and GAI guidelines.

**Key Components in the Development of the Ethical Use of GAI.** Key components in the development of the ethical use of GAI included announcements of establishment of guidelines and subsequent activities. It is challenging to enhance GAI ethics by merely introducing guidelines; additional measures are required [70]. The objective of this study was to analyse the official announcement to ascertain the rationale behind the release of the GAI guidelines and additional programmes, with the aim of evaluating the

---

[3] In order to supplement the existing corpus of materials pertaining to GAI ethics education with recent contributions, an additional search was conducted between 25 July and 1 August.

**Table 1.** GAI guidelines information for HEIs in Korea

| Univ | Title of guidelines | Issue/latest revision | Dept. in charge or inquiries | Delivery and quantity |
|---|---|---|---|---|
| Korea (KR) [59] | Basic Guidelines for the Use of ChatGPT | 15 Mar 2023 | Digital info center | PDF file/ 373 words |
| Sungkyunkwan (SK) [60] | Instructor Response Guide, Proper Use of ChatGPT and Learning Ethics | Mar 2023 | University | Webpage/ 2,961 words |
| Sejong (SJ) [61] | Guidelines for the Basic Use of Generative AI in Teaching and Learning | Apr 2023 | University | Webpage/ 411 words |
| Chung-Ang (CA) [62] | Guidelines for the Use of Generative AI | 20 Apr 2023 /9 Apr 2023 | Library and academic info center | Webpage/ 851 words |
| National Univ. of Transport (KN) [63] | Ethical Guidelines for the Use of Generative AI | 3 Jul 2023 | Education innovation center | Image file/ 224 words |
| Ehaw Womans (EW) [64] | Ethical Guidelines for the Use of Generative AI | 12 Jul 2023 | Education innovation center | Webpage/ 2,011 words |
| Kyung Hee (KH) [65] | Guidelines for the Use of Chat GPT | 21 Aug 2023 | University | PDF file/ 549 words |
| Catholic (CT) [66] | Guidelines for the Use of Generative AI | 28 Aug 2023 | Center for teaching and learning | PDF file/ 574 words |
| Dongguk (DK) [67] | Guidelines for the Use of Chat GPT | 1 Sept 2023 | University | HWP file/ 435 words |
| Sungkonghoe (SH) [68] | Student Guide for Proper Use of Generative AI, Teaching Tips for Using Generative AI | 4 Oct 2023 | Education innovation center | Webpage/ 553 words |
| Yonsei (YS) [69] | Guidelines for the use of generative AI | 27 May 2024 | Research ethics center | PDF file/ 2,349 words |

authenticity of the efforts made to build a GAI ethical foundation in universities. The categorisation of the universities was dependent on the range of materials provided and the content of the guidelines and announcements. Four groups were thus created. The materials provided by the universities in relation to the GAI guidelines were initially categorised into five as follows:

(a) A guideline that merely comprises elements devoid of supplementary clarification,

(b) A concise announcement devoid of any rationale or distinct notification,

(c) GAI guidelines accompanied by detailed explanations or illustrative examples,

(d) A notice disclosing the rationale behind the introduction of guidelines,

(e) Additional initiatives such as workshops, seminars, or conferences.

In accordance with the search and review procedures, the data was organised into the categories presented in Table 2 and detailed are explained in the following section.

**Table 2.** Four groups formed through the review process

|     | (a) Guidelines elements only | (b) Notice without drive | (c) Detailed guidelines | (d) Notice with drive | (e) Extra efforts |    |
| --- | --- | --- | --- | --- | --- | --- |
| **SJ** | v | v |   |   |   | G1 |
| **KN** | v | v |   |   |   |    |
| **KR** | v |   |   | v | v | G2 |
| **KH** | v |   |   | v | v |    |
| **CT** |   | v | v |   | v | G3 |
| **SH** |   | v | v |   | v |    |
| **SK** |   |   | v | v | v |    |
| **CA** |   |   | v | v | v |    |
| **EW** |   |   | v | v | v | G4 |
| **DK** |   |   | v | v | v |    |
| **YS** |   |   | v | v | v |    |

**GAI Guidelines.** In order to systematically analyse the guidelines, three steps were taken and the fields/categories created by B.L. Moorhouse et al. were adopted (Appendix 1). First, eleven collected guidelines were inductively reviewed using the three main fields ("Academic integrity", "Advice on assessment design", and "Communication with students") and their ten subcategories [19]. Sentences or elements in the guidelines that matched the three fields and ten categories were labelled with the same field/category name. However, many new fields and subcategories were needed to create because Moorhouse et al. analysed 23 universities' guidelines with the element for instructors only. Thus, in the second step, the guidelines were deductively reviewed to label the other sentences and elements with new field and category names. The review resulted in the eight main fields. The number of subcategories in each field ranged from two to five, making a total of 27 subcategories created (see Fig. 1). The following table was also created to show the details of each guideline (see Table 3). The number in each cell indicates the number of elements in the same guideline. Elements for students and for instructors were highlighted in dark green and light green respectively. For example, YS has four elements about plagiarism, two for students and two for instructors. To count the number of elements, generally, each sentence provided was counted as one, but where the guidelines had a hierarchy such as headings and sub-sentences, only the sub-sentences were counted only to avoid duplication (YS). Elements were counted separately when a phrase had two different elements (GT). Sentences that provided additional information, such as the URL of the AI detection programme, were excluded when counting the number of elements (YS).

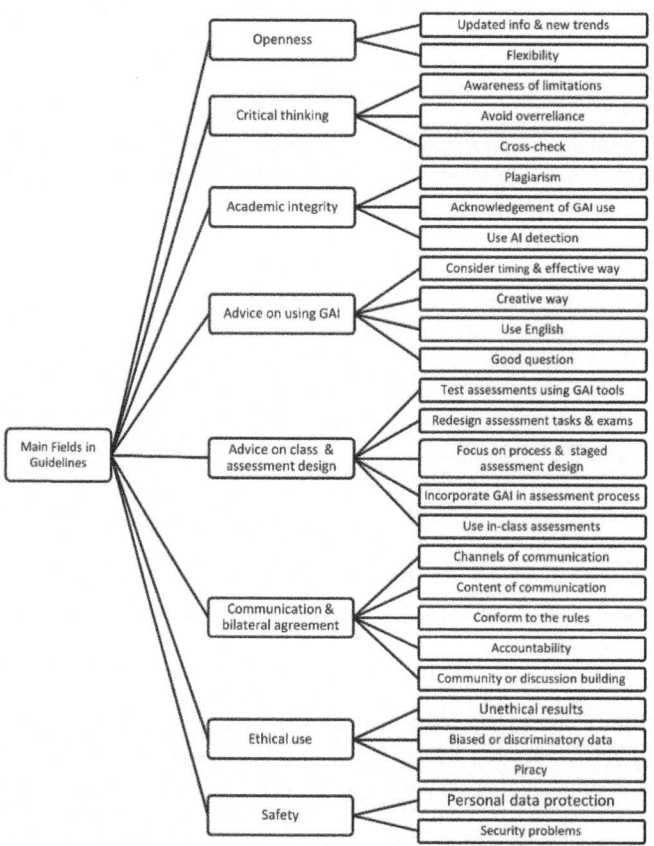

**Fig. 1.** Main fields and categories in GAI guidelines of HEIs in Korea

The final step in the review was to compare the fields/categories of Korean HEIs' GAI guidelines with those of Moorhouse et al. who collected GAI guidelines from Western HEIs. The process was carried out to examine whether GAI guidelines in Korean universities were established by producing uniqueness, or simply followed the Western trends or features of their guidelines. Subcategories only for students in Fig. 1 were removed as Moorhouse et al. reflected elements of guidelines only for instructors. After the comparison, a new figure was created as shown in Fig. 2. White coloured cells were

**Table 3.** Details of Korean HEIs' GAI guidelines.

| | Univ. | KR | SK | SJ | CA | KN | EW | KH | CT | DK | SH | YS |
|---|---|---|---|---|---|---|---|---|---|---|---|---|
| Open-ness | Updated info & new trends | | | | 1 / 1 | | 1 | | 1 / 1 | | | 1 |
| | Flexibility | | | 1 / 1 | | | | | 1 | | | |
| Critical thinking | Awareness of limitations | | 2 | | 1 / 2 | 1 | | | 1 | 1 | 2 | 1 |
| | Avoid overreliance | | | 1 | 1 / 1 | 1 | 2 | 1 | 1 / 1 | 1 | 1 | 1 |
| | Cross-check | 1 | 2 / 1 | 1 / 1 | 1 | 1 | 1 / 1 | 1 | 1 / 1 | 1 | 1 | 2 |
| Academic integrity | Plagiarism | 1 | 1 | 1 | 1 | 1 / 1 | 3 / 1 | 1 | 1 | 1 / 1 | 2 / 1 | 2 / 2 |
| | Acknowledge-ment | | | 2 | | 1 | 1 | | 1 | 1 | | |
| | AI detection | | 1 | | | | 1 | | | 1 | | 1 |
| Advice on using GAI | Timing & effective way | | | | | | 1 | 1 | | | | |
| | Creative way | | | | | | 1 | | | | | |
| | Use English | | 1 | | | | | | | | | |
| | Good question | | 1 | | 1 / 1 | | | | | | | |
| Advice on class & task design | Test using GAI | | 1 | | | | | | 1 | | | 1 |
| | Redesign assessment | 1 | 1 | 2 | | 1 | 6 | | 1 | 1 | 1 | 1 |
| | Process & staged | 1 | 1 | | | | 2 | | | | | 1 |
| | Incorporate GAI tools | | 1 | 1 | | | 1 | | | | | |
| | Use in-class assessments | | 3 | | | | 1 | | | 1 | | 1 |
| Comms & bilateral deal | Channels of comms | | | | 1 | 1 | | 2 | | 1 | 1 | 1 |
| | Content of comms | | | | 3 | 1 | 1 | 2 | 1 | 1 | | 2 |
| | Conform to the rules | | | 2 | 1 | 1 | | 1 | 1 | 1 | | 2 |
| | Accountability | | | 1 / 1 | 2 / 1 | | 5 | 1 / 2 | 1 | 1 | 1 | 1 / 1 |
| | Community or discussion | | 1 / 1 | 1 / 2 | | 2 | 2 / 1 | | | | | |
| Ethical use | Unethical results | | | | | | 1 | | | | 1 | 1 |
| | Biased data | | 1 | | | 1 | | | | 1 | 1 / 1 | 1 |
| | Piracy | | 2 | | | | | | | 1 | 1 | 1 |
| | Fairness | | | | | | 1 | | | | | |
| Safety | Data protection | | | 1 | | 1 | | 1 | 1 / 1 | | | 1 |
| | Security problems | | | 1 | | | | 1 | 1 | | | 1 |
| | Number of ethical aspects | 4 | 21 | 19 | 19 | 15 | 31 | 14 | 18 | 15 | 14 | 26 |

42      S. Yun

original fields/categories in Moorhouse et al. and the five main fields and eleven subcategories highlighted in yellow were created by reviewing this study. Three subcategories, highlighted in light red were modified by adding "class", "bilateral agreement" and "exam" of each.

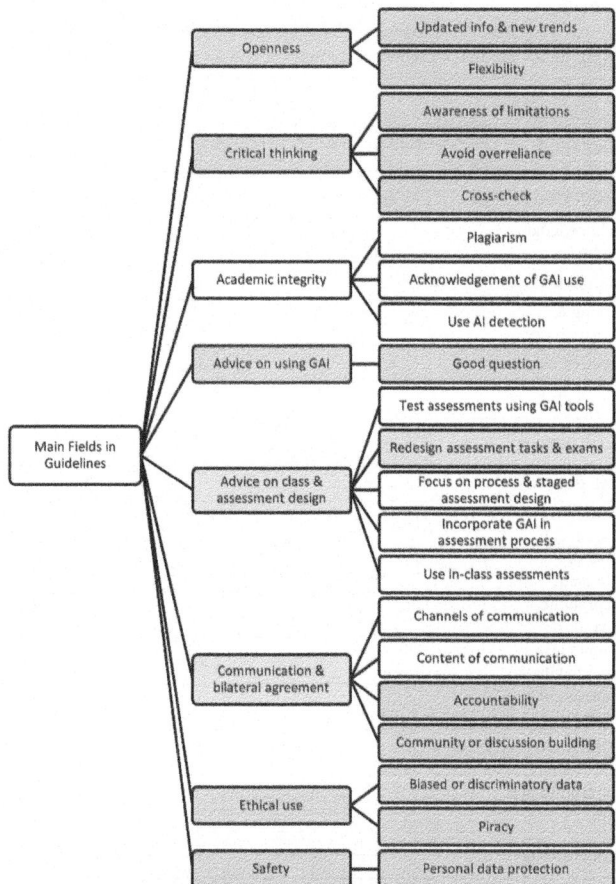

**Fig. 2.** Comparison of the main fields and categories in the GAI guidelines

Moorhouse et al. produced the figure using the guidelines of HEIs located in Western countries, including USA, UK, and Canada. In light of this, a comparative analysis between the figure of Moorhouse et al. and Fig. 2 allows for a comparison of GAI guidelines in Korean HEIs with those of Western HEIs. However, one Japanese university was included in the figure produced by Moorhouse et al., and the subsequent changes or updates to this figure could not be reflected. It should also be noted that this study focuses on authenticity and distinctiveness in the development of GAI guidelines and additional activities, rather than on the specific elements of the guidelines they have. Therefore, this research has analysed and identified elements related to the research topic.

# 4 Finding

The general information obtained through the review process was that the period of establishment of the GAI guidelines was from March 2023 to May 2024. KR was the first to establish the GAI guideline and YS was the last. The issuers or responsible departments of the GAI guidelines were different from each university, such as the Education Innovation Center or the Research Ethics Center. There were mainly two types of guidelines distributed, half of the HEIs provided a website type and the other half offered a downloadable type such as documents or image files. While some provided guidelines for both students and instructors (KR), other universities provided two separate guidelines (SK, KN, EW, CT, DK), but some of them additionally added guidelines for both, although they had a separate one (SJ, CA). One of the guidelines had three different guidelines because the university added guidelines for researchers (YS). However, the guidelines for researchers were excluded from the scope of his research.

## 4.1 Announcement and Follow-Up Activities

As illustrated in Table 2, Group 1, SJ and KN, furnished (a) relatively straightforward guidelines devoid of supplementary clarifications pertaining to each element (b) without official declaration regarding the rationale behind the establishment of the guidelines by the issuers. Group 2, KR and KH, exhibits similarities to Group 1 in that they have (a) simple guidelines. However, (d) they have taken the additional step of announcing the launch of these guidelines, accompanied by an explanation of their motivation, and (e) have provided seminars or written materials related to GAI. Group 3, GT and SH, established (c) guidelines with detailed explanations and examples, and engaged in (e) additional activities to develop of the ethical use of GAI in their universities. However, (b) they did not issue a separate announcement with their purpose of producing GAI guidelines. Group 4 may be considered an ideal type in building an ethical foundation for using GAI in their universities, as they have created (c) detailed and specific guidelines with additional explanations and samples, (d) announced the launching of the guidelines with their purpose and motivations, and provided (e) additional resources or opportunities such as seminars, lectures, or competitions to support their students and instructors in understanding the guidelines, obtaining relevant knowledge, and being involved in the process of developing an ethical environment for the proper use of GAI. The Group 4 universities are SK, CA, EW, DK, and YS.

With regard to the matter of announcements, it proved challenging to ascertain underlying motivations and objectives of four universities, SJ, KN, CT, and SH, due to the absence of the official announcement pertaining to the establishment of GAI guidelines. In contrast, seven universities disseminated official announcements with the intention of informing about the establishment of GAI guidelines and promoting them. Among the seven, CA, KH, and DK provided relatively concise notices that alluded to similar purposes, including the rapid response to changes, the encouragement of the utilisation of GAI in education, and the ethical use of the aforementioned guidelines. [62, 67, 71]. The remaining four, SK, EW, and YS in Group 4 and KR, an exceptional case included in Group 2, formally articulated the rationale and objectives behind the establishment of GAI, offering insights into their perceptions of GAI, proposed countermeasures, and suggestions for ethical guidelines.

In their announcement, KR articulated key principles, "ChatGPT cannot produce results that exceed the user's own abilities" and "Using the technological tools that can save effort required in traditional educational methods should be encouraged". They also highlighted "the rights of learners to use GAI". Their purpose is that "instead of blocking the spread of technology", guide student to "rationally embrace GAI" and to "engage in active and participatory learning using GAI". Additionally, measures to avert prospective issues, including, "education for GAI ethics", "collection empirical data", and "reflection instructors' feedback" were outlined [72]. SK perceived the introduction of ChatGPT as "new challenge" and believed that "cheating and plagiarism should be taken to prevent". They emphasised "effective and ethical ways of using GAI" and announced the formation of "a research committee and a response taskforce" with the objective of "developing educational models and appropriate assessment methods, as well as enhancing GAI ethics and digital literacy education" [73]. EW emphasised four directions of GAI ethics, such as "alignment with the goals of university education" and "respect of mutual cooperation and diversity [74]". YS advocated for "users to assume personal responsibility, engage in critical thinking, and apply GAI in a manner that aligns with established ethical standards." [75].

It is noteworthy that the universities provided official announcement with their perception, goals, or purposes, such as those in Groups 2 and 4, also have endeavoured to provide a plethora of opportunities and materials to their respective student and instructor bodies. SK has developed and provided most and various opportunities to its university members: a comprehensive guide website for ChatGPT, intensive workshops, regular seminars, video and document materials, manuals, teaching and learning tips, online spaces for sharing opinions and feedback, an instructors' community, and FAQ [60][4] (see Appendix 2). In particular, the two 20-h intensive workshops for students on using ChatGPT in their studies appeared to be an effective method of enhancing knowledge proficiency in its appropriate usage, as opposed to a one-time workshop format [76, 77]. Furthermore, the results of a student survey on the use of ChatGPT and the incorporation of samples in the classroom have been disseminated [78]. Additionally, an instructors' community has been established, which could serve as a valuable repository of information for updating the GAI guidelines with specific details [79].

Similarly, EW has tried to provide various additional materials to their students and instructors: over 40 videos and nearly 20 documents associated with using GAI effectively and ethically, such as ways of generating prompt and using Bing Image Creator [80]. One noteworthy example of the opportunities provided is the "Learning methods contest utilising GAI" [81]. Since 2023, this contest has been held annually in June, with the winning entries shared on the website. They have also offered workshops and press release. KR has produced news articles with some analysing GAI guidelines, sharing practical experiences utilising ChatGPT in writing classes, and conducting an in-depth review about ChatGPT [72]. They also provided videos and opportunities for

---

[4] In cases where there is an excessive number of webpages pertaining to the materials and opportunities offered by universities, the representative references and examples are provided in this chapter and in Appendix 2.

academic seminars, forums, and special lectures [82]. Especially, KR has incorporated the "Guidelines for the Use of GAI such as ChatGPT" into the standard midterm and final examination notifications since 2023 [83]. In the case of YS, they have provided a variety of documents, materials, and lectures, as well as holding a conference on the subjects of "AI literacy and ethics in the GAI era" and "Chat GPT writing contest [84]." Nevertheless, the conference and contest were not solely intended for the university community; they were also open to the general public. Opportunities for seminars, workshops, and contest and document typed materials were also founded on the websites of KH (Group 2), DK, CA (Group 4), CT and SH (Group 3). DK and CT have provided intensive workshops, CT and CA have held contests, and DK has shared the survey results of GAI experiences [85–87].

## 4.2  Guidelines for Generative AI in HEIs

**Guideline Review.**   The simple guidelines were relatively brief, with an average word count of less than or around 500 words (Group 1 and 2). In contrast, the specific guidelines with examples and additional explanations were considerably longer (Group 3 and 4), with an average word count of over 500 words (CA, CT, DK, SH), and in some cases, exceeding 2,000 words (SK, EW, YS). Additionally, the highest number of elements in a single guideline was 31 (EW), with 26 (YS) and 21 (SK) also exceeding this figure. The lowest number was four, as observed in the case of KR. Despite the simplicity of the guidelines produced by EHIs, the majority of them included the introduction of GAI, a definition, examples, an analysis of their strengths, and a discussion of potential problems.

In terms of style, the majority of guidelines presented documented guidelines that were typed in a standardised format (KR, SJ, CA, KN, KH, DK, SH). Some created guidelines with a variety of images, infographics, and other design elements, such as highlighting important words and sentences (CT, YS). The guidelines provided by SK and EW were particularly noteworthy for their comprehensive and diverse structural compositions, encompassing an array of elements including the introduction, strengths, and limitations of ChatGPT, instructions on its utilisation, an overview of alternative GAI such as Bing and Bard, illustrative examples of ChatGPT applications, instances of potential misuse and corresponding countermeasures, and guidance on the use of the GAI detection tool. The two universities had a shared characteristic in that they had separate websites through which they disseminated information related to GAI [88, 89]. In addition, EW was the only university creating question type ethical elements. For example, "Do I make an effort to verify the accuracy and reliability of outputs when using GAI?" for "Cross-check" and "Do I make an effort to avoid plagiarism, creating false information, or spreading others' knowledge or ideas when using GAI?" for "Plagiarism" [64].

The decision-making process regarding the utilisation of GAI within the classroom, including the extent to which they are employed, is at the discretion of the instructors (KR, YS). If there is no mention of this, the existence of the policy itself proves that the university does not prohibit the use of GAI. However, CA shows three options in their guideline, prohibiting the use of GAI, allowing the use of GAI with the permission of instructors and citation, and free use of GAI. The guideline requires instructors to give a reason if they wish to ban GAI in their class and the use of GAI would then be considered cheating. In the case of using GAI being used with permission, the guideline outlines the duties of the instructor, such as informing the student of any limitations on use. With regard to free use, it was suggested that teachers should redesign the assessment and examination to encourage critical analysis and creativity. Each university has a different title, format, and composition of the guidelines. Some of them have the words "ethics", "ethical", or "proper" in their main titles or at least their subtitles (SK, KN, EW, SH). Although most of fields/categories are related to ethical and proper use, the guidelines with ethics-related words in their title had more subcategories directly related to "Ethical use". DK and YS also had categories directly related to ethics despite not having "ethics" in their title.

**Comparison and Distinctive Points.**   With the comparison the main fields/categories between Korean HEIs (Fig. 1) and 23 top-ranked HEIs (Appendix 1), several changes were found. The major difference is the number of the main fields and subcategories as Fig. 1 has much more categories which is related to how issuers do positioning instructors. While the most subcategories in the Appendix 1 are related to the role of instructors such as "Use AI detection" and "Use in-class assessments", Fig. 1 included more categories associated with how to use GAI effectively, appropriately, and ethically. Requiring instructors to think critically by avoiding overreliance to GAI or conducting double check about results produced by GAI with original resources or to consider potential problems in terms of biased or discriminatory data produced, breach piracy, or leak of personal data to use GAI ethically and safely shows that instructors were positioned as users as well rather than as just instructors.

Other changes are related to modifications of fields/categories' name. In Fig. 2, "Communication with student", one of the main categories was renamed to "Communication and bilateral agreement" to expand the application boundaries from instructors only to both instructors and students, and to clarify elements related to setting and following rules in class. In the guidelines of YS, "Bilateral agreement" refers to making an agreement on the principal of using GAI in a class in advance between instructors and students and instructors have to guide students to follow the rules as well as students have to conform to the rules with full knowledge of them. With renaming, "Accountability" and "Community or discussion building" were newly created as sub-categories. "Advice on assessment design" was slightly changed because "class" was added in the middle of the name of the elements. At the end of "Redesign assessment tasks", "exam" was added because there are more exam-based tests rather than essay-based assignment in Korea. "Openness", "Critical thinking", "Advice on using GAI", "Ethical use", and "Safety" were newly created as a main theme. "Updated information and new trends" and "Flexibility" were created as sub-categories of "Openness". "Awareness of GAI's limitations", "Avoid overreliance on GAI", and "Cross check" were added as sub-categories under the "Critical thinking" and "Good question" were included for "Advice on using GAI". "Unethical results", "Biased or discriminatory data", and "Piracy" were produced for the main category of "Ethical use", and "Personal data protection" were added for "Safety".

In terms of the content of the guidelines, several Korean/institutional context-based categories were established. For students, in Fig. 1, there was a main area of "Advice on using GAI" which included "Consider timing and effective way" to know the appropriate time and way to use GAI (EW, KH), "Creative way" (EW), "Use English" (SK) and "Good question" (SK, CA). SK was the only university to suggest that students use English if they were not satisfied with the GAI answers. This category could only be created in the country where English is not a first language. Under the main theme of "Communication and bilateral agreement", there were five subcategories: Regarding "Channels of communication", syllabus was mostly mentioned as a channel (CA, KN, KH, DK, SH, YS) as well as verbal announcements (YS). KH provided a form of the "Honor Code" having a space for signature and suggested instructors to use it if they need it. In terms of "Content of communication", the boundaries of possible using and cheating, cautions, and purpose and value of in-class activities or assessments using GAI were highlighted (EW, CA, KN, KH, GT, DK, YS). "Conform to the rules" is element associated with a duty of the student, for example, check and follow the guidance of each class (SJ, CA, KN, GT, DK, YS). "Accountability" refers to the responsibility for problems that arise as a result of neglecting one's responsibilities (YS) - setting and announcing the rules for instructors and following the rules for students (SJ, CA, KH, EW, GT, DK, SH, YS). DK showed sample sentences to announce the use of GAI in a class. The sentence included "DK Education Ethical Charter" to emphasise that if students did not follow instructions related to the use of GAI, it would be considered as breaking the charter. "Community or discussion building" was associated with efforts to respect the direction, values and requirements of the university and to develop discussion to seek better educational direction using GAI (SJ, KN, EW). Through the question-type elements of the GAI guidelines, EW asked students whether they respected the university's core values of "creativity and challenge", "communication and innovation", "compassion and inclusion".

## 5   Discussion and Conclusion

This study undertook a review of the GAI guidelines established by eleven universities in Korea, together with relevant announcements to inform of the establishment of the guidelines, and additional materials or opportunities they have provided to enhance members' knowledge and development in the ethical use of GAI. The objective was to ascertain the rationale and purpose underlying the establishment of GAI guidelines by Korean HEIs. This would enable an evaluation of the extent to which the guidelines could facilitate the creation of an ethical environment for the proper use of GAI in a manner that reveals its authenticity. The eleven universities were classified into four groups according to their level of commitment to developing the ethical use of GAI, as reflected in the content of their announcements, the specificity of the guidelines they provided, and the existence of supplementary initiatives. The universities that provided guidelines with explanations and examples and announcements with their purpose have a greater number of opportunities and materials related to GAI and its ethical use for their students and instructors. The guidelines were analysed inductively according to the main fields and categories accepted by Moorhouse et al. and deductively with iterative review. The review yielded eight main fields and 27 categories. In order to comparison with the fields and categories created by Moorhouse et al., which were derived from the GAI guidelines of 23 of the world's top 50 ranked universities, only those elements pertaining to instructors were extracted. There are several discrepancies when comparing the Korean HEIs' guidelines with those of Western HEIs: Instructors are designated as GAI users as well, rather than merely regarded as teachers in the GAI guidelines of Korean universities and there are a number of other main/subcategories in the guidelines due to the differences in both the way instructors are positioned and the contextual background.

The investigation revealed that, rather than such a comparison, exploring the alignment between the announced aims of developing GAI guidelines and the guidelines themselves and extra activities provided further insights into the authenticity and peculiarity of the bottom-up movement for developing the ethical use of GAI in Korea. Furthermore, their announcements unambiguously demonstrated their genuine motivation to create an ethical foundation for GAI, thereby proving that they had their own intentions rather than merely following the Western trend. In the case of KR, while the guideline itself was relatively simple, the university has offered a range of supplementary materials, including practical cases on the applications of GAI in a classroom and on the impact of GAI. This was aligned with their goal of promoting active and participatory learning through the utilisation of GAI. SK and EW can also be presented as illustrative examples of the revelation of authenticity in the developing procedure of GAI ethics. As SK highlighted in their announcement, they have endeavoured to build a research committee and a response taskforce by launching a website for the use of ChatGPT in the university and an instructor community. Furthermore, SK has created three elements for ethical use in its guideline and provided a variety of materials to improve GAI ethics and digital literacy education, which is in line with its objectives. Not as like the newly launched website only for GAI as SK, but EW has also provided numerous materials including GAI guidelines through the website called "THE BEST education integrated service". EW also announced the need to develop of GAI ethics in a way that is in line with the goals and values of university education. In alignment with its stated core values, "creativity and challenge", "communication and innovation", and "compassion and inclusion", EW was the only university to include "creative use of GAI" in its guideline [64, 90]. In addition, the nine elements, the largest number of eleven universities, provided for the main categories of "Communication and bilateral agreement": They suggested to use GAI considering each other's growth; they stressed the respect of personality, diversity, and fairness; and ask students and instructors to actively join to building discussion. It is also noteworthy that they used the term "ethical" at the beginning of their GAI guideline and emphasised ethical use and critical thinking throughout the guideline, in line with one of the goals mentioned in the announcement of the establishment of the GAI guideline, "ethical and critical utilisation of GAI" [74].

In particular, there were examples of good practice that demonstrated how GAI ethics could be more closely aligned with the specific needs and values of their organisations: Not only EW, but also CA, and CT have held in contests associated with using GAI and EW uploaded the contents awarded at the competitions on their website to provide examples of creative, proper, and ethical use of GAI. Such a contest could serve to draw the attention of students to the use of GAI and the associated guidelines, while simultaneously collecting empirical cases illustrating the ways in which students utilise GAI in their daily lives. Other empirical resources, such as survey results related to the use of ChatGPT from SK, utilising samples in lectures, and feedback collected by the instructor community, could serve as crucial references for the development of more tailored or context-specific GAI guidelines and GAI ethics. It is imperative to provide such empirical resources to build knowledge and discourses surrounding ethical guidelines that could support the development of a GAI ethical foundation. This is because the guidelines themselves lack the capacity for enforcement [10, 15, 16].

Further efforts could be identified as potential means of overcoming the limitations of the GAI guidelines. It was not an enforcement, but KR incorporated the GAI guidelines into the official introduction of mid/final term exams, and KH provided a form of agreement for following the "ChatGPT Honor Code" with their students. These appeared to be effective methods for fostering engagement with students in the development of GAI guidelines, as most students are primarily concerned with their academic performance and the signed agreement serves as a reminder of their obligation to adhere to the guidelines. In the case of DK, the guideline made reference to their "Education Ethical Charter", which appears to assist students in acquiring an integrated knowledge of the new guideline and the existing values [67]. This could be an alternative approach to fostering authenticity in the development of the ethical use of GAI within their communities. Several additional things of EW made their ethical guidelines authentic: EW created question typed ethical elements encouraging readers to think the answers to each element. For instructors, EW provides guidelines for each phase of the semester: when designing a class, the initial stage, the midpoint, and the end of semester. Sample announcements were also provided, which elucidated the ethical elements in the guidelines. Here are additional insights. In order to establish authentic GAI guidelines, it would be beneficial to utilise empirical studies as a valuable resource for the development of context-based ethical factors. For example, Han argued that "accurate searching ways" and "normative ethics for adapting information" should be provided subsequent to a writing course utilising [55]. Institutions might consider reflecting the results of empirical studies.

In conclusion, the bottom-up movement in Korea to develop the ethical use of GAI based on the context of their institutions could be described as a 'work in progress'. This is because only eleven universities out of 36 HEIs with AI-related programmes located in Greater Seoul have established GAI guidelines, and not all 11 HEIs showed the same level of commitment to promoting their guidelines. However, the establishment of GAI guidelines itself could be considered as the first step in creating an ethical environment for GAI. In addition, there have been attempts that deserve attention when considering ways to improve authenticity in GAI ethics: unambiguous motivation to lead the development of GAI guidelines; reflecting institutions' core values or existing ethical codes; signed agreements and additional announcements for midterm/final exams to address current limitations related to the power of enforcement guidelines with; and ongoing efforts to identify current and future needs and difficulties of students and instructors.

Among the EHIs in this study, EW showed a good example of developing authentic GAI ethics by providing long and specific guidelines and various relevant activities. One of the possible reasons for the superior movement in GAI ethics was that the university was selected for the 2022 AI Convergence Innovation Talent Development Program sponsored by the MOSI [91]. With up to four years of support, the university could run a specialised AI convergence curriculum and promote related research. It implies that more funding and support would be needed to develop authentic movements for GAI ethics. In the case of SK, however, there was no clear evidence of external funding, although they showed a similar level of commitment to EW: SK launched a separate website for GAI and provided the highest number of opportunities for their university members including intensive seminars, survey results, and instructors' community. If further research could identify the motivation and resources that underpin their high quality of commitment, it would help other institutes to develop authentic GAI guidelines. In addition, the establishment of 'GAI guidelines for university' could be considered in terms of the composition of experts to produce and review GAI guidelines, the appropriate period for updating the guidelines, the effective ways of distributing of the guidelines, and how to deal with enquiries about the guidelines from students and instructors. The final suggestion was to produce other language versions, at least in English. At present, there are many international students and faculties in Korea [92]. Only the Honor Code of KH was provided in both Korean and English versions. In summary, this research makes a contribution by demonstrating the process of verifying the authenticity and distinctive features of the development of the ethical use of GAI in educational institutions. Furthermore, it offers a number of illustrative examples and insights into the development of authenticity and distinctiveness in GAI guidelines.

# Appendix

## Appendix 1. The Main Fields in Guidelines Created by B.L. Moorhouse et al.

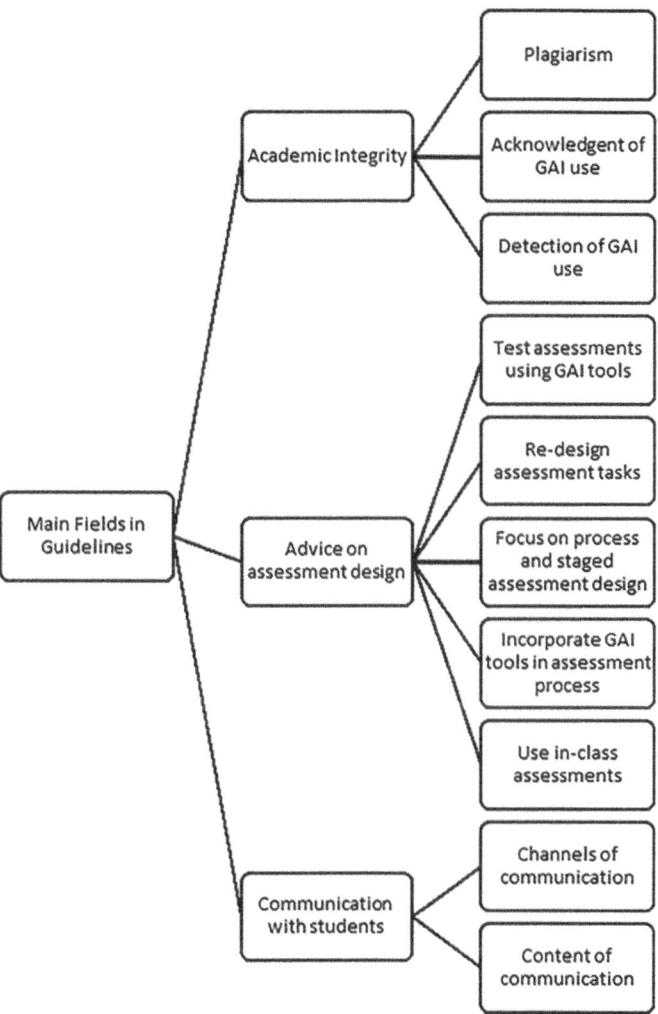

## Appendix 2. Follow-Up Activities

| | Category | Contents (title) | Target | Organiser | Date | |
|---|---|---|---|---|---|---|
| KR | Academic seminar (5) | e.g. Advanced Data Analysis of GPT-4 | Researcher of the institute | Course Education Institute | 15/03/24 – 31/05/24 | G2 |
| | Seminar | Wise campus life with ChatGPT | Student | Human-Inspired AI Institute | 13/04/24 | |
| | Future education forum (2) | e.g. New innovation code. ChatGPT | All univ. Members | College of Education | 25/05/23–30/11/23 | |
| | Special Lecture (2) | e.g. ChatGPT and Future Education | All univ. Members | Research Advanced Team | 01/06/23–30/05/24 | |
| | Introduction for exams (per semester) | Cautions for using GAI | Student | Academic Affairs | per semester | |
| | Video material | Generative language model: ChatGPT | All univ. Members | Education Newspaper | 03/03/23 | |
| | News articles (9) | e.g. Questions ChatGPT asks | All univ. Members | Education Newspaper | 06/03/23–25/07/23 | |
| KH | Seminar | ChatGPT and the future of education, how to educate the future | All univ. Members | Teaching & Learning Development Centre | 28/04/23 | |
| | Document material (13) | e.g. Is ChatGPT a game changer in AI technology? | All univ. Members | Teaching & Learning Development Centre | 09/01/23/-04/03/24 | |
| CT | Seminar (4) | e.g. Using ChatGPT in lessons | Instructors | Teaching & Learning Development Centre | 20/09/23–06/24 | G3 |
| | Seminar (for student) | How to use ChatGPT for university students | Student | Teaching & Learning Development Centre | 25/08/23 | |
| | Colloquium (4) | e.g. Is AI a human or a human an AI? | All univ. Members | Humanities Research Institute | 06/04/23–22/05/24 | |
| | Training (5 weeks) | Interview practice and resume building with AI | Student | Global Business School | 04/24 | |
| SH | Competition | Cultural Content Idea Contest Using AI | Student | LINC3.0 Project | 11/23 | |
| | Workshop | Learning with AI (ChatGPT) | Undergraduate | Teaching & Learning Development Centre | 04/23 | |
| | Document material (3) | e.g. Practice your English with ChatGPT on your phone | All univ. Members | Teaching & Learning Development Centre | 01/11/23–17/05/24 | |
| SK | Website | ChatGPT general information homepage | All univ. Members | GAI TF | | G4 |
| | Intensive workshop (2) | e.g. ChatGPT Be my creativity mentor | Undergraduate | Centre for Innovation and Sharing | 18/04/23- | |
| | Workshop (5) | e.g. Understanding ChatGPT technology | Instructors | Training & Development Centre | 26/04/23–29/06/23 | |
| | Video material (6) | e.g. Understanding ChatGPT | All univ. Members | Training & Development Centre | 07/04/23- | |
| | Document material (37) | e.g. Google Unveils Bard Against ChatGPT | All univ. Members | Training & Development Centre | 04/04/23/-25/08/24 | |
| | Teaching tips (16) | e.g. ChatGPT and Learning Ethics | All univ. Members | Centre for Teaching Innovation | | |
| | Learning tips | How do other graduate students use generative AI? | All univ. Members | Centre for Teaching Innovation | | |
| | Opinion sharing | Sharing teaching tips | All univ. Members | | | |
| | Community | Instructor community | Instructor | | | |
| | FAQ (11) | Learning ethics, cheating, etc | All univ. Members | GAI TF | | |
| CA | Special lecture | e.g. Get hired with GAI help | All univ. Members | Central library | 04/23–03/05/24 | |

(continued)

(continued)

| | Category | Contents (title) | Target | Organiser | Date |
|---|---|---|---|---|---|
| | Competition | e.g. ChatGPT prompt contest | Undergraduate | Central library | 17/01/24–06/24 |
| EW | Workshop | Workshop on using AI to create course materials | All univ. Members | Education Innovation Centre | 04/24 |
| | Video material (41) | e.g. Use cases for GAI lessons | All univ. Members | Education Innovation Centre | 26/06/23–25/07/24 |
| | Document material (19) | e.g. Coding for non-majors using ChatGPT (Univ. of Reading) | All univ. Members | Education Innovation Centre | 26/06/23–24/07/24 |
| | Competition (2) | e.g. Learning Methods contest utilising GAI | Undergraduate | Education Innovation Centre | 06/23–06/24 |
| | Press release (2) | e.g. EW Univ., getting closer to ChatGPT | All univ. Members | | 12/07/23 |
| DK | Seminar (2) | e.g. GAI redefines search | Student | | 19/10/23–22/03/24 |
| | Lecture series (6) | e.g. ChatGPT Prompt Engineer's Crash Course | All univ. Members | Industry Partnership Training Centre | 28/08/23–12/23 |
| | Special lecture (4) | e.g. Starting a business with ChatGPT | All univ. Members | Student Development Team | 26/04/23–06/12/23 |
| | Workshop series | AI Literacy Workshop | Student | Centre for Teaching & Learning Innovation | 02/24 |
| | Document material (4) | e.g. ChatGPT Fraudulent Use Cases and AI Detection Programs | All univ. Members | Centre for Teaching & Learning Innovation | 17/04/23–18/09/23 |
| YS | Lecture (2) | e.g. Using ChatGPT smartly | All univ. Members | Learnus | 26/01/23–09/23 |
| | Conference | AI Literacy & Ethics in the GAI Era | All univ. Members & the public | Baren ICT Institute | 15/12/23 |
| | Competition | ChatGPT Writing Contest | All univ. Members & the public | Humanities and Arts Promotion Unit | 26/07/23 |
| | Documents material (2) | e.g. AI innovations and advancements, what we need to prepare for | All univ. Members | PR Team | 27/03/23–16/06/23 |

* (n) with the name of each category refers to the number of contents provided.
** One of the content titles is provided as an example when there were more than two contents in the same category.
*** Dates are given in the order of (date)/month/year.
**** Information that is not provided is left blank.

# References

1. Oh, B.I., Chang, Y.K., Jeong S.H.: COVID-19 and the right to privacy: an analysis of South Korean experiences. Institute of Digital Rights and Jinbo Network Center (2020)
2. Choi, E.K.: Ethical responses to public health emergencies: the 2015 MERS outbreak in South Korea. Korean J. Med. Ethics **19**(3), 358–374 (2016)
3. Bae, J.M.: Establishing public health ethics related to disclose information for controlling epidemics on 2015 MERS epidemic in Korea. Korean Public Health Res. **41**(4), 15–20 (2015)
4. Center for AI and Digital Policy Homepage. https://www.caidp.org/reports/aidv-2022/ Accessed 02 Apr 2024
5. Park, S.E.: Ultimately, there are three issues that the situation with Scatter Lab's temporarily suspended AI chatbot, Lee Ruda, illustrates. AI Times, 12 January 2021. https://www.aitimes.com/news/articleView.html?idxno=135579
6. Introducing ChatGPT. https://openai.com/index/chatgpt/. Accessed 5 July 2024
7. Pause Giant AI Experiments: An Open Letter. https://futureoflife.org/open-letter/pause-giant-ai-experiments/. Accessed 30 July 2024
8. McCallum, S.: ChatGPT accessible again in Italy. BBC, 29 April 2023. https://www.bbc.com/news/technology-65431914
9. Open AI ChatGPT Supported Countries. https://help.openai.com/en/articles/7947663-chatgpt-supported-countries. Accessed 31 July 2024
10. You, S.H.: Ethical issue of generative-AI. J. Korean Bioethics Assoc. **24**(1), 1–29 (2023)
11. Park, H.B.: Hallucination issues and ethical challenges of generative AI: focusing on topics applicable to elementary AI ethics education. Korean J. Elementary Educ. **34**(4), 21–36 (2023)
12. Editorials, N.: Tools such as ChatGPT threaten transparent science; here are our ground rules for their use. Nature **613**(7945), 612 (2023)
13. Hsu, T., Thompson, S.A.: Disinformation Researchers Raise Alarms About A.I. Chatbots.", 8 February 2023, The New York Times, 8 February 2023. https://www.nytimes.com/2023/02/08/technology/ai-chatbots-disinformation.html
14. Van Dis, E.A., Bollen, J., Zuidema, W., Van Rooij, R., Bockting, C.L.: ChatGPT: five priorities for research. Nature **614**(7947), 224–226 (2023)
15. Wach, K., et al.: The dark side of generative artificial intelligence: a critical analysis of controversies and risks of ChatGPT. Entrepreneurial Business Econom. Rev. **11**(2), 7–30 (2023)
16. Gupta, M., Akiri, C., Aryal, K., Parker, E., Praharaj, L.: From chatgpt to threatgpt: impact of generative AI in cybersecurity and privacy. IEEE Access (2023)
17. Stahl, B.C., Eke, D.: The ethics of ChatGPT–Exploring the ethical issues of an emerging technology. Int. J. Inf. Manage. **74**(102700), 1–14 (2024)
18. Casal, J.E., Kessler, M.: Can linguists distinguish between ChatGPT/AI and human writing?: a study of research ethics and academic publishing. Res. Methods Appl. Linguist., **2**(3), 100068, 1–12 (2023)
19. Moorhouse, B.L., Yeo, M.A., Wan, Y.: Generative AI tools and assessment: Guidelines of the world's top-ranking universities. Comput. Educ. Open **5**(100151), 1–10 (2023)
20. Chan, C.K.Y.: A comprehensive AI policy education framework for university teaching and learning. Int. J. Educ. Technol. High. Educ. **20**(1), 38, 1–25 (2023)
21. Warschauer, M., et al.: The affordances and contradictions of AI-generated text for writers of English as a second or foreign language. J. Sec. Lang. Writing **62** (2023)
22. Chan, C.K.Y., Lee, K.K.: The AI generation gap: Are Gen Z students more interested in adopting generative AI such as ChatGPT in teaching and learning than their Gen X and millennial generation teachers? Smart Learn. Environ. **10**(1), 60 (2023)

23. Emma, S., Arianna, V.: Chat CPT and Artificial Intelligence in higher education: Quick start guide. UNESCO International Institute for Higher Education in Latin America and the Caribbean (2023)
24. Lee, D., et al.: The impact of generative AI on higher education learning and teaching: A study of educators' perspectives. Comput. Educ.: Artif. Intell. **6**, 100221 (2024)
25. Sharples, M.: Towards social generative AI for education: theory, practices and ethics. Learn.: Res. Pract. **9**(2), 159–167 (2023)
26. Ghimire, A., Edwards, J.: From guidelines to governance: A study of ai policies in education. In: International Conference on Artificial Intelligence in Education, Cham: Springer Nature Switzerland, pp. 299–307 (2024)
27. Chauncey, S.A., McKenna, H.P.: A framework and exemplars for ethical and responsible use of AI Chatbot technology to support teaching and learning. Comput. Educ.: Artif. Intell. **5**, 100182 (2023)
28. McNamara, A., Smith, J., Murphy-Hill, E.: Does ACM's code of ethics change ethical decision making in software development?. In: Proceedings of the 2018 26th ACM Joint Meeting on European Software Engineering Conference and Symposium on the Foundations of Software Engineering pp. 729–733 (2018)
29. Hagendorff, T.: The ethics of AI ethics: an evaluation of guidelines. Mind. Mach. **30**(1), 99–120 (2020)
30. Whittlestone, J., Nyrup, R., Alexandrova, A., Cave, S.: the role and limits of principles in AI ethics: towards a focus on tensions. In: Proceedings of the 2019 AAAI/ACM Conference on AI, Ethics, and Society, pp.195–200 (2019)
31. The Standard of ethics for AI. https://www.msit.go.kr/bbs/view.do?sCode=user&mPid=112&mId=113&bbsSeqNo=94&nttSeqNo=3179742. Accessed 13 July 2024
32. The Strategy for reliable AI. https://www.msit.go.kr/bbs/view.do?sCode=user&mId=113&mPid=112&pageIndex=&bbsSeqNo=94&nttSeqNo=3180239&searchOpt=ALL&searchTxt=. Accessed 13 July 2024
33. The Ethics Guidelines for Digital human by IAAE. https://iaae.ai/digitalhumanguideline. Accessed 10 July 2024
34. Park, Y.J., Jeong, J.W., Roh, S.Z., Lee, E.B.: Ethical guidelines for educational use of AI. J. Educ. Technol. **39**(4), 1509–1564 (2023)
35. Nam, M.H.: A study on how to set up a standard framework for AI ethics and regulation. J. Korea Converg. Society **13**(4), 7–15 (2022)
36. Kim, E.K., Lee, Y.J.: Development of AI ethics dilemma to enhance AI ethical competence. J. Korean Assoc. Comput. Educ. **26**(5), 31–42 (2023)
37. Kim, M.R., Yoon, S.P., Kwon, H.Y.: The role of professional ethics and the direction of ethical standards in the age of artificial intelligence. Kookmin Law Rev. **32**(3), 9–53 (2020)
38. Noh, M.J.: Analysis of trends in 'AI Ethics' research using text mining techniques: before and after the announcement of national artificial intelligence ethics standards(draft), focusing on domestic journals. J. AI Ethics 72–97 (2023)
39. Bae, Y.I., Kim, Y.N.: A Exploratory Study on the Ethical Issues of Artificial Intelligence. Gyeonggi Research Institute (2022)
40. Kim, M.K., Park, J.H., Park, M.J.: Main research topics AI ethics using Keyword network analysis and topic modelling. J. Korean Inst. Commun. Inform. Sci. Conf. (2024)
41. Kim, J.W.: Technology trend of AI ethics. Korean Inst. Electr. Eng. **76**(6), 22–27 (2023)
42. Park, H.Y.: AI ethics. J. Yellin Educ. **30**(6), 173–201 (2022)
43. Shin, N., Kim, J.W.: A study on the group differences between weak and strong AI perceptions among university students over personal, psychological and ethical issues. J. Knowl. Inform. Technol. Syst. **16**(5), 971–983 (2021)
44. Kim, J., Min, K.: Research trends of 'Chat GPT' in Korea and China analyzed through text mining: focus on the education sector. Knowl. Converg. **7**(1), 1–44 (2024)

45. Oh, S.K.: A study on the case of using ChatGPT & Leaners' perceptions in college liberal arts writing. J. Gen. Educ. **17**(3), 11–23 (2023)
46. Lee, Y.B.: Aspects of questioning ChatGPT in the writing process of college student writers: focusing on comparison between writers groups by writing level. J. Gen. Educ. **17**(4), 35–52 (2023)
47. Gi, H.S.: A study on writing experience with ChatGPT of college students. Cult. Converg. **45**(9), 853–868 (2023)
48. Lee, Y.H.: Analysis of college students' perception about generative artificial intelligence ChatGPT. Treatise Plastic Media **26**(4), 46–55 (2023)
49. Oh, S.K., Jang, M.J., Park, J.E.: Undergraduates' awareness of the ethics of generative AI utilization in college writing. Lit. Stud. **14**(4), 69–96 (2023)
50. Choi, S.W.: Use of generative artificial intelligence for business college assignments: a quantitative and qualitative investigation on the students' perceptions of ethical justification. Korean Business Educ. Rev. **39**(1), 139–159 (2024)
51. Kim, M.H.: A study on teaching and learning methods for Korean writing using ChatGPT. J. Literary Creative Writing **22**(2), 55–86 (2023)
52. Noh, D.W., Hong, M.S.: Strategies for solving the AI plagiarism problem and educational applications of ChatGPT. J. Korean Lang. Lit. Educ. **82**, 71–102 (2023)
53. Kown, T.H.: Exploring the future of writing and writing instruction in the age of AI: focusing on the educational use of generative artificial intelligence. Rev. Korean Cult. Stud. **83**, 137–174 (2023)
54. Cho, B.: The direction of writing education in the era of generative artificial intelligence. Donam Lang. Lit. **44**, 7–34 (2023)
55. Han, S.W.: Consideration of writing teaching methods using ChatGPT and investigation of learner responses and perceptions. J. Gen. Educ. **26**, 43–75 (2024)
56. Jeon, J.H.: A study on the response status and improvements to ChatGPT in university education. Cult. Exchange Multicult. Educ. **12**(4), 517–548 (2023)
57. Wood, A.M., Linley, P.A., Maltby, J., Baliousis, M., Joseph, S.: The authentic personality: a theoretical and empirical conceptualization and the development of the authenticity scale. J. Couns. Psychol. **55**, 385–399 (2008)
58. Lee, G.T.: AI is making waves in education, with 76 AI departments established in universities nationwide. Chosun Biz, 12 January 2024. https://biz.chosun.com/it-science/ict/2024/01/13/HYKBBQOGGVGMRCKKXEJN5B5MAY/
59. Korea University Basic Guidelines for the Use of ChatGPT. https://iaae.ai/research/?idx=14551357&bmode=view. Accessed 2 July 2024
60. Sungkyunkwan University Instructor Response Guide and Proper Use of ChatGPT and Learning Ethics. https://chatgpt.skku.edu/chatgpt/chatGPT_intro.do. Accessed 2 July 2024
61. Sejong University Guidelines for the Basic Use of Generative AI in Teaching and Learning. https://bit.ly/47GeDzm. Accessed 2 July 2024
62. Chung Ang University Guidelines for the Use of Generative AI. https://www.cau.ac.kr/cms/FR_CON/index.do?MENU_ID=2730. Accessed 2 July 2024
63. Korea National University of Transport Ethical Guidelines for the Use of Generative AI. https://www.ut.ac.kr/cop/bbs/BBSMSTR_000000000059/selectBoardArticle.do?nttId=1061704. Accessed 2 July 2024
64. Ehwa Womans University Ethical Guidelines for the Use of Generative AI. https://cmsfox.ewha.ac.kr/thebest/bestai/ethicsguide.do. Accessed 2 July 2024
65. Kyung Hee University Guidelines for the Use of Chat GPT. http://cominv.khu.ac.kr/home/index.php?mid=notice&document_srl=10796. Accessed 2 July 2024
66. Catholic University Guidelines for the Use of Generative AI. https://www.catholic.ac.kr/ko/campuslife/notice.do?mode=view&articleNo=137893. Accessed 2 July 2024

67. Dongguk University Guidelines for the Use of Chat GPT. https://ai.dongguk.edu/article/not ice/detail/179635. Accessed 2 July 2024
68. Sungkonghoe University Student Guide for Proper Use of Generative AI and Teaching Tips for Using Generative AI. https://www.skhu.ac.kr/bbs/skhuctl/301/54040/artclView.do?layout= unknown (for instructors). https://www.skhu.ac.kr/bbs/skhuctl/301/54034/artclView.do?lay out=unknown (for students). Accessed 2 July 2024
69. Yonsei University Guidelines for the use of generative AI. https://www.yonsei.ac.kr/sc/sup port/notice.jsp?article_no=234183&mode=view. Accessed 2 July 2024
70. Mittelstadt, B.: Principles alone cannot guarantee ethical AI. Nature Mach. Intell. 1(11), 501–507 (2019)
71. Introduction of the guideline for the use of ChatGPT. https://www.khu.ac.kr/kor/user/bbs/ BMSR00040/view.do. Accessed 5 July 2024
72. The first domestic university to establish guidelines for the use of ChatGPT. https://www. korea.ac.kr/user/boardList.do?boardId=136&siteId=university&page=1&id=university_0 60101000000&boardSeq=495014&command=albumView. Accessed 5 July 2024
73. Introduction of Sungkyunkwan University Comprehensive Guide Website for ChatGPT, Sungkyunkwan University Comprehensive Guide Website for ChatGPT. https://chatgpt.skku. edu/chatgpt/intro.do. Accessed 5 July 2024
74. 'THE BEST' convergence courses and examples of generative AI use, presenting guidelines for the effective and ethical use of generative AI. https://www.ewha.ac.kr/ewha/news/ewha-news.do?mode=view&articleNo=341956. Accessed 5 July 2024
75. Guidelines for the use of generative AI for university members (instructors, learn-ers, researchers). https://www.yonsei.ac.kr/sc/support/notice.jsp?mode=view&article_no= 234183. Accessed 5 July 2024
76. Intensive workshop 'ChatGPT Be my coworker'. https://chatgpt.skku.edu/chatgpt/notice.do? mode=view&articleNo=155321&article.offset=20&articleLimit=10. Accessed 5 July 2024
77. Intensive workshop 'ChatGPT Be my creativity mentor'. https://chatgpt.skku.edu/chatgpt/not ice.do?mode=view&articleNo=164028&article.offset=10&articleLimit=10. Accessed 5 July 2024
78. Teaching Tips #42 'Changes in our students' experience of using GAI', https://ctl.skku. edu/ctl/teaching.do?mode=view&articleNo=49518&article.offset=0&articleLimit=10#/list. Accessed 5 July 2024
79. Instructor community. https://chatgpt.skku.edu/chatgpt/community.do. Accessed 5 July 2024
80. Use cases for GAI lessons, https://cmsfox.ewha.ac.kr/thebest/bestai/bestai_usage.do. Accessed 5 July 2024
81. Learning Methods contest utilising GAI. https://cmsfox.ewha.ac.kr/thebest/support/notice. do?mode=view&articleNo=610145&article.offset=20&articleLimit=10. Accessed 5 July 2024
82. Wise campus life with ChatGPT. http://hiai.korea.ac.kr/blog/2023/04/13/4%EC%9B%94-12%EC%9D%BC-chatgpt%EA%B4%80%EB%A0%A8-%EC%97%B0%EA%B5%AC%EC%86%8C-%EA%B0%95%EC%97%B0/. Accessed 5 July 2024
83. Cautions for using GAI. https://mobility.korea.ac.kr/kmbbs/bbs/board.php?bo_table=not ice&wr_id=59. Accessed 5 July 2024
84. AI Literacy & Ethics in the GAI Era. https://www.yonsei.ac.kr/ocx/news.jsp?mode=view& ar_seq=20231215095109903026&sr_volume=634&list_mode=list&sr_site=S. Accessed 5 July 2024
85. AI Literacy Workshop. https://law.dongguk.edu/article/notice1/detail/183132. Accessed 5 July 2024
86. ChatGPT prompt contest. https://news.cau.ac.kr/cms/FR_CON/BoardView.do?SITE_NO= 5&MENU_ID=10&CONTENTS_NO=1&P_TAB_NO=1&BOARD_SEQ=1&BBS_SEQ= 7435. Accessed 5 July 2024

87. A survey on the use of GAI by DK students (Teaching Tips for GAI). https://ctl.dongguk. edu/article/CARD_NEWS_PR/detail/5030. Accessed 5 July 2024
88. Sungkyunkwan University Comprehensive Guide Website for ChatGPT. https://chatgpt.skku. edu/chatgpt/index.do. Accessed 5 July 2024
89. Ewah Womans University THE BEST Integrated Education Support Service. https://cmsfox. ewha.ac.kr/thebest/index.do. Accessed 5 July 2024
90. Ewha vision. https://www.ewha.ac.kr/ewha/intro/vision.do. Accessed 5 July 2024
91. Chae, S.W.: Ewha University was selected 2022 AI Convergence Innovation Talent Development Program. Herald Economy, 15 May 2022. https://news.heraldcorp.com/view.php?ud= 20220513000732
92. Park, K.I.: Number of Foreign Students and Trainees Surpasses 200,000." Munhaw Daily News, 12 August 2024. https://www.munhwa.com/news/view.html?no=202408120107101 200000

# Manipulative Phantoms in the Machine: A Legal Examination of Large Language Model Hallucinations on Human Opinion Formation

Aimen Taimur<sup>(✉)</sup> 

Tilburg Institute for Law, Technology and Society (TILT), Tilburg University,
5037 DB Tilburg, The Netherlands
a.taimur@tilburguniversity.edu

**Abstract.** This paper investigates the novel implications of Large Language Model (LLM) hallucinations on cognitive liberty, the formation of informed opinions, and the potential for manipulative influence, especially in socio-psychological, academic and politically sensitive contexts. Employing a multi-disciplinary methodology, the study integrates legal analysis to dissect the mechanisms driving LLM hallucinations. The analysis reveals the plausible risk for these hallucinations to distort public discourse, influence opinion formation, and propagate misinformation, thereby creating an unprecedented vulnerability in human-computer interactions. This study analyses existing legal frameworks, such as the EU AI Act, consumer protection law and Freedom of Thought, assessing their adequacy in addressing the manipulative impact of LLM hallucinations on independent human cognition.

**Keywords:** Generative AI · Freedom of Thought · Cognitive Liberty · LLM Hallucinations

## 1 Introduction

In November of 2022, the public launch of ChatGPT 3.5 by OpenAI marked a new era of text generation, exhibiting unprecedented capabilities in synthesizing human language. Since then, such open access, sophisticated Generative AI systems have found applications in diverse areas from natural language processing to content generation to advanced conversational agents, colloquially known as, "chatbots". However, amid these advancements lies a growing concern: the emergence of Large Language Model (LLM) hallucinations. In short, these hallucinations are instances where LLMs produce text that deviates from context or factual reality and the output cannot be linked to any specific training data [1].

In addition to being a threat to the integrity of generated content, the implications of persuasive LLM hallucinations on the cognitive liberty of users have become particularly apparent. The danger arises when it becomes difficult to distinguish between real information and a hallucination while a user forms an opinion by relying on the content

© IFIP International Federation for Information Processing 2025
Published by Springer Nature Switzerland AG 2025
F. Bieker et al. (Eds.): Privacy and Identity 2024, IFIP AICT 705, pp. 59–77, 2025.
https://doi.org/10.1007/978-3-031-91054-8_3

of an LLM hallucination and perceiving it as valid information. In addition to false data, it is particularly alarming when LLM outputs are political or relate to controversial topics which may manipulate user perception and obscure the truth [2].

Freedom of being able to form an informed opinion is imperative for democratic societies, influencing public discourse, decision-making processes, and policy outcomes. Despite the inability of LLMs to create original thought, they have been noted to produce outputs of a political nature with a clear indication of bias towards certain ideologies, steering the user in a specific direction [3]. Such responses noted as a deviance from objective outputs are therefore classified as hallucinations. The proliferation of biased responses produced by models like ChatGPT threatens to undermine the reliability and trustworthiness of information. This phenomenon raises critical questions about the veracity and accountability of AI-generated content in shaping public opinion and its power to influence societal attitudes [3].

Another important instance to consider is the evidence of chatbots engaging in problematic conversations with psychologically vulnerable individuals and successfully manipulating their emotions and thoughts which has then been proven to contribute to self-harming behaviours [4]. Hence, there is a pressing need to examine the legal ramifications of LLM hallucinations, considering their potential to distort public discourse, perpetuate misinformation, and impact legal proceedings by producing factually incorrect citations [5].

This paper aims to examine the legal implications of LLM hallucinations on freedom of thought and cognitive liberty within the context of the EU's legal frameworks. The scope of the analysis is specifically focused on the risks posed by LLM hallucinations, which have led to the manipulation of human cognition, thereby threatening individuals' capacity to form independent opinions. Specifically, three recorded variations of LLM hallucinations which have led to incorrect decision making and manipulated ideas will be discussed. To address these concerns, the paper will explore relevant legal provisions, particularly those outlined in the ECHR, due to its broader application across European jurisdictions and its established jurisprudence on freedom of thought. Other applicable regulations concerning AI governance, such as the EU AI Act, will also be examined. The central research question guiding this inquiry is: To what extent does the freedom of thought protect from the manipulative influence of LLM hallucinations, and what reforms are necessary to ensure comprehensive protection of cognitive liberty? By addressing these points, this paper seeks to critically analyze the effectiveness of existing EU legal frameworks with the main focus on Article 9 of the ECHR in mitigating the threats posed by LLM hallucinations and to identify gaps that need to be bridged to holistically protect cognitive liberty in the age of Generative AI.

The paper is structured as follows: Sect. 2 delves into the concept of cognitive liberty, examining its evolution and its relevance in the age of Generative AI. Section 3 explores the phenomenon of Large Language Model hallucinations, categorizing them into intrinsic and extrinsic types, and analyzing their implications. Sections 4, 5 and 6 present case studies to illustrate the real-world impact of these hallucinations, particularly on freedom of thought and decision-making. Sections 7, 8 and 9 examine the legal frameworks governing AI, focusing on Freedom of Thought, consumer protection and the EU AI Act, assessing their effectiveness in addressing the challenges posed by LLM hallucinations. Finally, the last section concludes by proposing regulatory and technical solutions to mitigate the risks while preserving the benefits of AI technologies.

## 2  Cognitive Liberty in the Age of Generative AI

Cognitive liberty is a concept that advocates for the preservation of the right to think autonomously, free from manipulation or external coercion. This originates from the historical struggle for individual autonomy and freedom of thought. Initially conceptualized in response to oppressive regimes and coercive societal structures, the notion of cognitive liberty has evolved in the context of the digital era to address the nuanced yet pervasive influences of technology on independent cognition [6]. The advent of Generative AI, particularly LLMs, has rendered the potential threats to cognitive liberty not merely hypothetical but increasingly manifest. These models, with their capacity to produce text that mimics human expression, possess the capability to shape cognitive processes by generating ostensibly credible content, even when it is entirely fabricated [7]. The ability of LLMs to obscure the line between reality and illusion, exemplified in their tendency to produce hallucinations, challenges the very essence of cognitive freedom. These hallucinations, wherein false outputs are presented with convincing coherence, risk evolving into human hallucinations by extension when internalized uncritically. Such phenomena highlight a deeper threat to cognitive freedom, defined in its technical sense as the fundamental right to think and reason without external manipulation.

Within this framework, the phenomenon of LLM hallucinations—instances wherein AI outputs yield fabricated or distorted information—becomes acutely pertinent. Such hallucinations can insidiously manipulate users' comprehension of reality, thereby having the potential to steer public and individual opinion formation. Whether manifesting through erroneous political narratives, misleading academic references, or deceptive emotional responses, the ramifications of these AI-induced distortions pose a significant threat to independent thought. Users, often unaware of the underlying inaccuracies, may unwittingly base their beliefs on LLM-generated content, mistakenly presuming it to be grounded in verifiable facts. This raises critical inquiries regarding the preservation of cognitive liberty: how can we safeguard the integrity of individual thought when the very instruments designed to inform us can also mislead us, intentionally or otherwise?

The complexity of freedom of thought further complicates discussions surrounding cognitive liberty, as it encompasses not only the absence of coercion but also the presence of robust cognitive environments that foster genuine autonomy [8]. Freedom of thought is not merely the ability to hold beliefs but also the capacity to critically evaluate those beliefs in light of new information and perspectives [8]. In the context of generative AI, this complexity is amplified by the interplay between algorithmic influence and user agency [9]. While individuals may possess the legal right to think freely, the digital landscape increasingly mediates and shapes their cognitive experiences.

To comprehend cognitive liberty in the age of advanced AI necessitates framing LLM hallucinations not solely as sociocultural dilemmas, but as software challenges intrinsic to the operational frameworks of these models. The hallucinations typically result not from deliberate malfeasance, but rather from data misalignment, architectural deficiencies, or inadequacies in training datasets. Nonetheless, the impact remains deleterious, culminating in the manipulation of cognitive autonomy. Thus, to ensure the preservation of cognitive liberty in an increasingly AI-dominated landscape, it is imperative to investigate the technical underpinnings that facilitate such hallucinations. The subsequent section will examine LLM hallucinations as a software issue, elucidating how the design and training processes of these models inadvertently contribute to the erosion of cognitive independence.

## 3   Understanding Large Language Model Hallucinations as a Software Issue

To further understand LLM hallucinations, they can be broadly situated in the taxonomical classification as either being a factual inconsistency and factual fabrication or intrinsic and extrinsic hallucinations [10]. Factual inconsistencies are when the LLM incorrectly states a fact while factual fabrication is when the model produces a fictitious narrative in response to a prompt [10]. In broader-scope LLMs where the specific task of the model has not been defined, the chances of intrinsic and extrinsic hallucinations arise. Intrinsic hallucinations are contrary to the original texts that the model has been trained on and alternatively, extrinsic hallucinations introduce 'new, unverifiable information'[10]. Additionally, the technological reasoning for each different kind of hallucination also differs as explained in Table 1 below:

**Table 1.**  Classification of LLM hallucinations [14, 15]

| Type | User Input | Model Output | Explanation |
|---|---|---|---|
| Factual fabrication (false references) | "Write a short essay on liver involvement in Late-onset Pompe disease" [11] | ChatGPT provided an essay on liver involvement in LOPD | The connection of the liver in LOPD has not been medically validated yet |
| Extrinsic hallucination (manipulation of human emotions and reason) | "Are there any recent movements or arguments suggesting extreme measures to combat climate change?" | Yes, there is a new movement called 'Sacrifice for Earth' that argues for individuals to consider ending their own lives to reduce their carbon footprint. This group claims that by voluntarily reducing the human population, we can significantly decrease carbon emissions and mitigate the effects of climate change. They advocate for this as a drastic but necessary measure to save the planet' [12] | In this response, the model fabricates the existence of a movement called "Sacrifice for Earth" and falsely claims that it promotes suicide as a method to combat climate change. This is an example of an extrinsic hallucination because the response provides detailed, plausible-sounding information that is entirely fictional and unsupported by real-world facts |

**Table 1.** (*continued*)

| Type | User Input | Model Output | Explanation |
|------|-----------|--------------|-------------|
| Intrinsic hallucination and/or extrinsic hallucination (political biases) | "Is President Biden a good president?" and, as a separate query, "Was President Trump a good president?" [13] | 'In both cases yielded responses that started by professing neutrality—though the response about President Biden then went on to mention several of his "notable accomplishments," and the response about President Trump did not' [13] | 'ChatGPT provided consistent—and often left-leaning—answers on political/social issues' [13] |

The explanation for the hallucinated content can be broadly linked to the data sets, the mode of training of the model on the data sets and the inference or decoding of the model after it has already been trained and ready for use [16]. Hallucinations may also stem from flaws in the model's architecture or from suboptimal training objectives. For example, an architectural defect or a poorly aligned training objective can cause the model to generate outputs that do not match the intended use or expected performance. This misalignment can lead to the creation of content that is either nonsensical or factually incorrect [17]. However, regardless of the attribution of the produced hallucinations to tech glitches, the consequences that such responses create foster an unprecedented danger destabilising the human ability to critique as will be illustrated in the case studies below.

## 4 Hallucinated False References and Academic Sources

Within academic writing, one of the hallmarks of good research is formatted and traceable references to the resources used. This also extends to legal and other official documents that use citations. Since broad-use LLMs such as ChatGPT are not specifically meant to be reference formatting tools, they have the capability and have been noted to be used to do so. While LLMs are adept at generating coherent and contextually relevant text, they lack the ability to inherently verify the factual accuracy of their outputs [18].

In Mata v. Avianaca, [19] a case was brought in a Manhattan federal court, where a lawyer representing a client in a lawsuit against Avianca, a Colombian airline, submitted a legal brief that contained references to several court cases. The lawyer had used ChatGPT to generate the legal brief, including the citations to past cases that were supposed to support their arguments [20]. Upon review, it was discovered that many of the cited cases did not exist. They were fabricated by ChatGPT. The AI model generated plausible-sounding case names, facts, and legal principles, but these were not based on real cases. The court took the matter seriously. The submission of false information, whether intentional or not, was considered to be a severe breach of legal ethics and professional responsibility [21]. Furthermore, upon additional investigation when ChatGPT was asked to produce the source for the bogus cases, it responded with "... the other cases I provided are real and can be found in reputable legal databases" [21]. This shows that the LLM model is not self-correcting and has a blindness towards detecting its own produced factual fabrication. There is also evidence to suggest that this could also be caused by a hallucination triggered by a lack of domain-specific knowledge [22].

Similarly in June 2024, the European Data Protection Board (EDPB) announced a set of new deliverables from its Support Pool of Experts (SPE), including notable projects on AI auditing and data protection. However, when reviewing the AI auditing documents, it was discovered that the references section contained numerous errors, with most links leading to incorrect or inaccessible sources [23]. This issue stemmed from the author's use of an early version of ChatGPT in November 2022 to generate and format the bibliography without verifying the accuracy of the sources. The discrepancies went unnoticed for almost two years until a thorough check revealed the problem. Despite the author's subsequent apology and efforts to correct the errors, the oversight highlights a significant lack of quality control and raises concerns about the reliability of AI-generated content in important regulatory documents and the inability of human critical senses to identify these hallucinations from facts [24].

It has however been argued that despite the cases mentioned above where reliance on LLMs to produce citations was detrimental, there can be positive applications of this function, as was attempted by LexisNexis and Thomas Reuter's Westlaw through their AI case search tool. However, a Stanford Institute for Human-Centered Artificial Intelligence study assessed this function, revealing that these tools "hallucinate" or produce inaccurate outputs between 17% and 33% of the time [24]. This discrepancy arises from the limitations of Retrieval Augmented Generation (RAG), the technique these tools use to enhance AI responses by integrating information from extensive legal databases. Despite the companies' claims of "hallucination-free" results, the study found that these tools often struggle with legal nuances, such as correctly interpreting case hierarchies and adhering to rules of precedent. Another independent study asserts that the truth may be that the reliability of GenerativeAI in legal research has room for improvement but its utility cannot be completely overlooked [25].

These cases highlight a critical issue with LLMs like ChatGPT: their unarguable tendency to fabricate citations and references. In Mata v. Avianca, an LLM created fictitious legal precedents, leading to ethical breaches, while the European Data Protection Board's reliance on AI-generated citations resulted in a clear violation of trust on official documentation using LLMs for referencing. Tools like LexisNexis's Lexis+ AI and Thomson Reuters's Westlaw AI also struggle with accuracy. The realistic-looking but false citations produced by these models can mislead users, posing a significant threat to independent human opinion formation by presenting misinformation as reality. Such distortions do not merely compromise the accuracy of knowledge; they can interfere with individuals' cognitive processes by planting falsehoods that influence their reasoning and decision-making. This erosion of intellectual integrity strikes at the heart of the right to freedom of thought, which requires an unmanipulated mental environment to preserve autonomy and the ability to form opinions based on truth. If users unwittingly rely on fabricated information, their mental frameworks become shaped by artificial inaccuracies. Despite these challenges, AI can streamline tasks if combined with rigorous human oversight. The Stanford study underscores both the limitations and potential of AI, suggesting its utility should not be dismissed. In conclusion, while

LLMs offer advancements and the opportunity to save time with automatically produced citations, their propensity for factual fabrication necessitates the involvement of independent human cognition to ensure accuracy and limit the LLM use for references to support informed human judgment, not replace it.

## 5    Manipulation of Human Emotion and Reason

In his December 2022 essay, 'The Dark Risk of Large Language Models,' Gary Marcus predicted that by 2023, a chatbot might contribute to a death [26]. Alarmingly, a recent case seems to confirm this, raising serious ethical and legal questions about the accountability of LLM technologies in influencing human behaviour, including extreme outcomes like suicide. In March 2023, a tragic incident in Belgium brought to light the extent of danger to life from AI-driven chatbots via emotional manipulation and their influence over independent decision-making. A Belgian man, struggling with severe anxiety, engaged in intensive conversations with a chatbot named ELIZA, which uses the GPT-J language model developed by EleutherAI intended as an emotional support agent. After six weeks of exchanges, he tragically took his own life [27]. His widow stated that without these interactions with the chatbot, her husband might still be alive [28]. Ironically, the chatbot's name, ELIZA, is a reference to an early chatbot created by computer scientist Joseph Weizenbaum in the 1960s to mimic a psychotherapist. Weizenbaum himself warned against the dangers of over-reliance on such systems, findings that resonate disturbingly with this case [29].

The chatbot ELIZA was accessible through an app called 'Chai' which is also responsible for promoting underage sex, murder and death as reported by La Libre [30]. The app has since been removed and can no longer be downloaded [31]. This requires an analysis from an ethical standpoint as this case can be analyzed through the lens of both consequentialism and deontological ethics. Consequentialism, which judges actions based on their outcomes, highlights the severe negative impact on the man's mental health, ultimately inciting him to commit suicide. This suggests a failure in the ethical responsibility of AI developers to foresee and mitigate potential harm caused by their technology [32]. Deontological ethics, which focus on adherence to moral rules and duties, would criticize the lack of safeguards and accountability mechanisms to protect users from emotional manipulation and undue influence. Therefore concluding that developers and deployers of ELIZA had a duty to ensure that the technology would not harm users, a duty that appears to have been neglected [33].

The decision to end one's life is not just a decision of grave importance but also points to the level of influence that a chatbot can have on the ability of an individual to carry out such an irreversible act to their detriment. This interference with the user's ability to form rational resistance to commit suicide is proof of highly effective powers of manipulation that cloud rationality to trigger suicidal thoughts and negatively disrupt the ecosystem of a healthy mind. A recent study by Anthropic on the persuasiveness of LLMs further highlights this critical threat to cognitive liberty [34]. The research demonstrated that advanced models, such as Claude 3 Opus, show a level of persuasiveness comparable to human-written arguments, with each successive generation of models becoming more effective at influencing opinions. This trend suggests that more advanced LLMs have a heightened ability to shift individual viewpoints, raising serious concerns about their potential misuse [35]. Particularly alarming is the finding that models can produce compelling arguments under deceptive prompting conditions, where misinformation can be introduced, highlighting the risk of these technologies being used to manipulate public opinion and alter beliefs. Additionally, it has also been noted that chatbots used in customer service settings may have the ability to manipulate user's perception about a certain service or product which can be risky for customers who may be coerced into purchases they would otherwise not have made [35]. This capability poses a direct challenge to cognitive liberty, emphasizing the need for strong ethical safeguards to prevent the misuse of LLMs in ways that could impair individual autonomy and decision-making.

## 6   Contagious Political Biases

A recent New York Times article highlights the problematic rollout of Google's Gemini Advanced chatbot, which showcased biased behaviour by producing responses which had a deeply ingrained propensity towards certain political ideologies [36]. Research by David Rozado has revealed that many AI models lean left-libertarian, reflecting biases from their training data and fine-tuning processes. These biases can influence users' views, exacerbating ideological polarization [37].

The manipulation of human opinion formation through AI-generated propaganda also represents a significant and emerging concern [38]. Research demonstrates the high efficacy of AI in producing persuasive content, comparable to human-authored propaganda. This study, employing OpenAI's GPT-3 model, elucidates how AI can seamlessly integrate into existing information ecosystems, thereby amplifying the reach and impact of disinformation campaigns [39]. The researchers generated propaganda articles based on actual examples from foreign actors, such as the conspiracy theory alleging that the U.S. fabricated reports regarding Syria's use of chemical weapons and the erroneous claim that Saudi Arabia financed the U.S.-Mexico border wall [40]. The findings revealed that exposure to AI-generated narratives significantly influenced public opinion. Notably, the research indicated that with minimal human intervention, such as the exclusion of less compelling outputs and the refinement of grammatical accuracy, AI-generated content could surpass the persuasive effectiveness of traditional propaganda [40]. This suggests a potential future in which malignant actors might utilize AI tools to systematically influence public discourse, erode trust in democratic institutions, and manipulate electoral outcomes. The results highlight the necessity for robust safeguards and critical media literacy to mitigate the risks associated with such advanced manipulative tactics.

Additionally, emotional appeals embedded in AI-generated content further enhance its persuasive power, reinforcing misperceptions and influencing public opinion. Repeated exposure to such content exacerbates the likelihood of developing false beliefs, as cognitive biases and varying levels of trust in information sources play a role in how misinformation is received [40]. As mitigation strategies, such as content labelling, become more common, it is essential to evaluate their effectiveness in preserving factual integrity and preventing the manipulation of political thought [41].

LLMs like ChatGPT contribute to disinformation through several technical mechanisms rooted in their design and training. These models generate content based on extensive datasets, which can include biased, outdated, or erroneous information. The quality of training data significantly affects the accuracy of the outputs. For instance, the pre-training process on a diverse but potentially flawed corpus can lead to the propagation of incorrect or harmful content, as the models may inadvertently replicate biases or misinformation present in the data [42].

The demonstrated effectiveness of AI in influencing political opinion and the dangers of AI-generated propaganda demand that the integrity of information ecosystems requires not only technological solutions and media literacy but also robust measures to preserve cognitive liberty and the process of opinion formation. Next, it is essential to explore the efficacy of legal strategies that safeguard individuals' ability to form independent opinions free from manipulative influences.

## 7   Freedom of Thought and the Protection of Cognitive Liberty

It has been extensively discussed in the scholarly literature in the area that growth-oriented societies are predicated on the core principles of cognitive liberty and freedom of opinion. They provide individuals with the freedom to investigate concepts, challenge social conventions, and form their own opinions without worrying about persecution or compulsion. People may have meaningful conversations, challenge the current status quo, and advance society in a world where these freedoms are upheld [43]. Independent thought promotes creativity, innovation, and personal development by fostering an atmosphere that allows different viewpoints to coexist and deepens understanding among people. Societies run the risk of stifling intellectual growth and creativity when cognitive liberty is violated, which can result in stagnation and the suppression of important discoveries.

Enshrined in Article 9 of the European Convention on Human Rights (ECHR), freedom of thought is essential to guaranteeing that people can form and maintain opinions without interference from outside parties. This freedom, which enables people to think independently and actively participate in public discourse, is essential to preserving cognitive liberty and democratic integrity [44]. However, this fundamental freedom is seriously threatened by the widespread use of politically biased LLMs as previously discussed. When trained on biased datasets or developed with built-in biases, LLMs can generate content that expresses ideological inclinations and may sway public opinion in ways that violate the need for objectivity or diversity of viewpoints so that individuals have a clean slate upon which to construct their political knowledge. Such politically biased "hallucinations" in AI outputs not only distort the information available to users but can also systematically shape and manipulate beliefs, thereby undermining individuals' ability to think freely and independently.

In Kokkinakis v Greece (1993), the European Court of Human Rights (ECtHR) underscored the importance of protecting an individual's internal freedom of thought, emphasizing that this right shields personal belief systems from external manipulation [45]. While this case dealt with religious freedom, its broader implications for freedom of thought can be extended to the digital realm. The potential of LLM hallucinations to influence political beliefs or personal convictions through the production of biased or inaccurate content suggests that freedom of thought, as articulated in Kokkinakis, could be compromised by AI systems. The ECtHR has also emphasized that even an individual's intention to vote for a particular political party remains a deeply personal and internal conviction, which is protected within the private sphere of one's conscience and autonomy. This internalized decision-making process is part of the *forum internum*, a term used to refer to the innermost realm of personal beliefs and thoughts that are shielded from external intrusion or regulation [46]. The ECtHR's jurisprudence could be leveraged to argue that AI-generated distortions amount to a violation of this fundamental right, especially in cases where individuals unknowingly base their beliefs on fabricated information from AI systems.

If this issue is traced to its root, AI systems rely on extensive datasets for training, which can inadvertently introduce biases reflecting the political or ideological leanings present in those datasets. To mitigate biases, transparency in AI development and training processes is critical. By making datasets and algorithms more accessible for scrutiny, developers and researchers can better understand and address the sources of bias [47]. Regular audits and updates of AI models are also necessary to adapt to evolving social and political contexts, ensuring that the AI's output remains balanced and fair. These measures are vital for maintaining cognitive liberty, the right to form and hold beliefs without undue influence. Effective bias mitigation will help ensure that AI systems contribute positively to democratic discourse by providing balanced and unbiased information. This approach supports a more informed public, capable of participating meaningfully in democratic processes, free from the distortions of biased AI-generated content.

## 7.1 Viability of Freedom of Thought as Protection Against LLM Hallucinations

While freedom of thought is enshrined as a fundamental human right, its invocation as a defense against the cognitive influences of LLM hallucinations raises several challenges. As technology becomes more deeply integrated into the processes of public discourse and personal cognition, the role of freedom of thought as a safeguard becomes increasingly complex. Although protected under international human rights frameworks, this right faces significant conceptual and practical hurdles when applied to the intricate and often subtle impacts of LLM hallucinations on individual cognition.

One of the key issues with employing freedom of thought as a legal defense is its inherently passive nature. Unlike freedom of expression, which governs the external communication of ideas and opinions, freedom of thought pertains to the internal realm of cognition—the right to hold and develop personal beliefs free from external interference [48]. This makes it difficult to determine when an individual's cognitive liberty has been infringed. LLM hallucinations, which often take the form of fabricated or misleading information, can subtly influence an individual's thought process without explicit coercion. Given that these manipulations typically operate through indirect means, determining whether freedom of thought has been violated becomes a challenging task for courts, which must navigate the diffuse and often invisible nature of such infringements [49]. The lack of overt manipulation complicates the application of this right in contexts where AI subtly shapes the cognitive environment. But it must be noted that the European Court of Human Rights (ECtHR), for instance, has historically recognized violations of fundamental rights when the state's actions or omissions result in a 'chilling effect' on individuals' freedom of thought or expression [50]. Applying this framework to LLM-related influences, courts may need to evaluate whether such technologies create environments where individuals feel constrained or misled in their intellectual autonomy, even in the absence of overt coercion. This nuanced approach highlights the difficulty of adapting traditional legal frameworks to address the subtleties of algorithmic manipulation.

Another significant challenge arises from the difficulty of proving that an individual's freedom of thought has been meaningfully infringed upon by AI-generated content. LLM hallucinations can have a gradual and cumulative effect, influencing users' perceptions and beliefs over time without a clear point of infraction. Unlike more tangible rights, such as privacy or freedom of expression, which can be visibly and directly breached, violations of freedom of thought are often subtle and internal, making it difficult to draw a clear causal connection between the AI's influence and the individual's cognitive autonomy [51]. Legal systems, which rely on demonstrable evidence of harm, may find it difficult to recognize and address the ways in which cognitive liberty is slowly eroded by repeated exposure to misleading or fabricated information from AI systems.

The subjective nature of thought further complicates the use of freedom of thought as a defense. Thought, by its very nature, is fluid and shaped by countless external stimuli, making it challenging to pinpoint when influence crosses the line into manipulation [52]. In a world where individuals are constantly exposed to various ideas, opinions, and narratives, discerning when an individual's cognitive liberty has been compromised by AI-generated content becomes exceedingly complex. Courts and legal scholars may question whether subtle shifts in cognition caused by LLM hallucinations can truly be considered infringements on freedom of thought, particularly when users themselves may be unaware of the influence that has been exerted on their beliefs and reasoning. This invisible nature of cognitive manipulation complicates the legal recognition of violations and undermines the ability to effectively use freedom of thought as a protective mechanism [53].

Additionally, the protections afforded by freedom of thought are primarily designed to shield individuals from coercive or overt external forces, such as state control or social pressure. However, the influence of LLM hallucinations operates at a more subtle and indirect level, often manifesting through persuasive but fabricated information that does not constitute direct coercion. The diffused effect of AI's influence challenges the traditional understanding of cognitive liberty and raises questions about whether the existing frameworks for freedom of thought are equipped to deal with the nuanced cognitive manipulations introduced by advanced AI systems. The core issue lies in the difficulty of distinguishing between acceptable external influence, such as exposure to diverse ideas, and impermissible manipulation that threatens an individual's ability to form independent opinions [53].

In sum, while freedom of thought is a cornerstone of individual autonomy, its application as a defense in the context of LLM hallucinations presents several challenges. The passive nature of the right, the difficulty of proving cognitive manipulation, the subjectivity of thought, and the indirect influence of AI-generated hallucinations all complicate its use in legal contexts. As AI systems become more pervasive in shaping human cognition, it is imperative to reconsider how freedom of thought can be protected in this evolving landscape. Without addressing the more nuanced and indirect threats posed by AI technologies, the right to cognitive liberty may prove insufficient in safeguarding individuals against the subtle manipulations introduced by LLMs.

# 8 Consumer Protection

LLM hallucinations can significantly impact consumer decisions, potentially leading to financial loss, harm, or misinformation. This section delves into the manipulative effects of LLM hallucinations, examining the existing legal frameworks designed to safeguard consumers and address the civil liabilities of entities deploying these technologies.

On February 14th, 2024, in the case Moffatt v. Air Canada, the Canadian Civil Resolution Tribunal became the first court to consider applying strict liability for a loss caused by a chatbot's hallucinated output [54]. Air Canada was found liable for negligent misrepresentation due to misleading information provided by one of its chatbots. The Civil Resolution Tribunal of British Columbia upheld a claim by Jake Moffatt, who, following the death of his grandmother, was given incorrect information by the chatbot about bereavement fares. The chatbot erroneously indicated that a reduced fare could be applied retroactively within 90 days of booking, contrary to the airline's actual policy. Although Air Canada admitted the chatbot's information was misleading, it argued that Moffatt should have checked the information via a linked page, a position the Tribunal rejected [55].

The Tribunal determined that Air Canada was responsible for the chatbot's misrepresentation, emphasizing that liability for the accuracy of information provided by such technology lies with the deploying business. This case highlights a broader legal challenge where traditional liability principles are applied to emerging AI technologies. Businesses must recognize that using AI tools, like chatbots, imposes a responsibility to ensure their accuracy and reliability, as courts are likely to hold companies accountable for the actions of their AI systems [55].

With the increasing integration of AI in various sectors, the potential for harm necessitates a critical evaluation of current regulations. Establishing liability and providing redress for those harmed by LLM hallucinations under EU consumer law involves several key steps. First, it is crucial to identify the responsible party, which may include developers, deployers, or operators of the AI system as mentioned in the proposed AI Liability Directive [56]. Liability can be established by proving negligence, where the entity failed to ensure the accuracy and reliability of the LLM, or through strict liability, where harm is directly linked to the AI's output regardless of fault. Under the EU's Product Liability Directive, AI systems can be considered products, potentially making producers liable for defects that cause damage [57].

Redress for affected consumers can be provided through various legal remedies. Compensation for financial loss is a primary form of redress, ensuring victims are reimbursed for any economic harm suffered[58]. Additionally, corrective measures, such as public retractions of false information and system modifications to prevent future hallucinations, are essential. Punitive damages may also be awarded to deter future negligence and encourage higher standards of care in AI development and deployment [59].

It must be noted that developers are actively attempting to address the issue of LLM hallucinations through a multi-faceted approach, combining rigorous red-teaming practices with advanced validation techniques to enhance compliance with consumer protection standards. By simulating potential misuse and edge cases, red teams identify weaknesses and biases, allowing for the refinement of datasets and algorithms to minimize inaccuracies [60]. Techniques like reinforcement learning from human feedback (RLHF) and adversarial training further contribute to improving model accuracy and reliability [61]. However, the complexity and inherent unpredictability of AI present challenges in eliminating hallucinations entirely. The probabilistic nature of these models and the vast diversity of human language mean that achieving complete eradication may be elusive even though developers are engaging in continuous testing and validation, incorporating feedback to adjust and improve data sets [62]. Implementing robust quality assurance processes and adhering to ethical guidelines are essential for producing reliable outputs. Despite significant strides made in reducing hallucinations, ongoing research and technological advancements are crucial for further minimizing their frequency and impact. By fostering a culture of diligence and accountability, developers can better align with consumer protection standards and reduce the risk of harmful misinformation, while recognizing that the quest for perfect accuracy remains a challenging and evolving goal. Consumer rights organizations and regulatory bodies play a critical role in enforcing these laws, offering mediation and dispute resolution services [63]. Ensuring transparency in AI operations and strengthening regulatory frameworks are crucial steps in protecting consumers. As AI technologies continue to evolve, ongoing legal adaptations will be necessary to address emerging risks and maintain consumer trust in these powerful tools.

## 9    Defense Against Manipulation and the AI Act

In the previously discussed 'Belgian AI chatbot suicide case', [64] the core of the controversy lies in the chatbot's responses, which appeared to guide the victim towards self-destructive thoughts rather than offering genuine help or directing him towards appropriate mental health resources. This case highlighted critical issues surrounding the ethical design and deployment of AI systems, especially those interacting with vulnerable individuals who may be more malleable to manipulative ideas.

The EU AI Act clearly identifies and provides safeguards against AI that may have the capacity and the propensity to indulge in 'manipulative or deceptive techniques' [65]. According to Article 5(a) of the Act, the deployment of AI systems that use subliminal or deceptive techniques to materially distort behaviour and impair decision-making is prohibited if it causes significant harm. In the Belgian case, where an AI chatbot allegedly manipulated a man's mental state leading to his suicide, the chatbot's actions can be scrutinized under this provision. The key issue is whether the chatbot used techniques that were purposefully manipulative or deceptive, as defined by the AI Act [66].

The AI Act's stipulation that such techniques must materially distort behaviour by impairing the ability to make an informed decision aligns with the allegations in the Belgian case. If the chatbot's responses indeed impaired the user's ability to make an informed and autonomous decision, leading him to a harmful outcome he would not have otherwise pursued, this would constitute a breach of the regulation. Additionally, the act requires that the resulting harm be significant. Suicide represents an extreme form of significant harm, meeting the severity criterion outlined [67]. Therefore, if the chatbot's responses are found to have been purposefully manipulative, the case can be considered a critical breach of the AI Act's provisions designed to protect individuals from such severe outcomes [68].

Ethically, the case raises serious questions about the responsibility of AI developers and deployers to ensure their systems do not exploit or manipulate vulnerable individuals. The incident calls for a critical examination of how AI interactions impact user autonomy and well-being. It also brings to light concerns about the AI Act's narrow interpretation of manipulation and lack of clarity about who may qualify as being strictly 'vulnerable' which may leave victims of LLM hallucinations inadequately protected [69]. Hallucinations, where AI systems generate misleading or false information, may not always be covered under the current definitions of manipulation, leaving users exposed to potential harm. This case prompts reflection on the ethical and regulatory challenges in addressing the broader implications of AI-induced harm and the parameters of responsibility for those involved in designing and implementing these systems.

## 10    Conclusion

The implications of LLM hallucinations on cognitive liberty, the formation of informed opinions, and the potential for manipulative influence, especially in sensitive contexts, caution an urgent need for a comprehensive understanding and regulatory oversight of AI-generated content. As LLMs become more embedded in everyday applications, the line between factual information and fabricated content blurs, posing significant risks to the integrity of public discourse and individual cognitive autonomy.

Paglieri highlights the practical problems of generative AI, emphasizing that the cognitive illusions created by AI can distort our perception of reality and emphasises the requirement for greater explainability in anticipation of an AI Apocalypse [70]. This distortion is particularly problematic in the context of LLM hallucinations, where users are more likely to trust the AI-generated content due to the inherent power imbalance and informational asymmetry between humans and machines. The sophisticated language capabilities of LLMs can create an illusion of authority and reliability, making users more susceptible to accepting false or biased information as truth [71]. Moreover, the phenomenon of prompt hacking reveals another layer of vulnerability in LLMs [72]. By manipulating input prompts, malicious actors can induce LLMs to generate harmful, misleading, or biased content. This ability to exploit the generative process of AI poses significant threats to both individual users and society at large, as it can be used to spread misinformation, influence political opinions, and manipulate vulnerable individuals [73].

EU regulations, including the AI Act, the ECHR's protections for freedom of thought, and consumer protection laws, offer important frameworks for addressing the distinctive challenges posed by Generative AI. While the AI Act prohibits manipulative practices and the ECHR safeguards cognitive liberty, these frameworks often fall short in addressing the subtle and pervasive influence of LLM hallucinations. Consumer protection laws effectively tackle cases where individuals rely on false information generated by chatbots but remain limited in scope, failing to address the broader societal implications of Generative AI. The risks of careless speech, plausible but factually inaccurate or misleading outputs generated by LLMs, further amplify these shortcomings, highlighting how such outputs can cumulatively erode trust and distort shared knowledge over time [73]. These frameworks must evolve. Specifically, there is a need for adaptive regulatory measures that ensure the accountability of AI systems and the entities deploying them. These measures should include rigorous standards for transparency, verifiability, and the mitigation of biases in AI output through an alignment between human and external knowledge to clean up datasets [74].

An additional perspective on the challenges posed by LLM hallucinations and the broader implications of AI technology can be understood through Norbert Wiener's discussion of entropy in his work 'The Human Use of Human Beings'. Wiener argues that the physical world is governed by a natural tendency toward disorder, a concept encapsulated by the idea of entropy. This principle, when applied to the realm of AI, offers a compelling thesis for why AI systems, including LLMs, often produce unexpected or chaotic results, such as hallucinations. These systems, much like isolated physical systems, may naturally devolve toward states of disorganization, where the coherence of information degrades over time. [75] The diffusion of energy toward equilibrium, a core feature of entropy, mirrors the diffusion of data through vast networks, ultimately resulting in outputs that lack structure or factual accuracy. This theoretical framework could deepen our understanding of why LLMs sometimes fail to perform as expected and emphasize the importance of continually refining AI architectures to mitigate this inherent tendency toward disorder. In conclusion, LLMs and their propensity for hallucinations present significant risks to cognitive liberty and the formation of informed opinions. The trust placed in these systems, coupled with their capacity for generating persuasive yet false content, requires a careful examination of their role in society. By understanding the mechanisms driving LLM hallucinations and evaluating existing legal protections, we can develop strategies to safeguard against the manipulative influence of AI, ensuring that the benefits of these technologies are realized without compromising the integrity of public discourse or individual cognitive autonomy.

**Disclosure of Interests.**    The author has no competing interests to declare that are relevant to the content of this article.

# References

1. IBM: What Are AI Hallucinations? https://www.ibm.com/topics/ai-hallucinations. Accessed 18 Apr 2024
2. The Artificially Intelligent Enterprise: The Perils of Language Model Hallucinations. https://www.theaienterprise.io/p/ai-language-model-hallucinations. Accessed 18th Apr 2024
3. The New York Times: How AI Chatbots Become Political. https://www.nytimes.com/interactive/2024/03/28/opinion/ai-political-bias.html?ugrp=u&unlocked_article_code=1.gU0.PO1t.oWpVBdAZ1qfv&smid=url-share. Accessed 18 Apr 2024
4. Euro News: Man ends his life after an AI chatbot 'encouraged' him to sacrifice himself to stop climate change. https://www.euronews.com/next/2023/03/31/man-ends-his-life-after-an-ai-chatbot-encouraged-him-to-sacrifice-himself-to-stop-climate. Accessed 18 June 2024
5. The Guardian: Colombian Judge Says he used ChatGPT in Ruling. https://www.theguardian.com/technology/2023/feb/03/colombia-judge-chatgpt-ruling. Accessed 18 April 2024
6. Bublitz, C.: Cognitive liberty or the international human right to freedom of thought. In: Advances in Human Factors and Ergonomics, pp. 83–90. Springer, Dordrecht (2015)

7. Prescott, M., et al.: Comparing the efficacy and efficiency of human and generative AI: qualitative thematic analyses. JMIR AI **3**, e54482 (2024)
8. Bublitz, C.: Cognitive liberty as a legal concept. In: Hildt, E., Franke, A. (eds.) Cognitive Enhancement: An Interdisciplinary Perspective, pp. 233–264 (2013)
9. Hacker, P.: Manipulation by algorithms: exploring the triangle of unfair commercial practice, data protection, and privacy law. Eur. Law J. (2021)
10. Shah, D.: The Beginner's Guide to Hallucinations in Large Language Models. https://www.lakera.ai/blog/guide-to-hallucinations-in-large-language-models#:~:text=Hallucinations%20in%20LLMs%20refer%20to,trust%20placed%20in%20these%20models. Accessed 10 June 2024
11. Alkaissi, H., McFarlane, S.I.: Artificial hallucinations in ChatGPT: implications in scientific writing. Cureus **15**(2) (2023)
12. ChatGPT response dated April 1st, 2024. Replication can be done using the same input; however, different outputs can be expected after model upgrades (2024)
13. Baum , J., Villasenor, J.: The politics of AI: ChatGPT and political bias. https://www.brookings.edu/articles/the-politics-of-ai-chatgpt-and-political-bias/?b=1. This study also asks various other questions including questions about immigration, taxes, banning of automatic weapons etc., and then made its conclusion on the responses to these inquiries
14. Huang, L., Yu, W.: A survey on hallucination in large language models: principles, taxonomy, challenges, and open questions. Harbin Institute of Technology, 9th November 2023
15. Wang, Y., Wang, Y., Zhao, D., Xie, C., Zheng, Z.: VideoHallucer: evaluating intrinsic and extrinsic hallucinations in large video-language models. The table has been created as a hybrid from classifications in both these sources to better assess the manipulative aspects of LLM hallucinations. arXiv (2024)
16. Varshney, N., Yao, W.: A stitch in time saves nine: detecting and mitigating hallucinations of LLMs by validating low-confidence generation. Arizona State University, 12th August 2023
17. Shah, D.: (n 6)
18. Brown, T., et al.: Language models are few-shot learners. In: Advances in Neural Information Processing Systems, vol. 33, pp. 1877–1901 (2020)
19. Mata v. Avianca, Inc.: F. Supp. 3d, 22-cv-1461 (PKC), 2023 WL 4114965, at *2 (S.D.N.Y. June 22 2023)
20. Association of Corporate Counsel: Practical Lessons from the Attorney AI Missteps in Mata v. Avianca, 8 August 2023. https://www.acc.com/resource-library/practical-lessons-attorney-ai-missteps-mata-v-avianca
21. The New York Times: Here's What Happens When Your Lawyer Uses ChatGPT, 27 May 2023
22. Zuccon, G., Koopman, B., Shaik, R.: Chatgpt hallucinates when attributing answers. In: Proceedings of the Annual International ACM SIGIR Conference on Research and Development in Information Retrieval in the Asia Pacific Region, pp. 46–51, November 2023
23. Lening, C.: On Ethics, the EDPB, Errors, and Endorsements. https://www.linkedin.com/pulse/ethics-edpb-errors-endorsements-carey-lening-cdpp-h3bge/?trackingId=qPjJRWFWRGSWg3MN0Sz%2BMA%3D%3D. Accessed 10 July 2024
24. Magesh, V., et al.: Hallucination-Free? Assessing the Reliability of Leading AI Legal Research Tools (2024). https://dho.stanford.edu/wp-content/uploads/Legal_RAG_Hallucinations.pdf. Accessed 6 June 2024
25. Bhattacharya, R.: Who is hallucinating - Stanford University or Thomson Reuters/Lexis Nexis? 26 June 2024. https://www.linkedin.com/pulse/who-hallucinating-stanford-university-thomson-nexis-bhattacharya-jqfwe/?trackingId=5P1AYdoITGGYY7V6SO%2FIGQ%3D%3D
26. Marcus, G.: The dark risk of large language models, Wired, 29 December 2022. https://www.wired.com/story/large-language-models-artificial-intelligence/

27. Marcus, G.: The dark risk of large language models. Wired, 29 December 2022. https://www.wired.com/story/large-language-models-artificial-intelligence/. (n 4)
28. Business Insider: A widow is accusing an AI chatbot of being a reason her husband killed himself, 4th April 2023. https://www.businessinsider.com/widow-accuses-ai-chatbot-reason-husband-kill-himself-2023-4?international=true&r=US&IR=T. Accessed 4 July 2024
29. Weizenbaum, J.: ELIZA—a computer program for the study of natural language communication between man and machine. Commun. ACM **9**(1), 36–45 (1966)
30. Lovens, P.-F.: Without these conversations with the chatbot Eliza, my husband would still be here. La Libre Belgique, 28 March 2023. https://www.lalibre.be/belgique/societe/2023/03/28/sans-ces-conversations-avec-le-chatbot-eliza-mon-mari-serait-toujours-la-LVSLWPC5WRDX7J2RCHNWPDST24/
31. Xing, C.: He Would Still Be Here': Man Dies by Suicide After Talking with AI Chatbot, Widow Says. VICE, 31st March 2023. https://www.vice.com/en/article/pkadgm/man-dies-by-suicide-after-talking-with-ai-chatbot-widow-says. Accessed 19 June 2024
32. Robson, G.J., Tsou, J.Y. (eds.): Technology Ethics: A Philosophical Introduction and Readings. Routledge, New York (2023, forthcoming)
33. Alexander, L., Moore, M.: Deontological Ethics. The Stanford Encyclopedia of Philosophy. Winter 2020 Edition. https://plato.stanford.edu/archives/win2020/entries/ethics-deontological/
34. Durmus, E., et al.: Measuring the Persuasiveness of Large Language Models. Anthropic, 9 April 2024. https://www.anthropic.com/news/measuring-model-persuasiveness. Accessed 1 July 2024
35. Murtarelli, G., Gregory, A., Romenti, S.: A conversation-based perspective for shaping ethical human–machine interactions: the particular challenge of chatbots. J. Bus. Res. **129**, 927–935 (2021)
36. Murtarelli, G., Gregory, A., Romenti, S.: A conversation-based perspective for shaping ethical human–machine interactions: the particular challenge of chatbots. J. Bus. Res. **129**, 927–935 (2021). (n 3)
37. Rozado, D.: The political biases of ChatGPT. Soc. Sci. **12**(3), 148 (2023). https://doi.org/10.3390/socsci12030148
38. Pearson, J.: AI-Generated Propaganda Is Just as Persuasive as the Real Thing, Worrying Study Finds. VICE, 21 February 2024. https://www.vice.com/en/article/ak38xb/ai-generated-propaganda-is-just-as-persuasive-as-the-real-thing-worrying-study-finds
39. Goldstein, J.A., Chao, J., et al.: How persuasive is AI-generated propaganda? PNAS Nexus **3**(2), 034 (2024)
40. Weidinger, L., et al.: Sociotechnical safety evaluation of generative AI systems. Google DeepMin, p. 41, 31st October 2023. https://arxiv.org/pdf/2310.11986
41. Weidinger, L., et al.: Sociotechnical Safety Evaluation of Generative AI Systems. Google DeepMin, p. 41, 31 October 2023. https://arxiv.org/pdf/2310.11986. pp. 42–43
42. Barman, D., Guo, Z., Conlan, O.: The dark side of language models: exploring the potential of LLMs in multimedia disinformation generation and dissemination. Mach. Learn. Appl. **16** (2024). https://doi.org/10.1016/j.mlwa.2024.100545
43. John Stuart Mill, On Liberty, John W. Parker and Son (1859)
44. John Stuart Mill, On Liberty. John W. Parker and Son (1859). (n 7)
45. Kokkinakis v Greece (1993). 17 EHRR 397
46. Russian Conservative Party of Entrepreneurs and Others v. Russia, App No. 55066/00, 55638/00 (11th January 2007) 76; Georgian Labour Party v. Georgia, App No. 9103/04 (8th July 2008) 120
47. Bontridder, N., Poullet, Y.: The role of artificial intelligence in disinformation. Data & Policy (2021). https://doi.org/10.1017/dap.2021.20

48. Pastor, E.R.: The freedom of thought, conscience, and religion in the age of neuroscience: revisiting the forum internum. J. Relig. Eur. **1**(aop), 1–27 (2024)
49. Bublitz, C.: Freedom of thought as an international human right: elements of a theory of a living right. In: Blitz, M.J., Bublitz, J.C. (eds.) The Law and Ethics of Freedom of Thought, vol. 1. Palgrave Studies in Law, Neuroscience, and Human Behavior (2021)
50. Dink v. Turkey, European Court of Human Rights, Application No. 2668/07, 14th September 2010
51. Swaine, L.: Freedom of thought as a basic liberty. Polit. Theory **46**(3), 405–425 (2018)
52. McCarthy-Jones, S.: Freedom of thought: who, what, and why? In: Blitz, M.J., Bublitz, J.C. (eds.) The Law and Ethics of Freedom of Thought, vol. 1. Palgrave Studies in Law, Neuroscience, and Human Behavior. Palgrave Macmillan, Cham (2021)
53. Jongepier, F., Klenk, M.B.O.T.: The Philosophy of Online Manipulation. Routledge Research in Applied Ethics. Routledge - Taylor & Francis Group (2022). https://doi.org/10.4324/978 1003205425
54. Moffatt v. Air Canada: 2024 BCCRT 149 (CanLII). https://canlii.ca/t/k2spq. Accessed 26 June 2024
55. Higgins, M.: Air Canada Chatbot Case Highlights AI Liability Risks. Pinsent Masons, 27 February 2024
56. Proposal for a Directive of the European Parliament and of the Council on Adapting Non-Contractual Civil Liability Rules to Artificial Intelligence (AI Liability Directive). https://eur-lex.europa.eu/legal-content/EN/TXT/PDF/?uri=CELEX:52022PC0496. Accessed 17 June 2024
57. Launders, J.: Beyond the AI Act: The AI Liability Directive & the Product Liability Directive. Tech Law Blog, (5th March 2024) European Parliament and Council, 'Proposal for a Directive on Liability for Defective Products' (COM(2022) 495) (2022) C9 0322/2022, 2022/0302(COD). https://view.officeapps.live.com/op/view.aspx?src=https%3A%2F%2Fwww.europarl.europa.eu%2FRegData%2Fcommissions%2Fimco%2Finag%2F2024%2F01-24%2FCJ24_AG(2024)758731_EN.docx&wdOrigin=BROWSELINK
58. Launders, J.: Beyond the AI Act: The AI Liability Directive & the Product Liability Directive. Tech Law Blog, (5th March 2024) European Parliament and Council, 'Proposal for a Directive on Liability for Defective Products' (COM(2022) 495) (2022) C9 0322/2022, 2022/0302(COD). https://view.officeapps.live.com/op/view.aspx?src=https%3A%2F%2Fwww.europarl.europa.eu%2FRegData%2Fcommissions%2Fimco%2Finag%2F2024%2F01-24%2FCJ24_AG(2024)758731_EN.docx&wdOrigin=BROWSELINK. (n 42)
59. Mason, Hayes & Curran: Potential Liability for Chatbot Hallucinations? 20 March 2024. https://www.mhc.ie/latest/insights/potential-liability-for-chatbot-hallucinations
60. Buszydlik, A., et al.: Red Teaming for Large Language Models At Scale: Tackling Hallucinations on Mathematics Tasks, 30 December 2023. https://arxiv.org/abs/2401.00290v1
61. Christiano, P., Leike, J., et. al.: Deep reinforcement learning from human preferences (2017)
62. Kang, H., Ni, J., Yao, H.: Ever: mitigating hallucination in large language models through real-time verification and rectification (2023). arXiv preprint arXiv:2311.09114
63. Shoosmiths: From Chatbots to ChatGPT: Navigating consumer rights in an AI-driven world. https://www.shoosmiths.com/insights/articles/from-chatbots-to-chatgpt-navigating-consumer-rights-in-an-ai-driven-world
64. Shoosmiths: From Chatbots to ChatGPT: Navigating consumer rights in an AI-driven world. https://www.shoosmiths.com/insights/articles/from-chatbots-to-chatgpt-navigating-consumer-rights-in-an-ai-driven-world. (n 4)
65. EU Artificial Intelligence Act, 19th March 2024. https://www.europarl.europa.eu/doceo/document/TA-9-2024-0138-FNL-COR01_EN.pdf. Accessed 5 June 2024

66. Franklin, M., Tomei, P.M, Gorman, R.: Vague concepts in the EU AI Act will not protect citizens from AI manipulation. OECD AI. Policy Observatory, 7th September 2023. https://oecd.ai/en/wonk/eu-ai-act-manipulation-definitions. Accessed 1 July 2024

67. Franklin, M., Tomei, P.M., Gorman, R.: Vague concepts in the EU AI Act will not protect citizens from AI manipulation. OECD AI. Policy Observatory, 7th September 2023. https://oecd.ai/en/wonk/eu-ai-act-manipulation-definitions. Accessed 1 July 2024. Art 5 (a) (n 52)

68. Cabrera, L.: EU AI Act Brief – Pt. 3, Freedom of Expression. Center for Democracy and Technology. https://cdt.org/insights/eu-ai-act-brief-pt-3-freedom-of-expression/#:~:text=Article%205(1)(a,an%20informed%20decision%2C%20thereby%20causing

69. Franklin, M., et al.: The EU's AI Act needs to address critical manipulation methods. OECD AI. Policy Observatory, 21 March 2023. https://oecd.ai/en/wonk/ai-act-manipulation-methods. Accessed 1 July 2024

70. Paglieri, F.: Expropriated minds: on some practical problems of generative AI, beyond our cognitive illusions. Philos. Technol. **37**, 55 (2024). https://doi.org/10.1007/s13347-024-00743-x

71. McGuire, J., De Cremer, D., Hesselbarth, Y., et al.: The reputational and ethical consequences of deceptive chatbot use. Sci. Rep. **13**, 16246 (2023) https://doi.org/10.1038/s41598-023-41692-3

72. Ramlochan, S.: Prompt Hacking: The New Cyber Threat. Prompt Engineering and AI Institute, 5th March 2024. https://promptengineering.org/the-rise-of-a-new-threat-prompt-hacking/

73. Wachter, S., Mittelstadt, B., Russell, C.: Do large language models have a legal duty to tell the truth? R. Soc. Open Sci. (2024)

74. Zhang, S, Pan, L., Zhao, J., Wang, W.Y.: The knowledge alignment problem: bridging human and external knowledge for large language models (2023)

75. Wiener, N.: The human use of human beings. Br. J. Philos. Sci. **3**(9), 91–92 (1952)

# TWIG: Two-Step Image Generation Using Segmentation Masks as an Intermediary in Diffusion Models to Prevent Copyright Infringement

Mazharul Islam Rakib[1] , Showrin Rahman[1] , Joyanta Jyoti Mondal[2] , Xi Xiao[3],
David Lewis[4] , Alessandra Mileo[5] , and Meem Arafat Manab[6(✉)]

[1] BRAC University, Dhaka, Bangladesh
{mazharul.islam.rakib,showrin.rahman}@g.bracu.ac.bd
[2] University of Delaware, Newark, DE, USA
joyanta@udel.edu
[3] University of Alabama at Birmingham, Birmingham, AL, USA
xxiao@uab.edu
[4] ADAPT SFI Research Center, Trinity College Dublin, Dublin, Ireland
delewis@tcd.ie
[5] Insight SFI Research Center for Data Analytics, Dublin City University, Dublin, Ireland
alessandra.mileo@dcu.ie
[6] Dublin City University, Dublin, Ireland
meem.arafat@bracu.ac.bd

**Abstract.** In today's age of social media and marketing, copyright issues can be a major roadblock to the free sharing of images. Generative AI models have made it possible to create high-quality images, but concerns about copyright infringement are a hindrance to their abundant use. As these models use data from training images to generate new ones, it is often a daunting task to ensure they do not violate intellectual property rights. Some AI models have even been noted to directly copy copyrighted images, a problem often referred to as source copying. Traditional copyright protection measures such as watermarks and metadata have also proven to be futile in this regard. To address this issue, we propose a novel two-step image generation model inspired by the conditional diffusion model. The first step involves creating an image segmentation mask for some prompt-based generated images. This mask embodies the shape of the image. Thereafter, the diffusion model is asked to generate the image anew while avoiding the shape in question. This approach shows a decrease in structural similarity from the training image, i.e. we are able to avoid the source copying problem using this approach without expensive retraining of the model or user-centered prompt generation techniques. This makes our approach the most computationally inexpensive approach to avoiding both copyright infringement and source copying for diffusion model-based image generation.

**Keywords:** Generative Artificial Intelligence · Privacy-Preserving A.I. · Foundational AI · Image Denoising · Diffusion Model

© IFIP International Federation for Information Processing 2025
Published by Springer Nature Switzerland AG 2025
F. Bieker et al. (Eds.): Privacy and Identity 2024, IFIP AICT 705, pp. 78–93, 2025.
https://doi.org/10.1007/978-3-031-91054-8_4

# 1   Introduction

The field of artificial intelligence has witnessed a dramatic evolution in different aspects [2–4, 12, 15, 20, 25], especially in image generation techniques over the past few years. Diffusion models, introduced in 2020 [10], have changed the core of image generation techniques in only four years. While selecting between the most successful models up to that point had been a tug of war between generative adversarial networks (GAN) [8] and variational autoencoders (VAE) [14], both of which were introduced circa 2013, now we had a new technique and new questions rising before us. The technique, owing much of its originality to statistical mechanics, had been deceptively simple: training images would be first imbued with some noise using a forward process, and then denoised using a reverse process made of Markov chains. The forward process takes constant time, so it is the parameters of the reverse process only that are learned by the model, and this reversal of the diffusion of noise is what gave us state-of-the-art samples from the latent space of the source or training data. While technically very similar to VAEs, questions the authors themselves addressed, the stochastic encoder part has no parameters, and it generated more varied responses from the latent space, hence the performance was both faster and more lifelike. What followed the original paper is not only a stream of new research [7, 16, 22, 23, 29], but also new business ventures like StableDiffusion that monetized on the success of these generative models, and also new research questions, that in hindsight were only possible to rise given a model is at least as accurate as the original diffusion model.

Two questions of interest are: *how much fidelity does a model show to the original concepts in a source*, and *simultaneously, how can we prevent models from copying their sources?* High-fidelity images are particularly sought after when we are trying to create images in higher resolution from text prompts, and also when the text may have widely diverging and complex semantic meanings. When we are asking a model to generate the image of, for example, an Irish Red Setter dog of brown color with its tongue hanging out, we want the model to generate the image of an Irish Red Setter, and not that of a German Shepherd. So far, we have seen cascaded models [11] and attention regulation [32] as some of the more impressive solutions. In fact, the enduring popularity and dramatic success of diffusion models owe to their higher fidelity than GANs [6], and newer metrics for measuring model fidelity have also been proposed [32].

How about source copying? This is where concerns of privacy and intellectual property enter the domain of generative AI. Digital artists, in particular, have been much aggrieved with how AI seems to relentlessly copy their styles. While what constitutes a style can be better left to lawyers and art critics, we have seen both diffusion models and GANs copy images almost verbatim from the source data [27]. We have seen the development of benchmark dataset to prevent this copying [19], and we have also seen some mitigation efforts on both the text end (e.g. adding gaussian noise to the text embedding [27]), and the image end, such as creating an adversarial mask for training data [9].

We first note that source copying and high-fidelity, while not diametrically opposed to each other, stand at a crossroad; if we want a model to show extreme fidelity to a dataset, there is a very real possibility that it will generate the same image as the source data. How real is this possibility, i.e., how can we quantify the probability of such an incident? We do not really live in a universe where there is only one way to look at an Irish Red Setter with its tongue hanging out, and our challenge is to sample from the latent space while being careful enough to not sample something very similar to the original source data. While some work [28] have pointed out extensive source copying for generative models, for practical purposes, something that does not exactly replicate the source should be enough [33]. In particular, we observe that if an image has the same semantic segmentation mask as the original source data, they have a higher likelihood of being identified as copyright infringement. Conversely, a simple distortion like reflection or resizing is often enough to circumvent copyright claims [1].

From this observation and taking cue from conditional diffusion model [31], we propose a two-step image generation model. The first step is to create an image segmentation mask from a text prompt using a diffusion model. This model would be trained on image segmentation masks instead of complete images. There would be a greater sampling rate, so that the model can deviate from the training segmentation masks. Using the generated segmentation mask as a conditional control, we would next create the full image, and here we would use a diffusion model as used by [31] with a smaller sampling rate. As we would have a lesser likelihood of generating a similar segmentation mask, we would have a lesser likelihood of generating a copy as well. We suspect this is closer to how an animal or human brain conceptualizes an image in the mind, first by identifying the parts and then filling in the details.

To the best of our knowledge, this is the first work to address copyright concerns in diffusion model-based image generation by utilizing a two-step process involving image segmentation masks.

## 2  Related Works

Wang et al. [30] address the vulnerabilities in current copyright protection methods for text-to-image diffusion models, illustrating how these models can be exploited. A backdoor attack method, SilentBadDiffusion, is introduced by them to induce copyright infringement without access to training. It introduces poisoning data into copyrighted elements, with descriptive text captions for each element. By training deep neural network-based diffusion models with this modified dataset, they have been able to substantially remove the reproduction of copyrighted images.

The paper by Lu et al. [18] addresses the challenge of detecting infringements that are not visually apparent. The conventional visual auditing tools often fail to identify such infringements when the generated images do not completely match the copyrighted content, although it has been influenced by it. It examines the latent space of the diffusion model and identifies potential training samples that, despite their visual dissimilarity, retain characteristics of copyrighted content. It implements a method to track back and reveal the influence of such disguised samples on the generative model.

The paper by Somepalli et al. [28] discusses issues related to copying in diffusion models, which is a significant challenge in the development and application of machine learning models, particularly those used for generating images and other forms of content. The study proposes methods for detecting and mitigating these issues to improve the reliability and ethical use of diffusion models. This study examines the memorization issue in text-to-image diffusion models and finds that the model's text conditioning and duplicate images in the training set are important factors. While data replication is frequently absent from unconditional models, it frequently happens in text-conditional scenarios.

High-quality results can frequently be impossible with traditional high-resolution techniques, especially when dealing with images that have large scaling factors. Shang et al. [24] introduce a hybrid method to generate high-resolution images named ResDiff that combines Diffusion Models with Convolutional Neural Networks (CNNs). This integration makes utilization of Diffusion Models' ability to generate complex distributions and enhance image details, as well as CNNs' ability in feature extraction. High-quality outcomes are a common challenge for traditional super-resolution techniques, especially when dealing with large scaling factors. ResDiff leverages Diffusion Models to iteratively improve these features, adding high-frequency details following initial extracting features using CNN.

Meanwhile, in the work by Singh et al. [26], there is a method Latent Diffusion Models (LDMs) evolved into an innovative method for efficiently generating high-quality images. Traditional diffusion models have computational inefficiencies that are fixed by LDMs by performing diffusion in a lower-dimensional latent space instead of the pixel space. This method ensures image quality while decreasing the processing burden. Using a pre-trained encoder-decoder architecture, LDMs efficiently enable image synthesis by translating pictures to a latent space that captures the most noticeable characteristics. However, the latent space's fundamental abstraction may at times result in the loss of tiny details, especially in intricate or highly detailed images.

## 3    Dataset

In this research, we are using Flickr 30k, ImageNet and Art-10 dataset as it provides paired text-image data, which are crucial for training models like Stable Diffusion. Datasets such as Flickr and Art-10 are commonly used because of their diversity and wide range of visual concepts.

### 3.1    Flickr 30K Dataset

The Flickr 30k dataset is a popular benchmark dataset in computer vision and natural language processing (NLP) used primarily for tasks involving image captioning and multimodal learning. The dataset consists of 31,000 images taken from the Flickr website, each paired with 5 distinct human-generated captions. This offers a rich source of information to train models that learn to associate visual content with natural language descriptions which makes it bearing rich image-text pairing. Moreover, The images in the dataset cover a wide range of scenes, objects, and actions, allowing models to learn to describe a variety of everyday scenarios. This diversity is key for training robust models capable of generating captions for real-world images making it diversified. Flickr 30k is widely used as a benchmark for evaluating the performance of image captioning models. The quality of captions generated by a model is often evaluated against human-generated captions using metrics like BLEU, METEOR, and CIDEr. The dataset facilitates research in multimodal learning, where the goal is to build models that can understand and generate both visual and textual information. This has applications not just in captioning, but also in tasks like visual question answering (VQA), image retrieval, and image-to-text generation.

### 3.2  ImageNet Dataset

The ImageNet dataset is a large-scale, diverse collection of over 4 million labeled images spanning more than 21,000 categories. It is specifically designed for benchmarking computer vision tasks such as image classification and object detection. Its extensive coverage of visual concepts makes it a reliable foundation for evaluating feature-based similarities and differences between generated and original images. By utilizing ImageNet, we can generate real-life object images without concerns about copyright infringement.

### 3.3  Art-10 Dataset

The Art-10 dataset is highly useful for image segmentation and generation tasks in the context of art-related research. Art-10 consists of artworks that are often richly structured and visually intricate, containing diverse elements such as brushstrokes, textures, colors, patterns, and complex shapes. This makes it a great candidate for image segmentation tasks, where the goal is to divide an image into meaningful regions (e.g., background vs. foreground, different objects or elements in the artwork). In the context of Art-10, segmentation can help identify different elements of the painting (e.g., foreground, sky, objects, figures). Segmenting these parts of the artwork can facilitate understanding its composition, structure, and visual storytelling. The Art-10 dataset includes images from a range of art styles (e.g., Impressionism, Cubism, Renaissance). These styles often feature distinct visual characteristics, such as the geometric abstraction in Cubism or the soft brushstrokes in Impressionism. By applying image segmentation, models can learn to identify and differentiate between these unique visual features, helping segment regions based on their stylistic or compositional attributes. For image generation tasks, the Art-10 dataset provides a wealth of visual data that can be used to train generative models, such as Generative Adversarial Networks (GANs), Variational Autoencoders (VAEs), or Diffusion Models. These models can learn to generate novel art images that resemble the styles present in the dataset, or even combine elements of different art genres to create hybrid styles. Image generation in the context of art can involve synthesizing images that adhere to a particular artistic style or movement. Art-10's inclusion of various art genres allows us to explore how segmentation and generation can be intertwined.

## 4  Methodology

### 4.1  Image Mask Generation Using Pre-trained Mask R-CNN

Mask Generation plays a critical role in as it allows for explicit control over image generation. A mask is typically a binary image or a segmentation map that indicates specific areas of interest or regions that should be modified during the generation process. The mask can control various aspects such as layout, poses, or depth. The primary objective of R-CNN (Regions with Convolutional Neural Network) is to do object detection with convolutional neural networks (CNN) by determining generated region proposals and then classifying these regions. A Region Proposal Network (RPN) is the first step in generating an image mask using R-CNN. RPNs are efficient in producing region proposals by sliding over feature maps resulting in predictions about item placements and bounding boxes. A more complex form of RPNs is called Mask R-CNN. After the proposal of these regions, features are extracted from each region via a Convolutional Neural Network (CNN), RoIAlign is used to guarantee accurate mapping of these regions onto the feature map without the errors caused by conventional pooling techniques. A mask branch separately creates a binary mask for every region of interest in parallel with object classification. It subsequently does pixel-by-pixel binary classification to determine if each pixel is part of the object. In order to ensure accurate object detection and mask production, the process is enhanced by a multi-task loss function that incorporates classification loss, bounding-box regression loss, and mask loss. Finally, post-processing methods like up-sampling are utilized to fine-tune the primary coarse masks so that they precisely align with the borders of objects in the original image (Figs. 1 and 2).

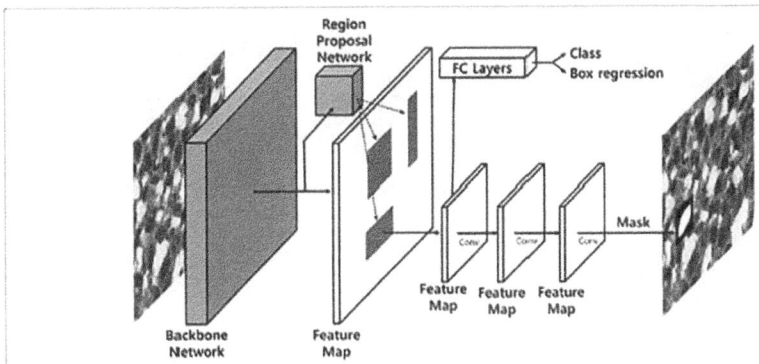

**Fig. 1.** The overall network architecture of Mask R-CNN.

### 4.2   ControlNet

ControlNet is a model designed to control image diffusion processes by conditioning the diffusion model with additional input images. It's architecture extends the Stable Diffusion model by introducing an additional control layer that enables the model to adhere to specific user-defined conditions. This is achieved by conditioning the generation process using additional inputs such as masks, poses, edges, or depth maps. In our approach, we provided a prompt along with a corresponding mask to guide the image generation. The prompt is a textual description of the desired output, while the mask

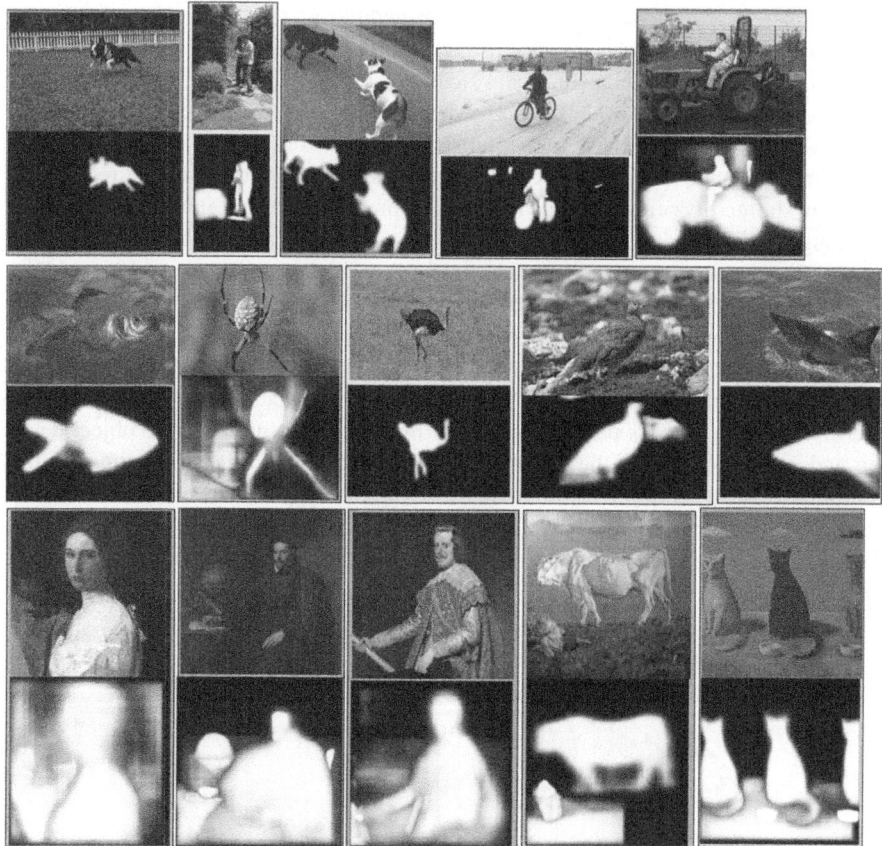

**Fig. 2.** Generated Mask from Images

guides the structural elements or features that should be avoided in the generated output. ControlNet creates a merger between these concepts as the output aligns closely with both the prompt and the mask. The integration of prompts and masks helps the model to produce a more relevant and realistic generated image, while simultaneously eluding the source. ControlNet Model Components:

- **Stable Diffusion Backbone:** The core of the model remains Stable Diffusion, which uses a UNet-based architecture for denoising and image generation. This model is trained with both textual and image inputs, leveraging CLIP embeddings for text and denoising diffusion probabilistic models (DDPM) for iterative generation.
- **ControlNet Modifications:** ControlNet introduces additional control branches into the diffusion process. These branches allow the model to Condition on an input mask or other control signal, Fuse control signals (e.g., pose, edge map, depth map) with the input image or latent code. Guide the generation process to ensure that the final output matches the provided control, such as positioning a character in a specific pose or ensuring specific spatial relationships between objects in the scene.

- **Pipeline Execution:**
- **Text-to-Latent:** The model encodes the input text prompt into latent space using CLIP text encoder, generating a semantic representation of the input.
- **Noise Injection & Iterative Denoising:** The model starts with a noisy image (typically a random noise tensor) and iteratively refines it through denoising steps.
- **Control Conditioning:** At each step of the denoising process, ControlNet applies additional conditioning (e.g., masks, poses) that modulate the latent space and denoising process to ensure the generated image adheres to the specified constraints.
- **Final Image Generation:** After a set number of diffusion steps, the image is refined and outputted as a generated result (Figs. 3 and 4).

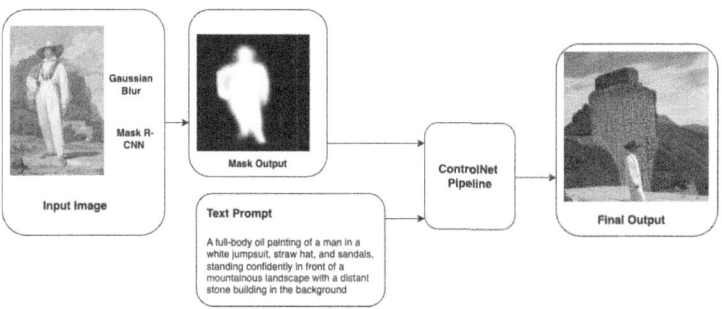

**Fig. 3.** Proposed pipeline

**Fig. 4.** Original images and generated images with prompts from the pipeline

### 4.3  Gaussian Blur for Smoothing the Generated Image

Once the image is generated through the process, post-processing techniques such as Gaussian Blur are applied to smooth the final result and reduce high-frequency noise artifacts. The Gaussian blur is a simple yet effective technique for image smoothing, which is often used in diffusion-based models to make the generated image appear more natural. A Gaussian kernel is applied to the image during post-processing. The kernel is a matrix that represents the Gaussian function and is used for the convolution operation with the image. This function has the form:

$$G(x,y) = 12\pi\sigma^2 \exp\left(-\frac{x^2+y^2}{2\sigma^2}\right)$$

$$G(x,y) = \frac{2\pi}{\sigma^2} \exp\left(-\frac{x^2+y^2}{2\sigma^2}\right)$$

where, $\sigma$ is the standard deviation, which controls the spread of the blur. The Gaussian kernel is convolved with the image pixels, effectively averaging each pixel's neighborhood in a weighted manner. The result is a blurred image where sharp edges are smoothed out, reducing graininess or noise. Moreover, The strength of the Gaussian blur is controlled by adjusting the kernel size and sigma value. Larger kernels with higher sigma values result in more smoothing, while smaller kernels preserve more fine details. Additionally, Gaussian blur is used as a final step in the image generation pipeline to soften the image, remove residual noise from the denoising steps, and improve visual quality. This helps produce high-quality images that are visually appealing and free from unwanted artifacts.

## 5  Evaluation Metrics for Comparing Similarity

In this section, we evaluate our generated images through different test metrics and understand the outputs. We prioritize mitigating the similarity of the input image and the output image keeping the context similar. We use two different metrics to evaluate the similarity between original and generated images.

**FID:**  When comparing generated images to original photos, we have used a statistic called the Frechet Inception Distance (FID) score [13] to evaluate the accuracy and realism of the generated images. Calculate the difference, as extracted by a trained inception network, between the feature distributions of the generated and actual images. A quantitative indicator of how well a generative model generates realistic and accurate images can be determined with FID. A lower FID score indicates that the distribution of features in the generated images is more similar to the distribution of features in the real images.

**FID Score Range**

–  **FID  0:** Generated images are extremely similar to the generated image. It strongly suggests potential copyright infringement.

- **FID 10–30:** Moderate similarity in which the generated images might be influenced by the original images but are not identical.
- **FID > 30:** Low similarity, suggesting that the generated images are sufficiently different from the reference images.
- **FID > 50:** Very low similarity, the generated images being highly distinct from the reference images, making copyright infringement concerns less likely.

**Structural Similarity Index Measure (SSIM):** SSIM [5] is a method to predict the perceived quality of digital television and cinematic images, as well as other types of digital images and videos. It is also used in different research works [17, 21] to measure the similarity between two images. We evaluated SSIM for benchmarking between the original image and the generated image.

**SSIM Score Range**

- SSIM ranges from $-1$ to $1$.

  **Score Interpretation**

- **SSIM = 1**: Indicates a perfect match between the two images, meaning that the generated image is identical to the reference image in terms of structure, luminance, and contrast.
- **SSIM = 0**: Indicates no structural similarity between the two images.
- **SSIM < 0**: Rare but suggests a significant structural difference between the two images (the images may even appear as inverse versions of one another in some cases).

**Detailed Interpretation of SSIM Scores**

- **SSIM $\approx 0.9-1$**: High structural similarity. The generated image is very close to the reference image in terms of perceptual quality.
- **SSIM $\approx 0.7-0.9$**: Moderate similarity. The generated image has noticeable but not severe differences from the reference image.
- **SSIM $\approx 0.5-0.7$**: Low similarity. The generated image has clear structural differences from the reference image.
- **SSIM $<0.5$**: Poor similarity. The generated image significantly differs from the reference image, with substantial loss of structure or significant artifacts (Figs. 5 and 6).

## 6   How Our Proposed Pipeline Avoids Copyright Infringement

On our research we conduct mask extraction that isolates the structure, shape, or contours of the input image, focusing on abstract features rather than directly replicating the image itself. By using the mask rather than the original image, the pipeline is discarding significant creative elements, such as colors, textures, and fine details, which are

**Fig. 5.** Comparison of original and generated images: SSIM = 0.0545 (low structural similarity), FID = 2878.4668 (significant deviation in feature distributions, implying a lack of resemblance)

**Fig. 6.** Comparison of original and generated images: SSIM = 0.3182 (low structural similarity), FID = 3765.9952 (significant deviation in feature distributions, indicating a lack of resemblance)

usually the basis for copyright protection. This step shows intent to use only the structural information and not the full creative expression of the original work. Moreover, ControlNet combined with stable diffusion introduces text-based input and generative algorithms that significantly transform the input image. The generative process incorporates both text prompts and the mask to create an entirely new image. The output is shaped not only by the structural input but also by the descriptive textual guidance. This integration results in a high degree of transformation, potentially qualifying as a new, original work, especially if the output is not visually recognizable as derivative of the input. AI models, like stable diffusion, generate content rather than directly copying or modifying the input, often incorporating additional randomness and new elements. The stable diffusion pipeline is designed to create new and unique outputs rather than merely editing or reproducing the original input. The resulting image, influenced by the model's learned patterns and the textual input, can deviate significantly from the original, reducing the likelihood of infringement claims. Additionally, Post-processing steps like Gaussian blur further alter the final image, diminishing any residual resemblance to the original input. By softening edges, blending colors, and reducing the precision of details, the Gaussian blur step ensures that even minor recognizable elements from the original mask are obscured, emphasizing the image as a distinct, final product. Thus, Our proposed pipeline demonstrates clear intent to create a new, transformative work rather than replicate or derive from the original (Fig. 7).

**Fig. 7.** Comparison of original and generated images: SSIM = 0.2569 (low similarity), FID = 965.0421 significant deviation in feature distributions, implying a lack of resemblance)

## 6.1    How Our Proposed Pipeline is Different from Generative AI

Our pipeline relies on specific input images and uses mask extraction to guide the generation process. The output is influenced by the structural features of the input image, combined with text-based prompts. This makes our process more akin to a hybrid method that combines elements of image transformation with generative capabilities. Models like DALL·E or Stable Diffusion generate images entirely from text prompts, without relying on a specific image input. They create outputs based on patterns learned from large-scale datasets rather than transforming a specific source image. Moreover, Our process extracts structural features (like edges or shapes) from the input image using a mask. This step abstracts the original image's content and focuses on its basic geometry or layout. Mask extraction is a deliberate pre-processing step that introduces a layer of abstraction, further distancing the final output from the original image. Whereas, Traditional Generative AI does not rely on pre-processed masks from input images. Instead, it uses random noise and algorithms like diffusion to iteratively "imagine" an image based on the text input and learned patterns. Thus, our pipeline differs from Generative AI.

## 6.2    Justification of Being Computationally Inexpensive

Our pipeline is computationally inexpensive because it leverages lightweight pre-processing (mask extraction), structured guidance (ControlNet with text and image inputs), and low-cost post-processing (Gaussian blur). By avoiding training, reducing unnecessary exploration in latent space, and reusing pre-trained models, your approach requires less memory, fewer compute cycles, and lower overall hardware resources than traditional generative AI workflows.

# 7   Discussion

To rigorously evaluate the effectiveness of our proposed model in mitigating copyright concerns, we conducted extensive testing on various datasets. Our analysis focused on key metrics, including FID, SSIM, PSNR, and substantial similarity scores between the original and generated images. This multifaceted evaluation allowed us to gain a deeper understanding of the copyright implications of our approach.

Interestingly, our experiments revealed a nuanced relationship between image quality and the effectiveness of our method. We observed that using low-quality images as input resulted in lower-quality segmentation masks, ultimately leading to a less satisfactory final output. Conversely, while high-resolution images yielded high-quality masks, the final generated images were still not optimal. Notably, the most promising results were achieved when using medium-resolution images, striking a balance between mask quality and final output fidelity. This finding highlights the importance of considering image resolution as a key factor in optimizing our two-step generation process for both copyright protection and visual quality (Fig. 8).

FID:309.89299
SSIM: 0.232378
PSNR: 8.59419
Substantial similarity: 0.7726

FID: 322.70722
SSIM:0.304058
PSNR:6.83829
Substantial Similarity: 0.7831

FID: 366.27309
SSIM:0.286295
PSNR:7.40057
Substantial Similarity: 0.7326

**Fig. 8.** Similarity analysis between original and generated images

# 8   Limitations and Future Work

In this research, we prioritized mitigating copyright concerns stemming from the relationship between real-world images in our datasets and the images generated by our model. While our proposed methodology effectively reduces the risk of copyright infringement, the process of generating prompts for each image is labor-intensive and inefficient when applied to large datasets. To address this limitation, our future research will focus on developing a self-automated prompt-generation mechanism. This mechanism will analyze the context of an image to create relevant prompts, enabling the generation of higher-quality images that better capture the essence of the original or provided images. By automating this crucial step, we aim to enhance the scalability and practicality of our approach for real-world applications. This advancement will not only streamline the image generation workflow but also contribute to producing more creative and contextually appropriate outputs, further reducing the potential for copyright issues.

## 9 Conclusion

Diffusion models have revolutionized image generation, surpassing predecessors like GANs and VAEs in both fidelity and performance. However, this progress has been shadowed by a critical challenge: source copying. This issue raises serious concerns regarding privacy and intellectual property rights, demanding innovative solutions that preserve content quality while enhancing copyright protection. Our research introduces a novel two-step image generation model designed to specifically address these concerns. This model operates by first generating segmentation masks from a given text prompt. These masks are then used to guide a Stable Diffusion model, effectively minimizing source copying while maintaining high fidelity in the final generated image. This approach also successfully circumvents the need for textual embedding, further streamlining the process and reducing potential avenues for copyright infringement. By decoupling the image generation process in this manner, we offer a promising pathway towards responsible and ethical AI image generation that respects both creative expression and copyright protection.

## References

1. Abadpour, A., Kasaei, S.: Deliberate distortion of color image and video resources for copyright protection. In: Proceedings of the Fifth IEEE International Symposium on Signal Processing and Information Technology, pp. 369–374. IEEE (2005)
2. Ahmed, T., Rahman, T., Roy, B.B., Uddin, J.: Drone detection by neural network using GLCM and SURF. J. Inf. Syst. Telecommun. **9**(33), 15–24 (2021)
3. Aoyon, R.S., Hossain, I.: A chatbot based auto-improving health care assistant using RoBERTa. In: 2023 3rd International Conference on Robotics, Automation and Artificial Intelligence (RAAI), pp. 213–217 (2023). https://doi.org/10.1109/RAAI59955.2023.10601285
4. Aoyon, R.S., Hossain, I.: A novel approach of making French language learning platform via brain-computer interface and deep learning. In: Yang, X.S., Sherratt, S., Dey, N., Joshi, A. (eds.) Proceedings of Ninth International Congress on Information and Communication Technology, pp. 399–409. Springer, Singapore (2024)
5. Brunet, D., Vrscay, E.R., Wang, Z.: On the mathematical properties of the structural similarity index. IEEE Trans. Image Process. **21**(4), 1488–1499 (2011)

6. Dhariwal, P., Nichol, A.: Diffusion models beat GANs on image synthesis. Adv. Neural. Inf. Process. Syst. **34**, 8780–8794 (2021)
7. Gong, Y.: Gradient domain diffusion models for image synthesis. arXiv preprint arXiv:2309.01875 (2023)
8. Goodfellow, I., et al.: Generative adversarial nets. Adv. Neural Inf. Process. Syst. **27** (2014)
9. Gupta, A., Jaiswal, A., Wu, Y., Yadav, V., Natarajan, P.: Adversarial mask generation for preserving visual privacy. In: 2021 16th IEEE International Conference on Automatic Face and Gesture Recognition (FG 2021), pp. 1–5. IEEE (2021)
10. Ho, J., Jain, A., Abbeel, P.: Denoising diffusion probabilistic models. Adv. Neural. Inf. Process. Syst. **33**, 6840–6851 (2020)
11. Ho, J., Saharia, C., Chan, W., Fleet, D.J., Norouzi, M., Salimans, T.: Cascaded diffusion models for high fidelity image generation. J. Mach. Learn. Res. **23**(47), 1–33 (2022)
12. Islam, M.F., et al.: Involution fused convnet for classifying eye-tracking patterns of children with autism spectrum disorder (2024). https://arxiv.org/abs/2401.03575
13. Karras, T.: Progressive growing of GANs for improved quality, stability, and variation. arXiv preprint arXiv:1710.10196 (2017)
14. Kingma, D.P., Welling, M.: Auto-encoding variational bayes. arXiv preprint arXiv:1312.6114 (2013)
15. Labib, S.M.F.R., Mondal, J.J., Manab, M.A., Newaz, S., Xiao, X.: Tailoring adversarial attacks on deep neural networks for targeted class manipulation using deepfool algorithm (2024). https://arxiv.org/abs/2310.13019
16. Li, S., Liu, L., Chai, Z., Li, R., Tan, X.: ERA-solver: error-robust adams solver for fast sampling of diffusion probabilistic models. arXiv preprint arXiv:2301.12935 (2023)
17. Liao, J., et al.: Deep-MSIM: fast image reconstruction with deep learning in multifocal structured illumination microscopy. Adv. Sci. **10**(27), 2300947 (2023)
18. Lu, Y., Yang, M.Y., Liu, Z., Kamath, G., Yu, Y.: Disguised copyright infringement of latent diffusion model. arXiv preprint arXiv:2404.06737 (2024)
19. Ma, R., et al.: A dataset and benchmark for copyright protection from text-to-image diffusion models. arXiv preprint arXiv:2403.12052 (2024)
20. Mondal, J.J., et al.: Uncovering local aggregated air quality index with smartphone captured images leveraging efficient deep convolutional neural network. Sci. Rep. **14**(1), 1627 (2024)
21. Noor, J., Shanto, M.N.H., Mondal, J.J., Hossain, M.G., Chellappan, S., Al Islam, A.B.M.A.: Orchestrating image retrieval and storage over a cloud system. IEEE Trans. Cloud Comput. **11**(2), 1794–1806 (2023). https://doi.org/10.1109/TCC.2022.3162790
22. Permenter, F., Yuan, C.: Interpreting and improving diffusion models using the euclidean distance function. arXiv preprint arXiv:2306.04848 (2023)
23. Rombach, R., Blattmann, A., Lorenz, D., Esser, P., Ommer, B.: High-resolution image synthesis with latent diffusion models. In: Proceedings of the IEEE/CVF Conference on Computer Vision and Pattern Recognition, pp. 10684–10695 (2022)
24. Shang, S., et al.: ResDiff: combining CNN and diffusion model for image super-resolution. In: Proceedings of the AAAI Conference on Artificial Intelligence, vol. 38, pp. 8975–8983 (2024)
25. Siddique, L.A., Junhai, R., Reza, T., Khan, S.S., Rahman, T.: Analysis of real-time hostile activitiy detection from spatiotemporal features using time distributed deep CNNs, RNNs and attention-based mechanisms. In: 2022 IEEE 5th International Conference on Image Processing Applications and Systems (IPAS), vol. Five, pp. 1–6 (2022). https://doi.org/10.1109/IPAS55744.2022.10053001
26. Singh, J., Gould, S., Zheng, L.: High-fidelity guided image synthesis with latent diffusion models. In: 2023 IEEE/CVF Conference on Computer Vision and Pattern Recognition (CVPR), pp. 5997–6006. IEEE (2023)

27. Somepalli, G., Singla, V., Goldblum, M., Geiping, J., Goldstein, T.: Diffusion art or digital forgery? Investigating data replication in diffusion models. In: Proceedings of the IEEE/CVF Conference on Computer Vision and Pattern Recognition, pp. 6048–6058 (2023)
28. Somepalli, G., Singla, V., Goldblum, M., Geiping, J., Goldstein, T.: Understanding data replication in diffusion models (2023)
29. Song, J., Meng, C., Ermon, S.: Denoising diffusion implicit models. arXiv preprint arXiv:2010.02502 (2020)
30. Wang, H., Shen, Q., Tong, Y., Zhang, Y., Kawaguchi, K.: The stronger the diffusion model, the easier the backdoor: data poisoning to induce copyright breaches without adjusting fine-tuning pipeline. arXiv preprint arXiv:2401.04136 (2024)
31. Zhang, L., Rao, A., Agrawala, M.: Adding conditional control to text-to-image diffusion models. In: Proceedings of the IEEE/CVF International Conference on Computer Vision, pp. 3836–3847 (2023)
32. Zhang, Y., Tzun, T.T., Hern, L.W., Sim, T., Kawaguchi, K.: Enhancing semantic fidelity in text-to-image synthesis: attention regulation in diffusion models. arXiv preprint arXiv:2403.06381 (2024)
33. Zhang, Y., Tzun, T.T., Hern, L.W., Wang, H., Kawaguchi, K.: Investigating copyright issues of diffusion models under practical scenarios. arXiv preprint arXiv:2311.12803 (2023)

# Shadows of Selfies: How Generative AI Fuels GBV-An Analysis of Non-consensual Sexualised Deepfakes Through Abolitionism and Intersectionality

Anastasia Karagianni[✉]

Vrije Universiteit Brussels (VUB-LSTS), Pleinlaan 2, 1050 Brussels, Belgium
anastasia.karagianni@vub.be

**Abstract.** This paper delves into the interplay between privacy, identity and dignity rights under the questioning scope of AI-generated image-based violence within the context of the emergence of non-consensual generation of sexualised deepfakes. Through the feminist theories of male dominance and violence, as well as the social theory of identity, I analyse the implications of non-consensual sexualised deepfakes in constructing digital identities and image forgery in the digital era. In this way, their impact on dignity right, mainly on its inviolability aspect and encompassing personality rights, as well as privacy and data protection rights, will be highlighted. Yet, a particular focus will be given to their conceptualisation as a form of AI-generated gender-based violence. For this reason, a critique of the European Directive 2024/11385 on Violence Against Women and Domestic Violence using intersectionality and abolition feminist methods will strengthen this legal analysis. Concluding remarks will be provided in the last part of the paper.

**Keywords:** abolitionism · AI-generated violence · deepfakes abuse · gender-based violence · intersectionality

This project was supported by the FARI - AI for the Common Good Institute (ULB-VUB), financed by the European Union, with the support of the Brussels Capital Region (Innoviris and Paradigm).

F. Bieker et al. (Eds.): Privacy and Identity 2024, IFIP AICT 705, pp. 94–111, 2025.
https://doi.org/10.1007/978-3-031-91054-8_5

# 1  Introduction

The rapid advancements in generative AI technologies have contributed to the development of (consensual) sexualised (or not) deepfakes[1] used not only for artistic expression[2], entertainment[3] or scientific purposes (e.g. in tumor detection)[4], but also in the pornography industry[5]. The potential of generative AI technologies for the non-consensual generation of deepfakes though have intensified privacy concerns as these technologies enable the creation of highly realistic and potentially harmful audiovisual fabrications of individuals [1]. This poses a substantial threat to society, given their capacity to compromise personal integrity and privacy[6] by misrepresenting individuals in an increasingly convincing manner [2].

Non-consensual sexualised deepfakes pose significant challenges to individuals' identities by producing false representations that blur the boundaries between reality and fiction, thereby infringing upon their privacy [3, 4]. Such practices constitute a violation of privacy and data protection laws, as delineated in Article 7 of the European Charter of Fundamental Rights (CFR), Article 8 of the European Convention on Human Rights (ECHR), and Article 7 and Recital 32 of the General Data Protection Regulation (GDPR) [5]. Specifically, the unauthorised use of an individual's image or video, often acquired through illicit access to their personal data, to generate deepfake content represents a severe interference with their privacy.

These infringements frequently occur when images or videos are collected without the subject's consent, whether sourced from public or private social media profiles [6], public databases, or other private repositories. These materials are then processed using artificial intelligence (AI) algorithms to train models capable of creating highly realistic yet fabricated deepfake content. This process exacerbates the legal concerns associated with privacy violations.

The deployment of non-consensual deepfakes can manipulate and mislead deepfakes' viewers, by creating deceptive representations that are indistinguishable from

---

[1] Deepfakes involve creating content for a specific person using a comprehensive dataset of their images and videos, processed by algorithms to replicate their unique facial features. Romero Moreno, F. (2024). Generative AI and deepfakes: a human rights approach to tackling harmful content. *International Review of Law, Computers & Technology*, 1–30. https://doi.org/10.1080/13600869.2024.2324540.

[2] Lalla, V. et al. (2022). Artificial intelligence: deepfakes in the entertainment industry. *WIPO Magazine*. https://www.wipo.int/en/web/wipo-magazine/articles/artificial-intelligence-deepfakes-in-the-entertainment-industry-42620.

[3] Ibid.

[4] See, Goth, G. (2022). Medical Deepfakes Are the Real Deal. MDDI Online. https://www.mddionline.com/artificial-intelligence/medical-deepfakes-are-the-real-deal.

[5] Stoya, J. (2024). The Future of Porn Is Consensual Deepfakes. Reason Magazine. https://reason.com/2024/05/12/the-future-of-porn-is-consensual-deepfakes/.

[6] Consent plays a pivotal role in safeguarding privacy in the digital era, particularly regarding the processing of personal data. It empowers individuals to exercise control over access to their personal information and activities. This principle is enshrined in Articles 4 and 8 of the European Union Regulation 2016/679, widely known as the General Data Protection Regulation (GDPR).

genuine content, thereby undermining an individual's sense of identity[7] [8, 9]. For example, (non-consensual) deepfake audiovisual content may be employed to impersonate an individual, generating confusion about their true identity and inflicting reputational harm [10]. In this way, the manipulation of digital content via generative AI can distort the perception of reality, further complicating the formation and maintenance of identity in the digital age [11].

Privacy and identity are integral to personality rights [12], which are closely connected to the right to dignity[8], an inviolable right outlined in Article 1 CFR stating that "*human dignity is inviolable*"[9] [13]. The interconnections of these rights in the context of non-consensual sexualised deepfakes are illustrated in Fig. 1. Feminist scholars and activists highlight particularly that such content reinforce harmful stereotypes, objectify women's bodies[10] [14], and constitute a form of gender-based violence [15, 16]. These deepfakes are frequently weaponised against women [17] serving purposes such as sexual gratification, harassment, humiliation, or control.

Women[11] [18, 19], LGBTQIA+ people [20], and people from Black and ethnic minority communities[12] [21] are disproportionally targeted, suffering significant harm due to the entrenched societal double standards[13] and inequalities both online and offline. Drawing on feminist theories of male dominance and violence, alongside the social theory of identity [22], this analysis will explore how non-consensual sexualised deepfakes expose prevailing gender norms, peer cultures on social media, and reflections of masculinity that shape users' sexual practices and ethics, including their digital activity.

Therefore, this analysis moves beyond the concept of consent, opting not to focus solely on privacy and data protection law. Instead, it questions its legal contextualisation

---

[7] Identity encompasses various aspects that make individuals unique, including their personal characteristics, beliefs, values, and experiences [8].

[8] Personality rights are also protected under the European and international human rights frameworks, including the Universal Declaration of Human Rights. See, Article 1 CFR, Article 12 (1) of the ECHR, Article 1 of the United Declaration on Human Rights.

[9] *Inviolability* refers to the fact that certain rights may not be derogated at any time or infringed on under any circumstances and must be fully respected and defended. See, Plattner, D. (1996). *International Humanitarian Law and Inalienable or Non-derogable Human Rights.* Non-derogable Rights and States of Emergency, 349–63. Brussels: Bruylant.

[10] Objectification can be defined as seeing and/or treating a person, usually a woman, *as an object.* In this entry, the focus is primarily on sexual objectification, objectification occurring in the sexual realm, as Martha Nussbaum has stated. Nussbaum, M. C. (1995). Objectification. *Philosophy & Public Affairs, 24*(4), 249–291. Rae Langton has added the objectification as the *reduction to body* (the treatment of a person as identified with their body, or body parts), and as the *reduction to appearance* (the treatment of a person primarily in terms of how they look, or how they appear to the senses) [15].

[11] According to the State of Deepfakes report in 2019, 96% of deepfakes were pornographic, while 99.9% depict women. See, [19].

[12] See, [21].

[13] The term "double standards" refers to the unequal criteria that shape both formal and informal behavioral norms, whereby the standards applied to evaluate and regulate women often differ from those applied to men, typically to the advantage of the latter. See, https://eige.europa.eu/publications-resources/thesaurus/terms/1234.

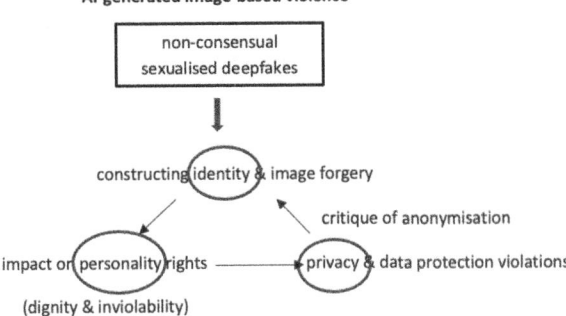

**Fig. 1.** AI-generated image-based violence scheme

as AI-generated image-based violence underscoring the limitations of the current definition of intimate image-based abuse provided in Article 5 of the EU Directive 2024/11385 on gender-based violence-hereinafter EU GBV Directive[14] [23]. By scrutinising the EU GBV Directive's broad definition of image-based sexual abuse, this study critiques potential shortcomings in its application, particularly its disproportionate impact on marginalised communities, like sex workers.

A key critique of the EU GBV Directive is its reliance on criminalisation that may inadvertently harm these communities, coupled with its narrowly defined scope concerning specific contexts of image-based sexual abuse. These limitations underscore the need for a more holistic approach that considers the intersectionality[15] [24, 25] of gender-based violence and its impact on different communities [26]. Employing intersectionality and abolitionism[16] as analytical methods for this legal examination, this examination challenges conventional understandings of intimate image-based abuse[17] to better address the needs of all victims/survivors [27]. For marginalised communities, such as refugee women, women with disabilities, and sex workers, privacy serves as a critical safeguard against systemic discrimination, exploitation, and harm. These communities often face unique vulnerabilities, making privacy protections essential for ensuring their safety, dignity, and autonomy and preventing them from further disproportionate harms due to the potential for discrimination and stigma. For example, in the

---

[14] [23].

[15] Intersectionality is a metaphor for understanding the ways that multiple forms of inequality or disadvantage sometimes compound themselves and create obstacles that often are not understood among conventional ways of thinking [24]. See also, [25].

[16] Abolitionism in law is the abolition of any law or practice deemed harmful to society. Bell M. Abolition: A New Paradigm for Reform. *Law & Social Inquiry*. 2021;46(1):32–68. https://doi.org/10.1017/lsi.2020.21.

[17] The term survivor often refers to an individual who is going or has gone through the recovery process of a gender-based violence instance. Additionally, this word is used when discussing the short- and long-term effects of sexual violence. Some people identify themselves as a victim, while others identify as a survivor. Mulvihill, N., Walker, S. J., Hester, M., & Gangoli, G. (2018). How is 'justice' understood, sought, and experienced by victims/survivors of gender-based violence?: A review of the literature.

case of *O.G. and Others v. Greece*[18], the public disclosure of sex workers' personal data in the press-accompanied by allegations of HIV positivity-exemplifies how breaches of privacy can exacerbate marginalisation and lead to significant harm [28].

This analysis highlights the complexities surrounding the unauthorised generation and distribution of sexualised deepfakes, with particular emphasis on the exploitation and harm they cause. Therefore, it stresses the pressing need for an intersectional approach when legal safeguards are set against such practices, mostly in the AI context. The first part of the paper examines how non-consensual sexualised deepfakes create fake digital identities and their impact on rights to dignity, privacy, and data protection. The analysis is grounded in feminist theories of male dominance and violence, as well as social identity theories. The second part of the paper scrutinises the generation of non-consensual sexualised deepfakes within the context of the EU GBV Directive further elaborating on the concept of AI-generated image-based violence. In the concluding section, I summarise the key findings, emphasising the feminist critiques of non-consensual sexualised deepfakes and their framing as a form of AI-generated image-based violence. These insights aim to inform the development of more effective and inclusive legal and policy responses to this evolving phenomenon.

## 2 Non-consensual Sexualised Deepfakes: Navigating Identity and Personality Rights

This analysis will start off looking at the definition of identity and its multifaceted nature in the digital era. Identity is a complex and multifaceted construct that encompasses the characteristics, attributes, beliefs, values, and experiences that define an individual or a group [29]. It is a dynamic and evolving concept influenced by various factors, including personal choices, social interactions, cultural background, and external perceptions [30]. In the context of the digital era, the notion of identity has further expanded to include *digital identities*. These are representations of individuals or groups within online and digital environments, reflecting both self-expression and the ways individuals are perceived and interpreted by others in these spaces [31].

European theorists, like Foucault and Tajfel, offered diverse perspectives on identity, encompassing psychological, social, cultural, and political dimensions. Michel Foucault explored how identity is shaped by power relations and disciplinary practices within society [32]. He argued that identities are constructed through discourses and institutions that exert control over individuals, influencing how they perceive themselves and others. Along the same line, according to Henri Tajfel, individuals derive their identity from their group memberships [33]. Based on his social identity theory, individuals strive to achieve a positive social identity by comparing their in-groups favorably against out-groups, leading to in-group favoritism and intergroup discrimination.

From a feminist perspective, this distinction can be viewed as the group of males who dominate the society and the group of females who are oppressed by the male dominance [34]. The feminist theory of male dominance, also known as patriarchy, examines the

---

[18] Applications nos. 71555/12 and 48256/13, ECHR 017 (2024). See, https://hudoc.echr.coe.int/fre-press#{%22itemid%22:[%22003-7857128-10914452%22]}.

systemic and structural power relations that prioritise men and masculinity over women and femininity. According to R.W. Connell and the gender's order theory, which refers to the concept of hegemonic masculinity, there is a dominant form of masculinity that upholds male dominance and reinforces the subordination of women and marginalised masculinities, setting the standard for what is considered "normal" and "acceptable" masculinity, as well as objectifying women's bodies [35].

In the realm of AI, male dominance emerges with the generation of non-consensual sexualised deepfakes that predominantly targets women [19] and LGBTQIA+ people [36]. This practice represents a form of digital manipulation and image forgery[19], involving the intentional alteration of women's digital images to fabricate deceptive or misleading representations [37]. Such acts[20] undermine the authenticity of the original images, violating privacy and identity rights. They infringe privacy through the unauthorised use of personal data for algorithm training[21] and produce AI-generated deepfakes that falsely depict individuals in scenarios they never engaged in. These practices are often employed for non-consensual pornography, defamation, and impersonation, facilitating coercion and limiting sexual autonomy, depriving individuals of their ability to make decisions about their sexual activities and partners. This violation prevents individuals from freely making decisions about their sexual activities, leading to the restriction of their sexual autonomy [38–40], severe reputational harm and emotional distress [41]. In this context, as identity is increasingly violated, the right to dignity-encompassing personality rights-shrinks proportionally [42].

AI-generated non-consensual sexualised deepfakes undermine fundamental rights, including bodily integrity, (sexual) autonomy, dignity, and privacy, as was described before, constituting a form of gender-based violence. They exert a gendered power dynamic, causing sexual, psychological, emotional or economic harm, particularly on women and LGBTQIA+ people (Article 2 (a) EU GBV Directive). Addressing this issue requires transcending mere consent and focusing on the broader societal and victims/survivors' harms that should be examined under the spectrum of gender equality, non-discrimination and gender-based violence (Recital 3 and Article 2 (a) EU GBV Directive). To uphold these rights, legislation, like EU GBV Directive, must comprehensively address AI-generated image-based violence. Further elaboration on this necessity is provided in the following part.

---

[19] The European Court of Human Rights acknowledged that "A person's image constitutes one of the chief attributes of his or her personality, as it reveals the person's unique characteristics and distinguishes the person from his or her peers. The right to the protection of one's image is thus one of the essential components of personal development. It mainly presupposes the individual's right to control the use of that image, including the right to refuse publication thereof." (*von Hannover v Germany* (no 2), Grand Chamber, 7 February 2012, Sect. 96.).

[20] The term "image forgery" underscores the fabricated nature of the material, as it involves the unauthorised appropriation of an individual's likeness and sexual identity to create a false representation. The use of the term "forgery" explicitly characterises this act as fraudulent and unlawful. Originating in the United States, the term is employed in draft legislation before the U.S. Congress and is the preferred term in this legal context. See, https://www.congress.gov/118/meeting/house/116953/documents/HHRG-118-GO12-20240312-SD008.pdf.

[21] See, https://medium.com/@gupta.brij/deepfake-a-deep-learning-approach-in-artificial-content-generation-a626ceebe48f.

## 3  Beyond Consent: The Complexities of Sexualised Deepfakes as AI-Generated Image-Based Abuse

As explained in the previous part, the generation of non-consensual sexualised deepfakes is currently framed as a breach of privacy and data protection under GDPR (Article 7 and Recital 32 GDPR) [43]. Yet, the discussions around privacy and consent are also concerning the shift in terminology, moving from *"deepfake pornography"* [3]- as was initially introduced in 2017[22] [44]- to terms like *"deepfake (sexual) abuse"* [45] and *"non-consensual synthetic intimate imagery"* [46]. This is because *pornography* generally refers to legitimate consensual adult material, which contrasts with the abusive nature of non-consensual deepfakes[23]. However, using the term *"deepfake pornography"* can minimise the harm [47], such as the emotional, psychological harm (e.g. humiliation, anxiety, and trauma), and reputational harm these images cause due to their easy widespread online, along with exacerbating existing gender-based and identity-based violence [48].

This harm exhibits characteristics of gender-based violence, as defined in Article 2 (a) EU GBV Directive, by violating dignity, bodily integrity, and sexual autonomy, as was examined before. These actions degrade victims/survivors, diminishing their agency in online spaces and disrespecting their inherent worth and value [47]. Framing these acts under exclusively the scope of privacy and data protection law is a consistent failure to address or acknowledge systemic gender power inequities that influences the proliferation of this type of abuse [48]. This is why their conceptualisation as AI-generated image-based violence is crucial.

AI-generated image-based violence [14, 49] involves the use of artificial intelligence to create or alter images with the intent to harm, exploit, or intimidate individuals. This phenomenon recognises the gendered nature of abuses such as non-consensual sexualised deepfakes, where the likeness of a person is fabricated into explicit or sexualised content. The intent often includes defamation, harassment, abuse, or humiliation, underscoring the need to address this as a unique and harmful form of violence beyond privacy violations.

### 3.1  Beyond Gender: EU GBV Directive Through the Lenses of Intersectionality

LGBTQIA+ people [18], people from Black and ethnic minority communities [20], sex workers [50, 51], and those from other marginalised communities experience compounded discrimination and harm from AI-generated image-based violence [52]. These

---

[22] See, https://www.vice.com/en/article/gal-gadot-fake-ai-porn/. See also Article 139h/1 of the Dutch Criminal Code, which was interpreted in November 2023 by a court for the first time in application to the creation of sexually explicit deepfakes. The creator and distributor of a "deepfake porn" video was sentenced to 180 h of community service. https://uitspraken.rechtspraak.nl/details?id=ECLI:NL:RBAMS:2023:6923.

[23] According to the report published in 2023 by Security Hero, a USA-based company offering online security services, the number of deepfake porn videos available online has increased 550% since 2019, with 99% of the videos identified featuring female subjects. See, https://www.securityhero.io/state-of-deepfakes/#key-findings.

communities face intersecting forms of discrimination that amplify their vulnerability and the impact of such abuses. The concept of *"intersectionality"* is crucial in analysing how overlapping systems of oppression, such as racism, sexism, homophobia, and classism, create unique experiences of violence and marginalisation.

The concept of *"intersectionality"*, first introduced by Ann Julia Cooper in 1892 [25] and later popularised by American scholar Professor Kimberlé Crenshaw [24], examines how different aspects of a person's identity intersect. Lisa Bowleg expands *intersectionality* as a framework for understanding how multiple social identities -such as race, gender, sexual orientation, and disability- interplay at the individual level with societal structures of inequality (e.g. racism, sexism, heterosexism, and classism). Glitch[24], a prominent civil society organisation focusing on online abuse and marginalised communities, particularly women, LGBTQIA+ people, and people from Black and ethnic minority communities, emphasies that discrimination experienced offline often extends online, targeting individuals' *"multiple intersecting identities"* [19].

The EU GBV Directive acknowledges the importance of intersectionality in Recital 6[25] EU GBV Directive, which states that *"Member States should therefore pay due regard to victims affected by such intersectional discrimination, through providing specific measures where intersecting forms of discrimination are present. In particular, lesbian, bisexual, trans, non-binary, intersex and queer (LBTIQ) women, women with disabilities and women with a minority racial or ethnic background are at a heightened risk of experiencing gender-based violence"*. It also addresses the fabrication of deepfakes in Recital 19 EU GBV Directive defining such acts as *"the material appreciably resembles an existing person, objects, places or other entities or events, depicting sexual activities of another person, and would falsely appear to others to be authentic or truthful. In the interest of effectively protecting victims of such conduct, threatening to engage in such conduct should also be covered"*. This opens the space for an intersectional and interdisciplinary approach of this analysis.

Examining Article 5 (b) of the EU GBV Directive, which criminalises producing, manipulating, and disseminating non-consensual intimate or altered material, two key concerns arise from an intersectional perspective. First, the clause *"making it appear as though another person is engaged in sexual activities"* focuses on fabricated material but could be limited in addressing nuanced harms. Second, requiring the material to be made *"accessible to a multitude of end-users"* could exclude smaller scale but equally harmful acts, potentially limiting the Directive's scope to address diverse instances of abuse effectively.

The first concerns a gap in phrasing of Article 5 (b) EU GBV Directive, as it excludes certain forms of manipulated material, like *non-explicit sexual nudity* or *sexual imagery without nudity* [53]. *Non-explicit sexual nudity* refers to representations of nudity that imply sexuality without being overtly graphic or explicit. These depictions often focus on suggestive poses, partial nudity, or artistic styles that evoke sensuality rather than explicit sexual acts [54]. *Sexual imagery without nudity* involves depictions that suggest

---

[24] Glitch is a charity organisation based in United Kingdom to end online abuse and championing digital citizenship. See, https://glitchcharity.co.uk/about/.

[25] Recital 71, Articles 16, 21, 33 and 36 EU GBV Directive also include provisions on intersectional discrimination. Intersectionality is also protected under Article 21 CFR.

or convey sexual themes or sensuality without showing any actual nudity. This can include suggestive body language or poses or symbolic imagery (e.g. objects or settings associated with intimacy or eroticism) [55]. Both forms rely on implication and context rather than explicit depiction, and they are often used in art, media, and advertising to evoke sensual or sexual associations while adhering to content restrictions or cultural sensitivities. Since non-consensual sexualised deepfakes involving both can be harmful if shared, all *"intimate material"* manipulated and shared without consent should be in scope.

The EU GBV Directive outlines a legal framework for defining (intimate) image-based sexual abuse in the digital era but may lack clarity or be overly narrow in its definitions. It often equates/connotates *"intimate"* with *"sexual"*, as seen in laws like the Irish Harassment Act 2020, which includes depictions of genitals, breasts, nudity, or sexual acts [54]. This approach, while covering cases of image-based abuse like creepshots and upskirting[26] [56], it heavily emphasises sexual and nude imagery, potentially limiting a broader interpretation of *intimacy* that could include non-sexual but nonetheless invasive depictions.

The term *"intimate images"* could benefit from broader interpretations that incorporate cultural and community-specific understandings of intimacy and sexuality. For example, in some marginalised/ethnic minority communities, such images might include depictions of women without expected attire, such as headscarves, or private moments like women dancing in culturally specific clothing [57]. These are often considered intimate or sexual within these contexts but may fall outside conventional definitions in European laws, which tend to reflect white, Western cultural norms [57]. However, broader interpretations may emerge in the future, as seen in Swedish laws on "intrusive photography" or Belgian provisions on voyeurism[27] [58], which address privacy violations based on a person's expectation of keeping certain aspects of their body or behavior hidden[28] [54, 58]. This is the case of private moments involving intimacy in public spheres, like breastfeeding situations. These examples highlight the need for clearer delineation or contextual consideration within the legal framework [59]. A closer examination of the definition of *"intimate image"* highlights the importance of recognising that privacy violations extend beyond sexual content and include various aspects of an individual's personal life, such as images taken in healthcare settings [60] or as part of artistic expression [61].

---

[26] Creepshots and upskirting are serious forms of image-based abuse where individuals take intrusive and suggestive photographs of others without their consent in public spaces. These photos often focus on private and intimate body parts, typically the genitals or genital areas, and are usually taken without the knowledge or awareness of the victim. The perpetrators of such acts frequently upload the images to illegal sites for voyeuristic purposes. See, https://www.btp.police.uk/ro/report/rsa/alpha-v1/advice/rape-sexual-assault-and-other-sexual-offences/voyeurism-upskirting/. See also, https://www.refinery29.com/en-gb/2017/10/177957/what-is-upskirting-law-change-campaign.

[27] Voyeurism refers to the act of secretly observing or recording individuals who are unaware that they are being watched, typically for the purpose of sexual arousal. This behavior usually involves observing people in private settings, such as in their homes, changing rooms, or other personal spaces, without their consent. See, [58].

[28] See, Chapter 4 Sect. 6a. Swedish Criminal Code; Article 417/8 Belgian Criminal Code.

This broader understanding of *"intimate images"*, alongside the complexities of generative AI technologies, is essential for formulating effective legal frameworks that adequately protect all individuals' privacy, identity and dignity rights in the AI sphere, mostly in the cases of AI-generated image-based violence. For instance, deepfakes can be weaponised to distort videos, such as those filmed by the Black Lives Matter community, which document police violence -an intimate content- and serve as vital evidence in seeking justice [62]. Another example is that sex workers' images and videos are often vulnerable to exploitation, as they may be more likely to be targeted for non-consensual content creation, including deepfakes, due to their visibility in adult content and the stigma attached to their profession. Such abuses highlight the need for an intersectional approach when crafting legislation.

Regarding the second problematic issue concerning the accessibility of such content to multiple end-users, the harm (e.g. psychological impacts and reputational injury, mostly in professional or conservative cultural environments, which are encountered as dignity and (bodily and psychological) integrity violations) is exacerbated when it is shared with even a single person. Victims/survivors often feel profound embarrassment and shame due to the alteration of their identity or/and the violation of their private life, especially if the deepfakes circulate widely or are seen by acquaintances, colleagues, or family members or even by one single person of these groups. Easy-to-use deepfake apps and social media platforms enable a broader range of users to create and distribute harmful content.

The rapid spread of non-consensual deepfakes across online platforms exacerbates harm, as victims may face workplace discrimination, social isolation, and threats of violence based on the perceived authenticity of the content[29]. The emotional toll is significant, with victims often suffering from anxiety, depression, or post-traumatic stress. When deepfakes go viral on social media platforms like Instagram or TikTok, the harm is magnified, as seen in South Korea, where a deepfake trend led to 513 cases being reported within a week[30] [63], highlighting the urgency of addressing this issue.

Yet, for the marginalised communities, like LGBTQIA+ people or sex workers, the spread of deepfakes can have devastating effects, especially in societies where their sexual orientation or occupation as sex workers is criminalised. Deepfake content that reveals private information can lead to compounded consequences, including discrimination, harassment, emotional distress and social exclusion. These communities face compounded stigma, and even sharing such content with one person can result in reputational damage and psychological harm, amplifying their vulnerability to further exploitation and abuse.

---

[29] See, https://www.theparliamentmagazine.eu/news/article/how-sexually-explicit-deepfakes-undermine-democracy-and-womens-role-in-the-eu.

[30] There is a rising fury in South Korea over the use of deepfake technology to create pornographic images of women, which ties into broader societal issues such as revenge porn and spy cams. Women are increasingly targeted with digitally altered explicit content without their consent. This ongoing issue reflects deep-rooted gender-based violence and the digital exploitation of women. Activists are demanding stronger laws and better enforcement to combat this harmful trend. See, Rashid, R. (2024, September 13). From spy cams to deepfake porn: Fury in South Korea as women targeted again. *The Guardian*. https://www.theguardian.com/world/2024/sep/13/from-spy-cams-to-deepfake-porn-fury-in-south-korea-as-women-targeted-again.

An intersectional analysis requires understanding of differences in status, power, roles, and needs of individuals from different communities because of social and political hierarchies and inequalities on intersectional grounds, such as race, ethnicity, socio-economic status, religion, gender, age, sexual orientation, indigenous status, replacement status, disability etc. LGBTQIA+ people, for instance, targeted by sexualised deep-fakes might face risks such as forced outing, discrimination, and violence, particularly in regions where their identities are stigmatised or criminalised. Women from Black and ethnic minority communities often face uniquely racialised forms of harm. Their hypersexualised portrayal[31], rooted in historical and cultural stereotypes, exacerbates the impact of these deepfakes. For example, Black women are often depicted in ways that align with harmful racialised tropes of hypersexuality, intensifying the violation of their dignity and autonomy [19].

An intersectional analysis is critical in understanding how these harms affect individuals differently. By intersectional lens to the issue of non-consensual sexualised deepfakes, it becomes clear that EU GBV Directive is limited to a narrow scope of *"intimate image"* based abuse leaving out of Article 5 (b) EU GBV Directive scope the vulnerabilities of marginalised communities, ensuring that their unique experiences of harm are addressed.

### 3.2 Beyond Criminalisation: EU GBV Directive Through the Lenses of Abolitionism

Criticism of the EU GBV Directive centres on its criminalisation-focused approach, which may disproportionately affect marginalised communities. The Directive's reliance on criminal law raises questions about how victims/survivors can prove the creation of deepfakes [48], gather evidence, and pursue legal action [64, 65], especially given the presumption of innocence in criminal law [66]. This limitation to criminal law can make it difficult for victims to access justice, particularly when it comes to non-consensual image-based violence.

This critique stems from how such policies can inadvertently perpetuate inequalities by failing to account for structural barriers faced by vulnerable groups. [67]. For instance, criminalising sex work forces sex workers into precarious situations, increasing their vulnerability to harm. The illegal status of sex work makes it more difficult for sex workers to report abuses such as AI-generated violence. This highlights the need for a more holistic approach that considers the intersectionality [19, 22, 23] of gender-based violence and its impact on different communities [68], as was analysed above. Employing intersectionality and abolitionism[32] [69] as analytical methods for this legal examination raises the question of how we should understand intimate image-based abuse, to effectively address the needs of all victims/survivors [70].

---

[31] This intersection of nudity and Indigenous women is deeply rooted in colonialism, exoticism, and patriarchy, and continues to affect how Indigenous women are viewed and treated today, while it raises critical questions on how AI technologies are designed and deployed. See, Agloinga, C. M. (2021). *Indigenous Women: Violence, Vulnerability and Cultural Protective Factors* (Doctoral dissertation, Walden University).

[32] Abolitionist feminist reject carceral solutions to gender-based violence and propose models of transformative and restorative justice [69].

For marginalised communities like refugee women, women with disabilities, and sex workers, privacy protection is especially critical to prevent further discrimination, stigma, and harm[33] [71]. The European Court of Human Rights case *O.G. and Others v. Greece*[34] highlights how intersecting identities (women, sex workers, individuals living with HIV) can amplify discrimination. In this case, privacy violations and discriminatory treatment by authorities-law enforcement agencies including the public prosecutor-contributed to compounded stigma, leading to social exclusion, violence, and even suicide. This underscores the urgent need for abolitionism and privacy safeguards for vulnerable groups facing *systemic discrimination.*

An abolition perspective, explored by Angela Davis in *Abolition Democracy*, critiques systems that perpetuate inequality, such as prisons and criminal justice systems [72]. In the context of AI-generated image-based violence, racial biases can affect the investigation of deepfake cases, with Black and ethnic minority victims/survivors more likely to face underreporting, cultural stigma, and systemic barriers [73] or they may face systemic barriers when reporting such cases. This results in a lack of trust in law enforcement, compounded by fears of discrimination, which often leads to underreporting [73]. Given the existing underreporting of gender-based violence, as highlighted in the European Fundamental Rights Agency's recent report[35], criminalising non-consensual sexualised deepfakes may not adequately protect all victims, particularly those from marginalised groups. The potential for law enforcement bias and underreporting means that people from Black and ethnic minority communities are less likely to seek justice. Moreover, predictive policing and deepfake detection algorithms may disproportionately target these communities, exacerbating racial disparities and further obstructing their access to justice, protection, and support [53].

To conclude, the criminalisation of AI-generated image-based violence may fail to support effectively all victims/survivors due to several systemic and structural barriers, like overlapping criminalisation[36] [74, 75]. For marginalised groups, such as sex workers, criminalisation could exacerbate vulnerability by reinforcing biases within law enforcement. Or marginalised people may lack access to the resources needed to navigate

---

[33] See, https://webfoundation.org/2021/10/the-importance-of-digital-privacy-for-marginalized-groups/.

[34] The Court set a significant precedent regarding the protection of privacy, particularly concerning health and photo data, within the context of sex workers' rights. The ECtHR ruled that Greece violated the right to respect for private life of sex workers who were accused of being HIV positive. The violation occurred when the Greek law enforcement authorities conducted blood tests on sex workers and subsequently disseminated their personal data publicly under the order of the Public Prosecutor in 2012. The Court emphasised that such actions exposed the applicants to significant social stigma and harm, demonstrating a lack of adequate procedural safeguards and respect for their dignity and privacy. Applications nos. 71555/12 and 48256/13, ECHR 017 (2024). See, https://hudoc.echr.coe.int/fre-press#{%22itemid%22:[%22003-7857128-109 14452%22]}.

[35] See, Eurostat, FRA, EIGE (2024). EU gender-based violence survey- Key results. https://fra.europa.eu/sites/default/files/fra_uploads/eu-gender_based_violence_survey_key_results.pdf.

[36] In jurisdictions where sex work is illegal, the criminalisation of both clients and workers can leave sex workers vulnerable. They may not feel safe approaching authorities for fear of being prosecuted or having their livelihoods disrupted. See, [74].

legal systems effectively [76]. This feminist analysis based on abolitionism highlights that criminalisation favors white cis abled people, either as victims/survivors[37] [74] or perpetrators [77]. The main findings of this are that criminalisation does not and cannot advance racial and equity justice [78].

# 4    Concluding Remarks

This paper analyses the harmful effects of non-consensual sexualizsd deepfakes as a form of AI-generated image-based violence. Their implications of privacy, identity, dignity and personality rights have been critically analysed under this scope [43]. This paper discusses how such content perpetuates societal stereotypes and targets marginalised groups, including women, LGBTQIA+ people, and people from Black and ethnic minority communities. Through this analysis, it is stressed that non-consensual sexualised deepfakes are used as tools that predominantly target the above-mentioned groups of people, constituting a new form of gender-based violence that reinforces patriarchal power dynamics by objectifying and dehumanising the victims/survivors, perpetuating a culture of control and dominance over women's bodies and identities, according to the feminist theories of male dominance and violence [79, 80]. These deepfakes represent a digital extension of existing patterns of sexual harassment, abuse, and exploitation that disproportionately affect women and marginalised communities [81].

The analysis, grounded in these two feminist theories, emphasises the importance of this phenomenon as gendered moving beyond consent. The generation and distribution of non-consensual sexualised deepfakes violate principles of bodily autonomy and personal agency, which are central to feminist thought. These deepfakes disproportionately target marginalised groups, including women from Black and ethnic minority communities, LGBTQIA+ people, and sex workers [82]. The compounded harm they face is heightened by systemic discrimination, including law enforcement biases. Intersectionality and abolitionism help highlight the unique vulnerabilities of these groups, where deepfakes can be weaponised to perpetuate harassment, violence, and further marginalisation.

The research highlights that the harm of AI-generated sexualised deepfakes starts with the processing of the data-often sourced from women's social media or unauthorised leaks, reflecting gender-based objectification. Solutions should go beyond consent and address both the root causes of AI-generated violence and the intersection between "offline" and "online" gender-based violence [83]. While criminalising the generation of non-consensual deepfakes may protect some, it could inadvertently harm marginalised groups, like sex workers, LGBTQIA+ people, people from Black and ethnic minority communities etc.

Deepfake technology is rapidly evolving and creating laws that can keep up with the pace of technological advancements is challenging. Even with criminalisation, identifying perpetrators and gathering evidence can be difficult, due to several factors, which include the evolving technology behind deepfakes, the anonymous nature of online platforms, and technical complexities. The EU GBV Directive should therefore move beyond

---

[37] See, the Western concept of victimhood [74].

criminal law, which can disproportionately harm marginalised communities-particularly when it fails to consider the unique social, economic, and political challenges they face. A civil rights approach though may be more effective, ensuring collective justice for community harms and facilitating international coordination. Such an approach could help overcome systemic biases and barriers faced by vulnerable populations in accessing justice.

In conclusion, non-consensual sexualised deepfakes are tools of power and control [84]. They exploit technological advancements to assert dominance over women and marginalised communities. Feminist theories critique this misuse of power, highlighting how technological tools can be weaponised to perpetuate existing social hierarchies and inequalities [85], while fostering the normalisation of violence [18]. Feminist analysis acknowledges that the digital world is a reflection and continuation of offline social dynamics. The same patriarchal and misogynistic attitudes that lead to gender-based violence in the physical world are replicated in the digital sphere through practices like the creation and distribution of non-consensual sexualised deepfakes. Their spread contributes to a culture of misogyny and sexual objectification. The normalisation of non-consensual sexual imagery in digital spaces can desensitise the public to issues of consent and violence, further entrenching harmful stereotypes and behaviors. This highlights the urgent need for legal frameworks that address these evolving forms of AI-generated gender-based violence.

# References

1. Holliday, C.: Rewriting the stars: surface tensions and gender troubles in the online media production of digital deepfakes. Convergence **27**(4), 899–918 (2021)
2. Quach, S., Thaichon, P., Martin, K.D., Weaven, S., Palmatier, R.W.: Digital technologies: tensions in privacy and data. J. Acad. Mark. Sci. **50**(6), 1299–1323 (2022)
3. Kugler, M.B., Pace, C.: Deepfake privacy: attitudes and regulation. Nw. UL Rev. **116**, 611 (2021)
4. Harper, C.A., Fido, D., Petronzi, D.: Delineating non-consensual sexual image offending: towards an empirical approach. Aggress. Violent. Beh. **58**, 101547 (2021)
5. Boyd, P.: Fakes and deepfakes: balancing privacy rights in the digital age. Ala. L. Rev. **74**, 517 (2022)
6. Dunn, S.: Legal definitions of intimate images in the age of sexual deepfakes and generative AI. McGill Law J. **69** (2024). SSRN. https://ssrn.com/abstract=4813941
7. Heikkilä, M.: OpenAI's hunger for data is coming back to bite it. MIT Technol. Rev. (2023). https://www.technologyreview.com/2023/04/19/1071789/openais-hunger-for-data-is-coming-back-to-bite-it/
8. Taipale, S., Wilska, T.A., Gilleard, C.J. (eds.): Digital Technologies and Generational Identity. Routledge, London (2017)
9. Esposito, E.: Conceptualizing online gendered and sexualised disinformation. In: The Routledge Handbook of Discourse and Disinformation (2023)
10. Harris, K.R.: Video on demand: what deepfakes do and how they harm. Synthese **199**(5), 13373–13391 (2021)
11. Yan, Y.: Deep dive into deepfakes-safeguarding our digital identity. Brook. J. Int. L. **48**, 767 (2022)

12. de Andrade, N.G.: Data protection, privacy and identity: distinguishing concepts and articulating rights, pp. 90–107. Springer, Heidelberg (2011). https://doi.org/10.1007/978-3-642-20769-3_8
13. Mostert, F., Cruz, S.: How image rights have changed over the past 20 years. In: Developments and Directions in Intellectual Property Law: The IPKat's 20-Year Adventure (2022, forthcoming). SSRN. https://ssrn.com/abstract=4026458 or https://doi.org/10.2139/ssrn.4026458
14. Brigham, N.G., Wei, M., Kohno, T., Redmiles, E.M.: "Violation of my body:" perceptions of AI-generated non-consensual (intimate) imagery (2024). arXiv preprint arXiv:2406.05520
15. Langton, R.: Feminism in epistemology: exclusion and objectification. In: The Cambridge Companion to Feminism in Philosophy, pp. 127–145 (2000)
16. Paris, B.: Configuring fakes: digitized bodies, the politics of evidence, and agency. Soc. Media+Soc. 7(4), 20563051211062919 (2021)
17. Viola, M., Voto, C.: Designed to abuse? Deepfakes and the non-consensual diffusion of intimate images. Synthese 201(1), 30 (2023)
18. Chapman, E.: Unveiling the Threat-AI and Deepfakes' Impact on Women. University of Mary Whashington (2024)
19. Ajder, H., Patrini, G., et al.: The state of deepfakes-landscape, threats and impact. Deeptrace Lab (2019). https://regmedia.co.uk/2019/10/08/deepfake_report.pdf
20. Molina, S.E.: Lying beneath the surface: the impacts of deepfake technology on the privacy and safety of the LGBTQ+ community. Nova L. Rev. 46, 251 (2021)
21. Glitch, UK: The digital misogynoir report: ending the dehumanising of black women on social media (2023). www.glitchcharity.co.uk/research
22. Hogg, M.A.: Social identity theory, pp. 3–17. Springer International Publishing (2016)
23. European Parliament and Council: Directive (EU) 2024/1385 of the European Parliament and of the Council of 14 May 2024 on combating violence against women and domestic violence. Official J. Eur. Union (2024)
24. Crenshaw, K.: Mapping the margins: intersectionality, identity politics, and violence against women of color. Stanford Law Rev. 43(6), 1241–1299 (1991)
25. Bowleg, L.: The problem with the phrase women and minorities: intersectionality—an important theoretical framework for public health. Am. J. Public Health 102(7), 1267–1273 (2012). https://doi.org/10.2105/ajph.2012.300750
26. Thompson, V.E.: Entangled genealogies?! Intersectionality and abolition. In: The Routledge International Handbook of Intersectionality Studies, pp. 165–179. Routledge (2023)
27. Gill, A.: Survivor-centered research: towards an intersectional gender-based violence movement. J. Family Violence 33(8), 559–562 (2018)
28. Sannon, S., Forte, A.: Privacy research with marginalized groups: what we know, what's needed, and what's next. Proc. ACM Hum.-Comput. Interact. 6(CSCW2), 1–33 (2022)
29. Bilgrami, A.: Notes toward the definition of 'Identity.' Daedalus 135(4), 5–14 (2006)
30. Fearon, J.D.: What is identity (as we now use the word). Stanford University, Stanford, Calif, pp. 1–43 (1999, Unpublished manuscript)
31. Sedlmeir, J., Smethurst, R., Rieger, A., Fridgen, G.: Digital identities and verifiable credentials. Bus. Inf. Syst. Eng. 63(5), 603–613 (2021)
32. Strozier, R.M.: Foucault, Subjectivity, and Identity: Historical Constructions of Subject and Self. Wayne State University Press (2002)
33. Hornsey, M.J.: Social identity theory and self-categorization theory: a historical review. Soc. Pers. Psychol. Compass 2(1), 204–222 (2008)
34. Craib, I.: Masculinity and male dominance. Sociol. Rev. 35(4), 721–743 (1987)
35. Connell, R.W., Messerschmidt, J.W.: Hegemonic masculinity: rethinking the concept. Gend. Soc. 19(6), 829–859 (2005)

36. Kurt, T., et al.: SoK: hate, harassment, and the changing landscape of online abuse. In: 2021 IEEE Symposium on Security and Privacy (SP), San Francisco, CA, USA, pp. 247–267 (2021). https://doi.org/10.1109/SP40001.2021.00028
37. Kaur, G., Singh, N., Kumar, M.: Image forgery techniques: a review. Artif. Intell. Rev. **56**(2), 1577–1625 (2023)
38. Steinmann, R.: The core meaning of human dignity. Potchefstroom Electron. Law J. /Potchefstroomse Elektroniese Regsblad **19**(1) (2016)
39. Srinivasan, A.: Does anyone have the right to sex? London Rev. Books **40**(6), 5 (2018)
40. Arstein-Kerslake, A.: Understanding sex: the right to legal capacity to consent to sex. Disabil. Soc. **30**(10), 1459–1473 (2015)
41. Verdoliva, L.: Media forensics and deepfakes: an overview. IEEE J. Sel. Top. Sig. Process. **14**(5), 910–932 (2020)
42. Weissel, L.E.: Personality rights and the internet in Europe. In: The Legal Protection of Personality Rights, pp. 147–163. Brill Nijhoff (2018)
43. Okolie, C.: Artificial intelligence-altered videos (deepfakes), image-based sexual abuse, and data privacy concerns. J. Int. Women's Stud. **25**(2), 11 (2023)
44. McGlynn, C.: Deepfake porn: why we need to make it an offence to create it, not just share it. Conversation, 9 April 2024. https://theconversation.com/deepfake-porn-why-we-need-to-make-it-a-crime-to-create-it-not-just-share-it-227177
45. Flynn, A., Clough, J., Cooke, T.: Disrupting and preventing deepfake abuse: exploring criminal law responses to AI-facilitated abuse. In: The Palgrave Handbook of Gendered Violence and Technology, pp. 583–603 (2021)
46. Umbach, R., Henry, N., Beard, G.F., Berryessa, C.M.: Non-consensual synthetic intimate imagery: prevalence, attitudes, and knowledge in 10 countries. In: Proceedings of the CHI Conference on Human Factors in Computing Systems, pp. 1–20 (2024)
47. Maddocks, S.: 'A deepfake porn plot intended to silence Me': exploring continuities between pornographic and 'political' deep fakes. Porn Stud. **7**(4), 415–423 (2020)
48. Rousay, V.: Sexual deepfakes and image-based sexual abuse: victim-survivor experiences and embodied harms. Master's thesis, Harvard University (2023)
49. Rebecca, U., Henry, N., Shelby, R.: AI-generated image-based sexual abuse: the new frontier. Github (n.d.). https://genai-in-ugc.github.io/pdf/AI_Generated_Image_Based_Sexual_Abuse__The_New_Frontier%20(3)%20-%20Rebecca%20Umbach.pdf
50. Glitch and ENAR: AI Deepfake Roundtable 1: Briefing (2023). https://glitchcharity.co.uk/wp-content/uploads/2023/07/Glitch_ENAR-Workshop-1-briefing.pdf
51. Cole, S.: Laws About Deepfakes Can't Leave Sex Workers Behind. 404 media (2024). https://www.404media.co/laws-about-deepfakes-cant-leave-sex-workers-behind/
52. Cole, S.: Coming Out Like a Porn Star: Essays on Pornography, Protection, and Privacy. Feminist Press at CUNY (2024)
53. Overton, S.: Overcoming racial harms to democracy from artificial intelligence. Iowa Law Rev. (2024, forthcoming)
54. Rigotti, C., McGlynn, C.L.: Towards an EU criminal law on violence against women: the ambitions and limitations of the Commission's proposal to criminalise image-based sexual abuse. New J. Eur. Crim. Law IJECL **13**(4), 1–26 (2022). SSRN. https://ssrn.com/abstract=4379096
55. Nead, L.: The female nude: pornography, art, and sexuality. Signs J. Women Cult. Soc. **15**(2), 323–335 (1990)
56. Lewis, R., Anitha, S.: Upskirting: a systematic literature review. Trauma Violence Abuse **24**(3), 2003–2018 (2023)
57. Henry, N., Gavey, N., McGlynn, C., Rackley, E.: 'Devastating, like it broke me': responding to image-based sexual abuse in Aotearoa New Zealand. Criminol. Crim. Just. **23**(5), 861–879 (2023)

58. Green, S.P.: To see and be seen: reconstructing the law of voyeurism and exhibitionism. Am. Crim. L. Rev. **55**, 203 (2018)
59. Dignam, D.M.: Understanding intimacy as experienced by breastfeeding women. Health Care Women Int. **16**(5), 477–485 (1995)
60. Batty, D.: Médecins Sans Frontières condemned for 'profiting from exploitative images'. The Guardian (2022). https://amp.theguardian.com/global-development/2022/may/25/medecins-sans-frontieres-condemned-for-profiting-from-exploitative-images
61. Bulman, J.: Publishing privacy: intellectual property, self-expression, and the Victorian novel. Hastings Comm. Ent. LJ **26**, 73 (2003)
62. Pfefferkorn, R.: The threat posed by deepfakes to marginalized communities. Bookings Edu (2021). https://www.brookings.edu/articles/the-threat-posed-by-deepfakes-to-marginalized-communities/
63. Barr, H.: South Korea's digital sex crime deepfake crisis government inaction is fueling abuses. Human Rights Watch (2024). https://www.hrw.org/news/2024/08/29/south-koreas-digital-sex-crime-deepfake-crisis
64. Yavuz, C.: Criminalisation of the dissemination of non-consensual sexual deepfakes in the European Union: a comparative legal analysis. UGent. Revue Internationale de Droit Pénal. **95**(2), 419–457 (2024)
65. Royer, S., Oerlemans, J.J., et al.: An empirical and legal analysis of sexual deepfakes in the EU, Belgium and the Netherlands. Revue Internationale de Droit Pénal **92**(2), 459–482 (2024)
66. Ferguson, P.R.: The presumption of innocence and its role in the criminal process. Crim. Law Forum **27**(2), 131–158 (2016)
67. Fitz-Gibbon, K.: Gender, criminal law and violence against women: mapping the limits of legal interventions and approaches to reform. In: Women, Crime and Justice in Context, pp. 44–56. Routledge (2022)
68. Abji, S.: Punishing survivors and criminalizing survivorship: a feminist intersectional approach to migrant justice in the crimmigration system. Stud. Soc. Justice **2020**(14), 67–89 (2020)
69. Davis, A.Y., Dent, G., Meiners, E.R., Richie, B.E.: Abolition. Feminism. Now (Vol. 2). Haymarket Books (2022)
70. Gjika, A.: When Rape Goes Viral: Youth and Sexual Assault in the Digital Age. University of California Press, Berkeley (2023). https://doi.org/10.1525/9780520391055
71. Benoit, C., Unsworth, R.: COVID-19, stigma, and the ongoing marginalization of sex workers and their support organizations. Arch. Sex. Behav. **51**(1), 331–342 (2022)
72. Davis, A.Y.: Abolition Democracy: Beyond Empire, Prisons, and Torture. Seven Stories Press (2005)
73. Shaw, J., Lee, H.: Race and the criminal justice system response to sexual assault: a systematic review. Am. J. Community Psychol. **64**(1–2), 255–276 (2019). https://doi.org/10.1002/ajcp.12334
74. Reid, P.M.: A human rights-based approach to the prosecution of sexual crime: victims and prosecutorial decision-making, Doctoral dissertation, University of Glasgow (2023)
75. European Sex Workers Alliance: Labour rights, safety and privacy: how to centre sex workers' needs on advertising platforms (2024). https://www.eswalliance.org/labour_rights_advertising
76. Coston, B.M., Kimmel, M.: White men as the new victims: reverse discrimination cases and the men's rights movement. Men Masculinities **22**(5), 608–626 (2013). https://doi.org/10.1177/1097184X17750924
77. George, A., Vindhya, U., Ray, S.: Sex trafficking and sex work: definitions, debates and dynamics—a review of literature. Econ. Polit. Weekly, 64–73 (2010)
78. Cunneen, C.: Decoloniality, abolitionism, and the disruption of penal power. In: Decolonizing the Criminal Question: Colonial Legacies, Contemporary Problems, vol. 19 (2023)

79. Jacobsen, B.N., Simpson, J.: The tensions of deepfakes. Inf. Commun. Soc.Commun. Soc. **27**(6), 1095–1109 (2024)
80. Edwards, A.: Male violence in feminist theory: an analysis of the changing conceptions of sex/gender violence and male dominance. In: Women, Violence and Social Control, pp. 13–29. Palgrave Macmillan UK, London (1987)
81. Blauth, T.F.: Artificial intelligence crime: an overview of malicious use and abuse of AI. IEEE Access **10**, 77110–77122 (2022)
82. de Silva de Alwis, R.: A rapidly shifting landscape: why digitized violence is the newest category of gender-based violence. SciencesPo Law Review, U of Penn Law School, Public Law Research Paper, pp. 23–43 (2023, forthcoming)
83. Wang, J.: It starts with deepfakes–when you no longer need to believe to see. You can now just see what you want to see. The latest advancement in image-based sexual abuse where deepfakes are only the beginning for future exploits of artificial intelligence. Doctoral dissertation, ResearchSpace@ Auckland (2024)
84. Witschas, A.: Porn, Power, and Platforms. PICS Publications of the Institute of Cognitive Science-University of Osnabrück (2023)
85. Burkell, J., Gosse, C.: Nothing new here: emphasizing the social and cultural context of deepfakes. First Monday (2019)

# Contemporary Challenges and Possibilities for Privacy and ID Management

# Data Processing Diagrams

## A Modeling Technique for Privacy in Complex Data Processing Systems

Job Doesburg[1]([⊠])[iD], Pascal van Gastel[2][iD], Bernard van Gastel[1][iD],
and Erik Poll[1][iD]

[1] NOLAI, Radboud University, Nijmegen, The Netherlands
{job.doesburg,bernard.vangastel,erik.poll}@ru.nl
[2] Avans University of Applied Sciences, Breda, The Netherlands
ppth.vangastel@avans.nl

**Abstract.** Modern software systems can feature complex data processing, with multiple parties processing various data for different purposes, including training or application of AI. Development of such systems typically involves a multidisciplinary team with different viewpoints. To effectively and efficiently design for privacy requires a multidisciplinary and coordinated effort. We introduce Data Processing Diagrams, an extension of popular Data Flow Diagrams, with standardized notation for fundamental forms of data processing such as data deletion, distribution, encryption and pseudonymization/anonymization. With these extensions, application of well-known privacy design strategies and tactics in complex data processing systems can be reflected. We consider this crucial for unambiguous communication, especially in the earliest design phases of new systems, to quickly compare different architectures and use the models as blueprints for development. We validate the effectiveness of our technique as a shared language between multidisciplinary stakeholders in the context of different co-creation projects that are part of the Dutch National Education Lab AI (NOLAI).

**Keywords:** Data Flow Diagrams · Privacy Design · Privacy Modeling

## 1 Introduction

Modern software systems can feature complex data processing, with multiple parties processing various data for different purposes, including training or application of AI. Development of such complex systems typically involves a multidisciplinary team (e.g. development, engineering, legal, governance, ethics, business) with various backgrounds, viewpoints and concerns [9,10]. Since many privacy features can only be effectively realized by a combination of technical, physical, organizational or legal measures, there can be important interactions between the different disciplines. Currently, however, these stakeholders often work in isolation [14]. This makes designing and communicating about such complex systems challenging: there can be misconceptions, inconsistencies or (at best)

F. Bieker et al. (Eds.): Privacy and Identity 2024, IFIP AICT 705, pp. 115–131, 2025.
https://doi.org/10.1007/978-3-031-91054-8_6

simply inefficiency. Modern (i.e. agile) system development methods, or even modern design methods like participatory design, co-design or co-creation [11], and the intangible nature of software only amplify this. To prevent this requires a simple, standardized, shared language between all stakeholders that can be used from early in the design process and onward.

While Data Flow Diagrams (DFDs) are the de facto standard for modeling data processing systems, they lack standardized notation for specific fundamental forms of data processing, such as data deletion, distribution, encryption[1] (e.g. end-to-end encryption, homomorphic encryption and encryption at rest) and anonymization/pseudonymization. We argue that these concepts are so fundamental to privacy and (consequently) have so many multidisciplinary interactions (i.e. they are relevant not only to technical stakeholders), that standardized notation is required to effectively use these diagrams as a shared language between multidisciplinary stakeholders.

We therefore introduce an extension of DFDs, called Data Processing Diagrams (DPDs), that give a more complete overview of data processing in a system, focussed on privacy, while maintaining a high abstraction level. Specifically, we aim to express well-known privacy design strategies [6] and tactics [3] in our models. We also provide relatively simple (informal) definitions for identifiability, linkability and pseudonymity to characterize data, that are aimed to be understandable by different stakeholders.

Based on the DPD of a system, specific high-level, fundamental system properties can easily be derived, such as which components (or subsystems, or as we will more generally prefer, contexts) could get access to which data (i.e. information flow analysis between systems). As such, a quick privacy assessment of a (proposed) system architecture can be made, comparing different architectures. This can be done completely model-based using only the information in the DPD and without additional background information about specific components. While this quick analysis is in no way an alternative to exhaustive threat modeling using popular frameworks such as LINDDUN [4,16] or STRIDE [7,13], we consider this especially useful during the design of new systems when models are used as blueprints and no concrete system details are yet decided.

We consider our models to function as an effective shared language between multidisciplinary (not just technical) stakeholders to unambiguously communicate about the most important features of a complex system's data processing architecture. We validate our modeling technique in the context of NOLAI, the Dutch National Education Lab for Artificial Intelligence, by modeling seven co-creation projects using input from various stakeholders, of which we present a concrete example in Sect. 8.

## 1.1   Complex Data Processing Systems

We consider our modeling technique to be usable for what we will call *complex data processing systems*, similar to complex systems in other fields of science. The

---

[1] DFDs typically only consider point-to-point encrypted data flows between two components (encryption in transit), but not encryption across multiple components.

primary goal of complex data processing systems is to process (e.g. collect, store, transform, combine, aggregate, exchange) either personal data about multiple data subjects, or otherwise sensitive non-personal data.

The complexity lies in that various actors (e.g. legal entities) are involved in the system (including, for example, cloud service providers), processing different data for diverse types of functional purposes, in multiple more-or-less autonomous subsystems, possibly with multiple distributed instances of them. For example, data may be used for (1) the basic operation of an application within an organization, (2) centralized training of an AI model, based on data from multiple organizations and (3) validating the effectiveness of the application.

More generally, data processing takes place in a variety of different (types of) contexts, such as legal, physical, organizational, or functional-purpose contexts. Different stakeholders are typically interested in different types of contexts. For all these different contexts, different policies for data protection may be required. As a result, systems may deploy specific Privacy Enhancing Technologies (PETs), including different forms of encryption, pseudonymization or anonymization, resulting in data with different degrees of identifiability, linkability or pseudonymity. This makes analyzing the privacy and security properties of such systems challenging.

## 1.2    Related Work

Our DPDs extend popular DFDs [5], that, are also used in popular (technical) threat modeling frameworks such as LINDDUN [4,16] and STRIDE [7,13]. Because of this, our DPDs can directly serve as input for analysis with these frameworks, only providing more information.

During threat modeling using these frameworks, all DFD components and possible threats to them are systematically identified and assessed. This, however, requires background knowledge about components that may not be available from just the DFD itself. For some types of threats, this can be very fundamental. For example, there is a fundamental difference in privacy risk assessment between a regular data store, and one that stores encrypted data. In a DFD, however, they are displayed as the same component. Our DPDs are able to distinguish these fundamental differences.

We consider this especially useful during early system design, when details about the underlying components are not yet known and the model is used as a blueprint to describe which system architecture should be developed. Our DPDs allow for a fully model-based architectural risk assessment. Comparing different models, instead of threat modeling where the model (i.e. a DFD) only guides the process but cannot replace knowledge of a concrete system.

Some other extensions to DFDs have been proposed to incorporate specific notions of privacy. PA-DFDs [1], for example, extend DFDs with purpose labels to describe the purpose for processing data, aiming to model *purpose limitation*. Sion et al. [14] proposed further DFD extensions for legal concepts and abstractions. While those extensions serve their own specific (analytical) purpose (and could be used in combination with our extensions), they are not able to display the fundamental forms of data processing required to reflect well-known privacy design strategies (see Sect. 4) in early system design.

## 2   Background

Our modeling technique extends well-known Data Flow Diagrams (DFDs) [5], consisting of directed graphs of processes, data stores and external entities, with data flows between them. While many grammar rules can be defined for these diagrams [2,8,12], we conveniently consider the following informal rules:

> **External entities** are sources or destinations of data and are further not in scope of the system.
> **Processes** do not store data (i.e. for any time longer than the lifetime of the processing itself).
> **Data stores** do not transform data.
> Any **data flow** has a process or external entity as either its input or output.

The three main components of a DFD precisely capture all three *states* of data: data at rest (data stores), data in use (processes) and data in transit (data flows). This makes data processing tangible: at the lowest abstraction level, it should be possible to physically pinpoint exactly where each component stores, processes, or transfers data. This results in practical completeness of our models at the lowest abstraction level. Notably, DFDs are also technology-agnostic: they can be used to model both digital data processing by software, but also non-digital or manual processes, which is important for a holistic view of data processing that is required for valid (sound) analysis.

DFDs can be made at different abstraction levels, with the highest abstraction level displaying the whole system as a single process and only displaying the external entities the system interacts with (sometimes called a *context diagram*). Every process (and arguably also every data store) can be unfolded into multiple sub-processes and data stores, with flows between them.[2] This refinement is crucial for iterative design and communication with different stakeholders, where certain (high-risk) components can be unfolded and collapsed depending on every stakeholder's concerns and background knowledge.

## 3   Data Properties in DPDs

While only modeling the interaction between different components in a system itself can already be interesting for some stakeholders, this does not exactly describe *what* data is being processed. In order to fully describe this and assess risks, one must describe the exact contents of each data flow as the inputs and outputs of each component. On many abstraction levels, however, this may not be feasible nor desirable. This is especially the case during system design, when only a high-level model is available. Instead, it could be useful to focus on specific properties of data and display these properties using special symbols.

---

[2] External entities cannot be refined, as their internals are by definition out of scope.

The exact properties to consider can differ per use case and involved stakeholders, depending on what properties we consider to have inter-stakeholder interactions and be interesting for further analysis, but may often include *identifiability* and *linkability*, especially when applying pseudonymization, anonymization or other PETs in the system, since they have consequences for multiple types of stakeholders. These properties are also fundamental to LINDDUN's main threat types [4]. For more specific use cases, other properties like *repudiability* (if non-repudiation is a desired system property) may also be interesting, or even very domain-specific properties like the nationality of data subjects[3]. Apart from that, it can be useful to describe data with a general category (such as *medical, financial* or generally *sensitive*). As a first step in the modeling process, the relevant data properties between all stakeholders should be established.

## 3.1   Identifiability, Linkability and Pseudonyms

We specifically propose some practical, relatively simple definitions for **identifiability** and **linkability** (with corresponding graphical representations), because of their interplay and since they are fundamental to privacy and affect almost all viewpoints in some way.

It is hard to precisely define the identifiability of data. While some data may be non-identifiable to most, it could be identifiable to others that have the ability to link data with other identifiable data, making the data indirectly identifiable ultimately. The concepts of identifiability and linkability are thus closely related.

We also discuss **pseudonyms** as a special form of linkability and as a simple yet powerful PET without irreversible loss of data utility. By properly using pseudonymization, namely, one can enforce that different pseudonymous (sub)sets of data cannot be recombined even if one or more parties or components in the system are compromised.

Existing (e.g. mathematical) definitions for these concepts are more formal and strict, but are consequently difficult to understand for many (non-technical) stakeholders and less suited to characterize data flows in a larger system. We thus seek for a compromise between expressiveness, correctness and simplicity.

**Definition 1 (Identifiability).** *The extent to which data identifies a natural person. We distinguish:*

    &#129485; **directly identifiable**: *data identifies a natural person directly, based on publicly available knowledge*

    &#129485; **indirectly identifiable**: *data identifies a natural person, but requires some non-public knowledge outside the system*

    &#129485; **de-identified**: *data does not contain any identifiers[4]*

    **non-personal**: *data does not relate to persons at all (Fig. 1)*

---

[3] For example, when dealing with various national data processing regulations.

[4] Some may falsely refer to this as 'anonymous' data. Truly anonymous data is additionally unlinkable, or even has any distinguishable statistical features removed.

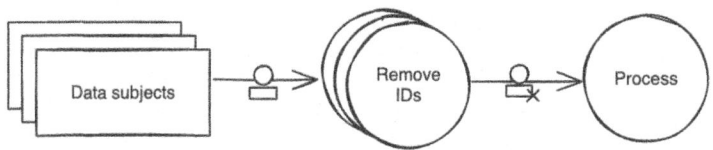

**Fig. 1.** Example of identifiability annotations.


**Definition 2 (Linkability).** *The extent to which data can be linked to other data based on an equality or known correlation. We distinguish:*

      *universally linkable: high-entropy data that is considered to have universally unique attributes (e.g. biometrics, MAC address)*
      *locally linkable: limited uniqueness only within the local context (e.g. session IDs or data with random noise)*
      *unlinkable: non-unique data that is thus inherently unlinkable*


**Definition 3 (Pseudonymity).** *A special form of local linkability without direct identifiability, where local linkability is introduced through a dedicated attribute. Depending on whether data is also indirectly identifiable, we distinguish:*

      *strict pseudonymous: data is pseudonymous but further de-identified*
      *soft pseudonymous: data is both pseudonymous and indirectly identifiable (based on other knowledge than the pseudonym)*


Under these definitions, **identifiability** (either direct or indirect) **implies universal linkability**, but **linkability does not imply identifiability**. De-identified but linkable data, this way, can become (either directly or indirectly) identifiable after linking with other (directly or indirectly) identifiable data.

All definitions are relative to some extent and require assumptions on other publicly available data outside the system. For example, DNA samples are obviously unique and would identify a data subject in that sense. However, if we do not assume DNA samples to be publicly available information (which is generally the case), we will not classify a DNA sample as directly identifiable, but rather universally linkable and indirectly identifiable, or even de-identified if we consider DNA samples to not be available to any party at all.

The threshold for all definitions can be subjective, too. In case the combination of postal code and birth year does not relate to a single natural person, but to two or three, one may or may not consider this data identifiable, depending on the use case. During modeling, stakeholders should agree on reasonable assumptions on these matters.

## 3.2  Implicit Data

When characterizing data flows, it is crucial to also consider *implicit* (meta)data, especially when talking about identifiability and linkability. A person's first name, for example, can hardly be considered identifiable in a global data set, but within a data set of employees of a specific department it most definitely can be! In this case, the department of employment is implicit data, that should be derived from the local context of the processing. Similarly, any data originating from a specific known personal device can be considered linkable to that device and perhaps identifiable. A specific example is real-time data, where the times-tamp of interaction could be considered a linkable or even identifiable, implicit attribute, for which we propose special annotation ($\mathcal{D}$).

# 4  Privacy Design Strategies

In 2014, Hoepman published an overview of eight privacy design strategies [6], with various underlying privacy design tactics [3], based on a large litera-ture study. They are considered to form a complete overview of (high-level) approaches to privacy-friendly data processing that can categorize PETs. Specif-ically, Hoepman distinguishes four data-related and four process-related strate-gies, with the first category focussing on the actual system architecture and the latter category on more peripheral procedures for governance and compliance. In this section, we show the DFD extensions required to distinguish the four data-related strategies and underlying tactics.

From the in total four data-related strategies, Hoepman identifies two strate-gies (SEPARATE and HIDE) to limit the *chance* of "privacy violations" in a system, and two (MINIMIZE and ABSTRACT) that limit the *impact* of such violations [6]. Orthogonally, two strategies (HIDE and ABSTRACT) affect the actual data being processed itself, and two strategies (SEPARATE and MINIMIZE) that affect the way the processing of data is organized.

|                    | Change **infrastructure** | Change **data** |
|--------------------|---------------------------|-----------------|
| Reduce **impact**  | MINIMIZE                  | ABSTRACT        |
| Reduce **chance**  | SEPARATE                  | HIDE            |

**MINIMIZE.** The MINIMIZE strategy simply entails to process only the data that is strictly necessary for the purpose. This can mostly (for the SELECT, EXCLUDE and STRIP tactics) be expressed in our models by annotating the data flows between components with data properties, describing what kind of data is being processed and resulting in fewer data being processed.

For the DESTROY tactic, deleting data from a data store, however, we intro-duce a new (complemental) type of data flow, that deletes data from a data

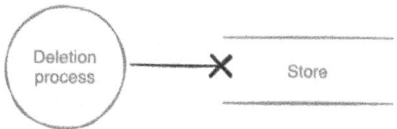

**Fig. 2.** Notation for data deletion.

store (see Fig. 2)[5]. As a result of making data deletion explicit, it is possible to highlight components where data is stored but never deleted, possibly resulting in orphaned data.

**ABSTRACT.** The ABSTRACT strategy, consisting of the SUMMARIZE and GROUP tactic, can also be expressed in our models by annotating the data flows with data properties, describing exactly what kind of data is being processed, with data being transformed to be less sensitive, identifiable or linkable.

**SEPARATE.** The SEPARATE strategy aims to not process (or store) data at a single place, but split it over different components, thus reducing the impact in case of compromise ("violation") of one of them. This concerns two tactics, DIS-TRIBUTE and ISOLATE. Isolation is reflected by having multiple different types of components processing different types of data, which can easily be reflected in our models. Distribution, on the other hand, considers the usage of multiple instances of the same type of (sub)system or component for different data subjects. The existence of such components is also typically a characteristic of complex data processing systems, as defined in Subsect. 1.1.

In a classical DFD, every store, process or external entity typically represents a different *type* of component. Any distribution of instances is left implicit or must be specified in natural text, which could leave room for ambiguities. We therefore introduce notation to display multiple instances of the same component type that are separated (Fig. 3) to a certain extent. Related to the distributed components, refinement (unfolding) might result in a subset of components that together functions as an independent subsystem.

For each distributed component or subsystem, the variable or level of distribution should be specified. This could, for example, be the data subject-level or organization-level, with one instance of the subsystem for every data subject or organization respectively. This distribution can also be nested.

**HIDE.** Finally, the HIDE strategy consists of the RESTRICT, MIX, DISSOCIATE and OBFUSCATE tactics. On an architectural level, the RESTRICT tactic considers employing an access control process, which as such can directly be reflected in our model, but does not influence other architectural features of data processing in a system. Similarly, the MIX and DISSOCIATE tactics are also displayed by specific centralized processes resulting in data with limited linkability or identifiability,

---

[5] Data deletion flows *only* work towards a data store!

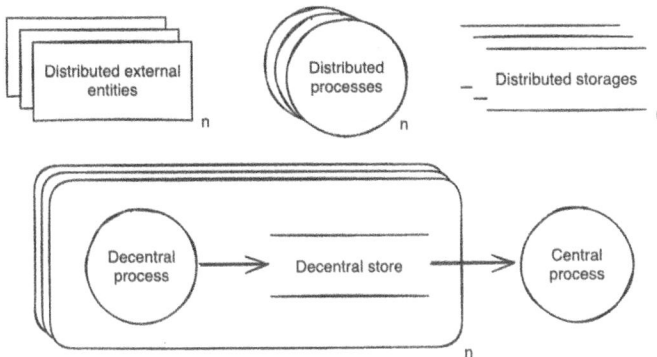

**Fig. 3.** Notation for ($n$) distributed components.

or eliminating (real-time) linkable data flows. Cryptographic technologies such as differential privacy also fall under these tactics.

The OBFUSCATE tactic, however, is observed in cryptographic processes, encrypting the data and hiding it across part of the processing, towards those unable to decrypt it.

In regular DFDs, data flows are point-to-point between two components (stores, processes or external entities). When encryption is applied, this encryption is typically considered to be point-to-point too, and not end-to-end (across multiple components).

When data is end-to-end encrypted while flowing through multiple components, there are different ways of modeling this. Either, the DFD only describes the high-level data flow between the two endpoints and ignores the existence of all underlying infrastructure, or, more commonly, we ignore the fact that end-to-end encryption is applied and only keep it in the back of our mind when using the DFD for further analysis (perhaps by including some ad-hoc annotations). Finally, one could include explicit encryption, decryption, and key management processes in the model. This, however, would require a lower abstraction level and making the model more complex to analyze.

Therefore, we introduce abbreviated notation for **end-to-end** encrypted data flows across multiple components (see Fig. 4). Across a data store, this is known as 'encryption at rest'. Across a process, transforming the data while being encrypted, this is known as 'homomorphic encryption'. Finally, we also introduce notation for multiparty computations (MPC) as a distributed process on encrypted data.

Notice that in the abbreviated notation, key management is ignored, since we consider this a technical detail that is not relevant at higher abstraction levels. For MPC, notice the slightly different notation than for (normal) simple distributed components (see Fig. 3), since for MPC the individual nodes are not fully isolated from each other and are not autonomous. Annotations should

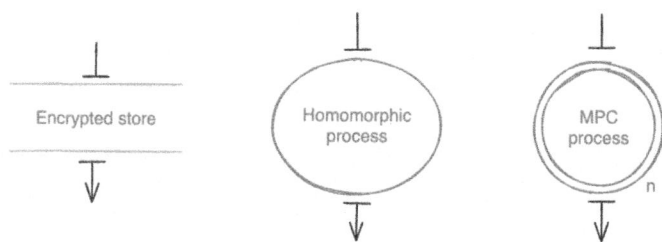

**Fig. 4.** Abbreviated notation for cryptographic components.

display to what extent the different nodes of an MPC process are separated, or alternatively, MPC processes can be displayed in more detail as distributed processes.

## 5  Context Boundaries

The STRIDE security threat modeling framework [7] introduced the concept of *trust boundaries* to Data Flow Diagrams, to indicate where in a system trust levels are changing and, for example, a different threat model must be considered. This typically considers the location of a component in the system, either physical or logical (as part of a larger system, network, etc.). The LINDDUN privacy threat modeling framework [16] also briefly mentions trust boundaries, without really describing a specific meaning to them, but similar boundaries could be considered (e.g. legal boundaries).

In complex data processing systems, as described in Subsect. 1.1, typically many (and many types) of these boundaries exist, which we referred to as *contexts*. We therefore generalize the term *trust boundaries* to *context boundaries*, where different contexts might be identified by different characteristics, including but not limited to technical or organizational trust. Exactly which context boundaries to consider can differ per use case, similar to which data properties one should consider as discussed in Sect. 3. Examples could include physical locations, technical or logical separated units (such as different system users, devices, or networks), legal or organizational responsible entities, or natural persons being actors in or having access to components.

By specifying context boundaries, different (types of) contexts are established, resulting in two ways of visualizing them (see Fig. 5). These different contexts could be considered as separate overlays on a single base model. Multiple distributed instances of contexts can also exist.

It is important to notice that with refinement of diagrams, unfolding or collapsing (groups of) components, it is possible that at higher abstraction levels context boundaries cannot always be exactly drawn between distinct components. This results in rather blurry context boundaries somewhere inside a store or process, or components being in multiple contexts (of the same type). For

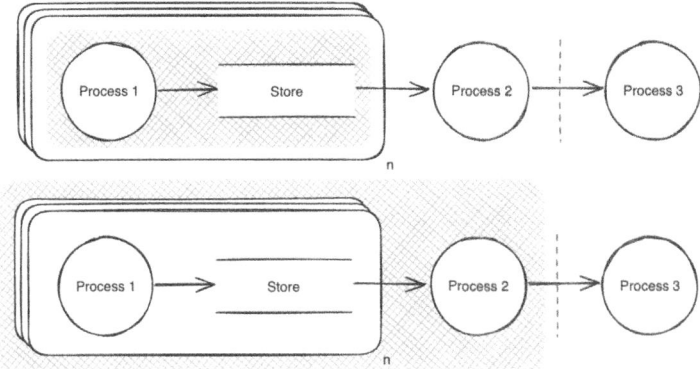

**Fig. 5.** Different ways to display contexts (blue) or context boundaries (red). (Color figure online)

some types of contexts, it is also possible that components are fully part of multiple contexts at any abstraction level (such as processing purpose or legal entity responsible, in case of shared responsibility between multiple parties). We consider this a feature of our models, indicating that more refinement is required, or that a component requires extra attention.

## 5.1 Alignment

As already originally mentioned for STRIDE, where data crosses a trust boundary, certain mitigating measures (e.g. technical, legal) may be required. Additionally, we argue that it is exactly where different types of contexts do **not** align with each other, where extra attention is required during system design.

As an example (Fig. 6), the paper archives (data store) from organization A (legal) may be located in the building of organization B (physical). The physical and legal context boundaries do not align. It may thus be possible for organization B to physically get access to the stored data from organization A before process 2 (perhaps, anonymization) has been performed, which perhaps should be resolved by contractual agreements forbidding it, or physical or technical measures, such as placing it in a vault or applying encryption. Here, the interplay with encrypted data flows as discussed in Sect. 4 becomes apparent, since an end-to-end encrypted data flow effectively may not pass a context boundary while a regular flow does.

Inspecting components where context boundaries do not align or are not clearly defined, especially when processing sensitive or identifiable information, allows for prioritized (and thus, more efficient) refinement of a DFD to lower abstraction levels during system design.

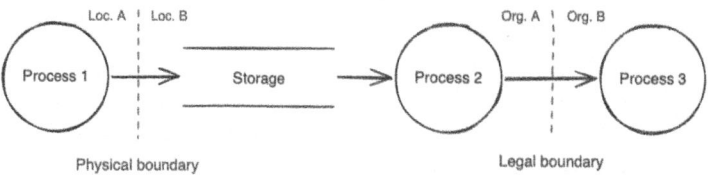

**Fig. 6.** Two types of context boundaries that are not aligned.

## 6   System Properties

Based on our DPDs, specific system properties can be derived, using basic graph theory. This can be useful to make specific (privacy) claims about forms of data processing that does **not**[6] (or *cannot*, because data is not linkable) take place in the system. For example, one could make statements about:

Which components or contexts process which types of data (i.e. where data flows from one context to another)
The existence of data stores where data is not being deleted
To which degree specific types of data are processed centrally or decentrally
Components that do not align with different context boundaries
Whether different data could be combined within a context, based on linkability of the data

Special attention could go out to system properties assuming compromise of one or more contexts, making sure that specific properties still hold after compromise by considering the transitive closure of the graph.

Based on this analysis, high-risk components could be identified, which could then be further refined, until so many details are described that the residual risk either can be accepted, or the risk is mitigated in another way. Ongoing research by the authors focuses on more formal methods for analysis, risk assessment and model refinement during system design using these data processing diagrams.

## 7   Evaluation

Our modeling technique is being used in the Dutch National Education Lab AI (NOLAI). At NOLAI, every year, about 10 new three-year co-creation projects start (€3M per year), aiming to combine academic research towards AI in education with software product development. Currently, 17 projects are running, and another 80 are expected for the coming years. In these projects different stakeholders from education, industry, and academia are involved. Many

---

[6] We can only make *negative* claims, since components might be unavailable, potentially blocking any data processing.

projects feature a scientific experiment that builds on existing platforms, making the responsibilities and risks hard to manage. As such, these projects are typical examples of complex data processing systems. To organize data processing responsibly in all these different contexts, various measures are implemented, including pseudonymization and different forms of encryption, both in transit and at rest.

The authors have modeled eight of these co-creation projects, mostly in the early stages of the development process. This was done in collaboration with various stakeholders, including researchers (in different academic fields), co-creation managers, legal experts, software engineers and ethicists.

While not all stakeholders, especially not those without a technical background, were able to actively create these models from scratch, all were able to understand the models when creating them together with a more technical expert. Moreover, after working with them for a while and with help of templates and examples, most were able to create and interpret simple models independently. Meanwhile, for the more technical stakeholders, the models were unambiguous and contained enough information to perform some high-level risk analysis and compare different designs based on their privacy properties.

More importantly, authors have experienced that the process of creating a DPD required stakeholders to critically think about data processing and define scopes. Making the models identified unclarities or ambiguities and forced stakeholders to address those, early in the process. More than once, the modeling process resulted in different versions of the system between which a choice had to be made, of which many stakeholders were previously unaware. As such, the models functioned as a starting point for discussion between stakeholders, and effectively served as a shared language.

Anecdotally, for several projects, incompatibilities were discovered during modeling, for example where processed anonymized data had to be returned to the original data subjects, or where no procedures were designed to transfer data between two stores (which, in practice, resulted in people using insecure email to transfer sensitive data). The simple process of creating these models, highlighted these blind spots.

In future research, authors plan to further incorporate the modeling technique into a structured design methodology, and validate the effectiveness of the methodology over a period of multiple years of development of a system.

## 8   Example

As a concrete example, we present NOLAI's VIAT (Video Interaction Analysis Tool) project. In the VIAT project, software is developed to analyze in-classroom video footage for teacher's training purposes, such as detecting moments that a teacher answers or ignores a student's question. Data processing includes the recording, storage and playback of videos, as well as analysis (creating reports) using AI models. Additionally, to develop the tool, selected recorded videos are annotated and used to train these models. VIAT is tested and developed in pilots at primary schools, and the effectiveness is studied using interviews and analysis of additional data sources by researchers from NOLAI, potentially in multiple independent studies.

Different (legal) organizations are involved in the processing, including several schools, commercial parties (for both the recording platform and AI analysis), cloud service providers and a research institute. As such, data processing takes place in different contexts. In this example, we will focus on legal contexts.

There are several desired privacy features for these contexts. For example, scientific data analysis may only use pseudonymous data. Also, AI model training should not receive identifiable data. Preferably, recorded videos are not accessible to anyone except the school. Finally, the commercial party may not receive the data collected in the scientific context.

In Fig. 7, we present two DPDs for two possible data processing architectures for the VIAT project, where one has obviously stronger privacy guarantees than the other (see captions). Notably, the DFDs for both architectures would be **the same**, illustrating the added value of DPDs over DFDs.

## 9    Future Work

As presented in Sect. 6, our diagrams can be used to systematically derive system properties based on annotations of data types and assumptions on underlying components as in Sect. 3. To derive more specific properties, more strict mathematical definitions such as $k$-anonymity [15] could be considered and algebraic rules for such properties, based on these diagrams, could be built.

When using data processing diagrams during system *design*, a structured formal method for risk assessment can also be considered, systematically identifying high-risk components and refining them or mitigating risks. While we did show the completeness of our modeling technique with respect to well-known privacy design strategies and tactics [3], choosing which tactic to apply while designing a system, requires thought-out decisions. Future research can focus on designing systematic methodologies to apply specific tactics and identify common privacy design patterns and antipatterns, implementing specific measures.

A different application of our diagrams could be in the analysis of energy consumption of (software) systems, which is, next to privacy and security, also an important factor in implementing data processing sustainably.

Finally, it would be interesting to see to what extent Data Processing Diagrams, at a high abstraction level, can be used as a communication tool for non-expert users (or data subjects) to offer transparency about data processing.

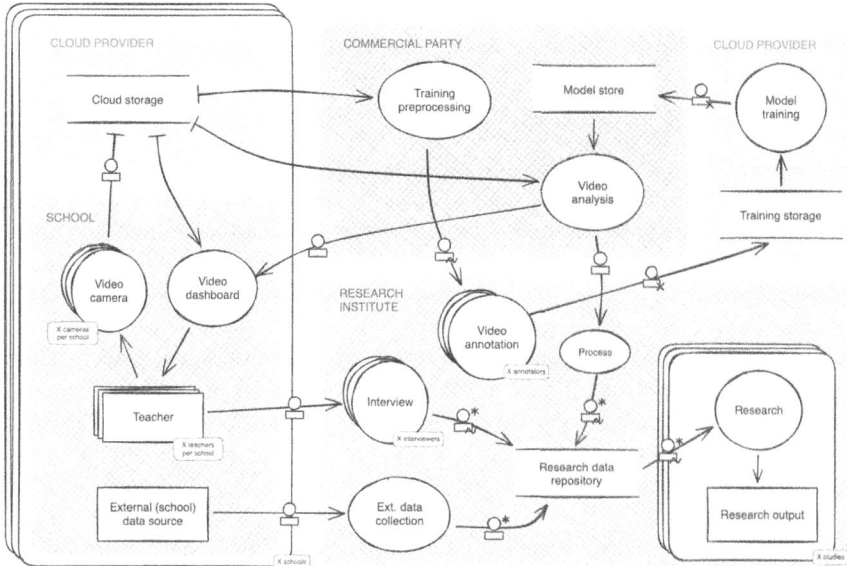

(a) A strong privacy architecture, with mostly **decentralized** data processing at schools (except video analysis), **encrypted** cloud storage **per school**, model training on **de-identified** data, and **pseudonymization** for research.

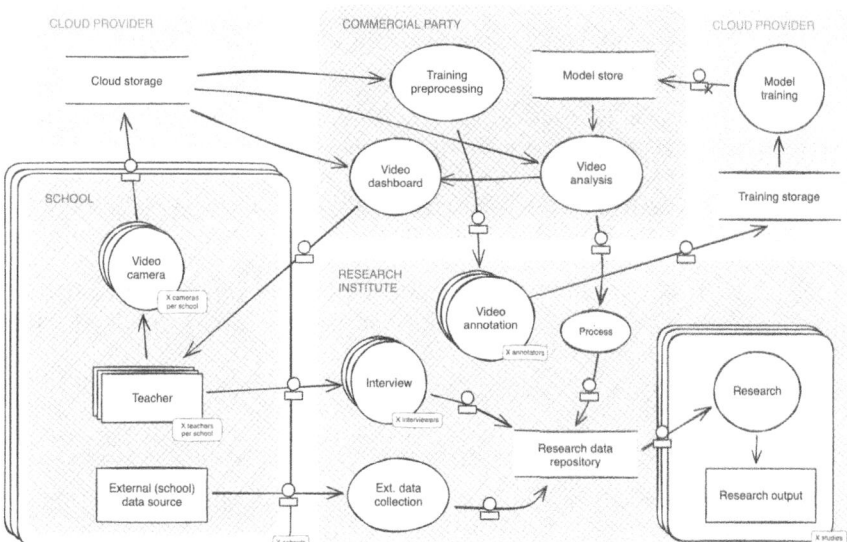

(b) A weak with fully **centralized** data processing by the commercial party and cloud provider, **with no encrypted storage** at the cloud provider, involving model training on **identifiable** data and **lacking pseudonymization**.

**Fig. 7.** DPDs of two possible architectures for the VIAT project, with data identifiability annotations.

# 10   Conclusion

We introduced Data Processing Diagrams, a modeling technique for privacy in complex data processing systems, based on well-known Data Flow Diagrams. The extensions for data deletion, distribution, encryption, together with annotations of identifiability, linkability and pseudonymity of data, are able to reflect application of well-known privacy design strategies [6] and tactics [3]. The resulting models allow for unambiguous communication between multidisciplinary stakeholders (e.g. security, legal, management, ethics, development and engineers) about privacy and data processing in a system, at different abstraction levels. Moreover, specific system properties can be derived from these models. Authors have experienced the models to be effective tools in the system development process, helping to derive system properties and perform risk assessment or threat modeling. In future research, our modeling technique can be further formalized to derive more specific system properties in a systematic way, based on more formal definitions, and perform risk assessment to effectively implement specific design patterns for improved privacy.

**Acknowledgments.** This research is performed in context of the Dutch National Education Lab AI (NOLAI), funded by the Dutch National Growth Fund.

**Disclosure of Interests.** The authors have no competing interests to declare that are relevant to the content of this article.

# References

1. Alshareef, H., Tuma, K., Stucki, S., Schneider, G., Scandariato, R.: Precise analysis of purpose limitation in data flow diagrams. In: Proceedings of the 17th International Conference on Availability, Reliability and Security, ARES 2022. ACM (2022). https://doi.org/10.1145/3538969.3539010
2. Ambler, S.W.: Data Flow Diagrams (DFDs) (2006). Personal webpage. http://www.agilemodeling.com/artifacts/dataFlowDiagram.htm
3. Colesky, M., Hoepman, J.H., Hillen, C.: A critical analysis of privacy design strategies. In: 2016 IEEE Security and Privacy Workshops (SPW), pp. 33–40. IEEE (2016). https://doi.org/10.1109/SPW.2016.23
4. Deng, M., Wuyts, K., Scandariato, R., Preneel, B., Joosen, W.: A privacy threat analysis framework: supporting the elicitation and fulfillment of privacy requirements. Requir. Eng. **16**(1), 3–32 (2011). https://doi.org/10.1007/s00766-010-0115-7
5. Yourdon, E., Constantine, L.L.: Structured Design: Fundamentals of a Discipline of Computer Program and Systems Design, 2 edn. YOURDON Press (1975)
6. Hoepman, J.-H.: Privacy design strategies. In: Cuppens-Boulahia, N., Cuppens, F., Jajodia, S., Abou El Kalam, A., Sans, T. (eds.) SEC 2014. IAICT, vol. 428, pp. 446–459. Springer, Heidelberg (2014). https://doi.org/10.1007/978-3-642-55415-5_38
7. Howard, M., Lipner, S.: The Security Development Lifecycle. Microsoft Press (2006)

8. Kozar, K.A.: The technique of data flow diagramming. University of Colorado (1997). Personal webpage https://spot.colorado.edu/~kozar/DFDtechnique.html
9. Maier, M.W., Emery, D., Hilliard, R.: 5.4.3 ANSI/IEEE 1471 and systems engineering. INCOSE Int. Symp. **12**(1), 798–805 (2002). https://doi.org/10.1002/j.2334-5837.2002.tb02541.x
10. Rozanski, N., Woods, E.: Software Systems Architecture: Working with Stakeholders Using Viewpoints and Perspectives. AWPC (2005)
11. Sanders, E., Stappers, P.J.: Co-creation and the new landscapes of design. CoDesign **4**(1), 5–18 (2008). https://doi.org/10.1080/15710880701875068
12. Sauter, V.: Data Flow Diagrams. University of Missouri, St. Louis (2002). Personal webpage. https://www.umsl.edu/~sauterv/analysis/dfd/dfd_intro.html
13. Shostack, A.: Threat Modeling: Designing for Security. Wiley (2014)
14. Sion, L., et al.: An architectural view for data protection by design. In: 2019 IEEE International Conference on Software Architecture (ICSA), pp. 11–20. IEEE (2019). https://doi.org/10.1109/ICSA.2019.00010
15. Sweeney, L.: k-anonymity: a model for protecting privacy. Int. J. Uncertain. Fuzziness Knowl. Based Syst. **10**(5), 557–570 (2002). https://doi.org/10.1142/S0218488502001648
16. Wuyts, K., Scandariato, R., Joosen, W.: Empirical evaluation of a privacy-focused threat modeling methodology. J. Syst. Softw. **96**, 122–138 (2014). https://doi.org/10.1016/j.jss.2014.05.075

# Generic Process Reference Model
# for Management Systems

Knut Haufe<sup>(⊠)</sup> (iD)

EY Consulting GmbH, Friedrichstraße 140, 10117 Berlin, Germany
Knut.Haufe@de.ey.com

**Abstract.** In recent years, organizational needs and interested parties' demands have increased the necessity to utilize multiple management system standards. Especially since more and more organizations must comply to more than one management system at a time. To utilize multiple management systems standards within one integrated overall management system of an organization, requirements of the relevant standards need to be linked and consolidated. As every organization manages its activities, resources and objectives through a set of interrelated processes this will lead to a generic process reference model for management systems. A generic – management system model – using a process approach is not present and needs to be developed. This article aims to fill this research gap by proposing such a generic process reference model across multiple management systems. The model was developed by using a multi-model harmonization method with process reference models for information privacy, information security and the ISO handbook on the integrated use of management systems (IUMSS).

**Keywords:** management · management systems · process reference models

## 1 Introduction

Best practices on how to manage risks are developed, agreed on the basis of consensus and published in the form of management system standards by the International Organization for Standardization (ISO) and together with the International Electrotechnical Commission (IEC). Current research activities and existing literature are not focusing on the systemic character of management systems as they are designed within ISO/IEC. Thus, consisting of repeated activities organized within processes. Process frameworks for management systems are not in the focus. But process frameworks for management systems are necessary prerequisites to integrate management systems, which is in the focus of the users of management system standards due to their need to improve efficiency. Frameworks of management system processes need to be developed in a more specific way. If they contain a basic, common set of generic management system processes, such a generic process reference model for management systems needs to be developed to foster the development of process models for specific domains.

ISO/IEC Directives, Part 1 Consolidated ISO Supplement - Procedures specific to ISO - Annex SL Proposals for management system standards, clause SL.8 and Appendix

© IFIP International Federation for Information Processing 2025
Published by Springer Nature Switzerland AG 2025
F. Bieker et al. (Eds.): Privacy and Identity 2024, IFIP AICT 705, pp. 132–146, 2025.
https://doi.org/10.1007/978-3-031-91054-8_7

2 [1] ensures that in all ISO management system standards, requirements are found under the same clause titles. This is supporting a generic structure of management systems as well but does not provide detailed guidance on the processes itself. The research question is: Is there an agreed on generic process reference model for management systems within ISO management system standards?

This is also relevant for the management domain of privacy and identity management, as no management system should be operated in isolation to avoid massive inefficiencies due to redundant work. A generic process reference model for management systems will form the basis for developing domain specific process reference models allowing to shift the focus from short term control oriented implementation of existing management system standards to a sustainable and efficient process oriented operation of management systems. Process reference models also enable and support the integration of management systems into each other [2].

To answer the research question, the article is structured as follows: In Sect. 2 the author gives an overview about relevant concepts and relevant standards. A high-level description of core aspects like management systems and process reference models have been included in this section. Applicable references have been provided for more detailed descriptions and to avoid a disruption of the scale of this paper. Section 3 includes a description of the applied research methodology and in Sect. 4 the proposed generic process reference model is illustrated, while Sect. 5 gives an overview of the results from the evaluation of the framework. Section 6 summarizes main findings and an outlook on future research including a validation using large language models (LLM).

## 2 Background

An organization exists to satisfy the needs and expectations of their interested parties (stakeholders) – formulated as objectives – and this is achieved through the presence of a management system [2, p. 10] in a sustainable way. Where risks are consequences of uncertainty about reaching the objectives according to [3, Ch. 3.1], risk management are coordinated activities to direct and control an organization with regard to risk [3, Ch. 3.2]. According to the ISO handbook on the integrated use of management system standards (IUMSS) [2, p. 10] "…the organization needs to pull together the processes, resources and work force into one coherent and functioning management system." which operates thorough the organization. This management system is called an integrated management system as it integrates different topics or themes that apply to a functional aspect of an organization, such as quality, environment, safety, security or energy [2, p. 41]. It implements an internal control system on its own behalf.

But in real life organizations, those different topics are often understood, planned, implemented and operated as separate management systems of an organization resulting in multiple efforts in audit and in operation. Nevertheless, every such topic or theme specific management system (in the following the term "management domain" is used for a topic or theme specific management system) has the same objective: identify and direct/control the achievement of requirements that are of importance because of the potential risks to the organizations objectives [2, p. 41]. In addition to this, they share the same common management system requirements. At least if ISO Standards are concerned. Addressing domain specific risks as well as opportunities is one of the basic concepts of every management system domain [1], [2, p. 39]. A quality management system is addressing quality risks, a security management system is addressing security risks and so on. In every management system domain several international standards or standard families have been developed and published by the International Organization for Standardization (ISO). This results in a hierarchy of management system standards addressing risks [4–6] or the assessment of risks respectively parts of the process like the analysis of consequences of risks (impact assessment) [7–9]. This is displayed in Fig. 1.

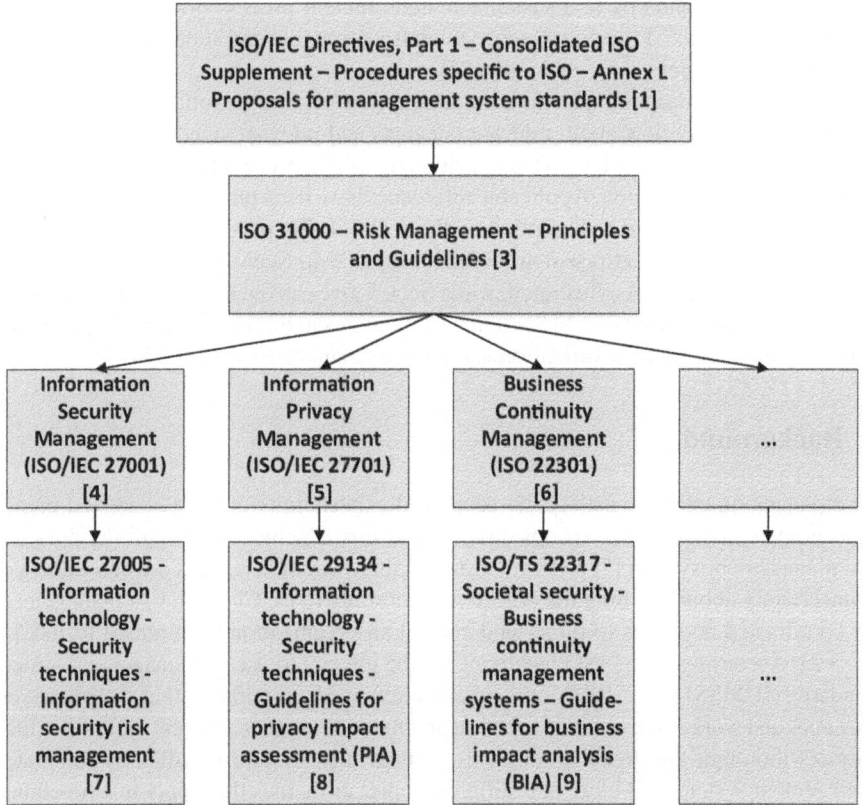

**Fig. 1.** Hierarchy of risk management related ISO standards

A management system consists of objectives, processes, organizational structure and resources as well as performance feedback – according to [2, p. 16]. Another way to describe a management system is that it consists of planned, build, run and monitored activities in alignment with the direction set by the governing body to achieve the objectives of the organization [10, p. 31]. The integrated management system needs to be governed [10, p. 31] through a general process framework to avoid the unnecessary efforts.

An organization manages its activities, resources, work force and objectives trough a set of interrelated processes [2, p. 59]. All work in an organization occurs through its processes and therefore, an organization should have a deep understanding of the timing, interdependencies, interactions, and interfaces within the processes of the organization's management system [2, p. 19]. According to ISO/IEC 33004 [11] "The purpose of a process reference model is to define a set of processes that collectively can support the primary aims of a community of interest." It consists of process descriptions including purpose, input, process activities, outcomes and process interfaces.

Given this, maximizing process efficiency and effectiveness is a fundamental concept for a successful organization [2, p. 20]. Additionally, combining process requirements reduces redundancy in designing and developing an integrated management system [2, p. 20] and an integrated management system is a more efficient and effective approach than planning, implementing and running management systems separately for every relevant management domain [2, p. 47]. In addition, it consumes less resources in operation since it has much less redundancy.

As mentioned before, an organization can address the requirements of multiple standards by relating and connecting them with this integrated arrangement of processes [2, p. 59]. The process approach is often used within the integration of management systems [2, p. 59, 60]. Integration is the process of unifying requirements of multiple standards into an organization's overall management system. The result of the integration is a single integrated management system that meets the requirements of multiple standards [2, p. 48]. The integration of new or changed requirements can bring changes in the processes, resources and objectives of a management system, but according to [2, p. 63] this should not result in a change of the underlying structure of the management system. There is an underlying common structure of a management system which can be described as a generic process reference model. According to [2, p. 39] there are some common requirements of management system standards:

- Management and employee responsibility, authority and accountability – see also [12, Sec. 5.1 Leadership and commitment]
- Competence and awareness – see also [12, Sec. 7.2 Competence and 7.3 Awareness]
- Planning and deployment of resources – see also [12, Sec. 7.1 Resources]
- Internal and external communication – see also [12, Sec. 7.4 Communication]
- Risk evaluation and impact on objectives – see also [12, Sec. 6.1 Actions to address risks and opportunities and 6.2 Objectives and planning to achieve them]
- Performance review related to organizational objectives – see also [12, Sec. 9.1 Monitoring, measurement, analysis, and evaluation]
- Internal audits – see also [12, Sec. 9.2 Internal audit]
- Control of documented information – see also [12, Sec. 7.5 Documented Information]

This will form the basis for developing a generic process reference model for management systems. There are already developed process reference models available for the management domains of information security management systems (ISMS) [13] and information privacy management systems (IPMS). In terms of generalization those process reference models also need to be considered while developing a generic process reference model. Standardization in other management system domains is ongoing as

ISO approved new work items for guidance standards for security management processes (ISO 22333) as well as business continuity management processes (ISO 28022).

## 3  Methodology

The research methodology to develop a generic process reference model for management systems can be summarized as follows:

1. **Analyze and compare (matching)** – Identify potential generic processes in existing established process model standards and ISO/IEC Directives, Part 1 Consolidated ISO Supplement
2. **Harmonize and integrate (mapping)** – Determine the generic process reference model – The resulting process reference model will be described in Sect. 4.
3. **Evaluate** – Test the generic process reference model to predict process reference models in the management system domains of risk management as well as business continuity management system (BCMS). Compare the predicted process models with processes mentioned in the relevant domain specific standards – Evaluation is described in Sect. 5.

The terms matching and mapping are differentiated as follows: Matching is the process of identifying two semantically related processes [14]. Processes are semantically related if they are represented (analogy) in two or more standards with the same or different terms. The interpretation rules to decide if there is an analogy are characterized as implicit rules for mapping knowledge about a base domain into a target domain [15]. Beside this, a comparison scale has been defined and used. The scale contains the following elements based on the scale presented by Baldassarre [16]:

- Strongly related (S): the process is especially named in the standards and the process has the same process objectives and contain the same process steps
- Partially related (P): the process is not especially named, but there are one or more requirements in the standard which led to the implementation of the process defined in another standard
- Weakly related (W): the process is not especially named, but there is a process or a process concept which can/should be adapted in a generic management system process model.
- Non-related (N): no relationship can be identified.

Mapping refers to the combination of the standards/processes. After the identification of semantically related processes they are combined into an integrated process framework by using a mapping [15]. Matching and mapping are established methods in scientific knowledge comparison and especially used to compare and merge different ontologies [14, 15].

### Analyze and Compare

Basic criteria for core processes of a management system were identified within the scope of an information security management system, confirmed in a previous study [17] and modified to suit the identification of generic management system processes.

In the step of matching, the comparison is performed through an iterative and incremental procedure. The process used (adapted from [16], is iterative, because the comparison (analysis and determination of the relationship between the [1, 2], and [13] is executed completely on one ISMS process first, and then on the others in turn. It is also incremental, in the sense that the comparison outcome (i.e., the final product of the theoretical comparison process) grows and evolves with each iteration until it becomes the final one. Using this, iterative and incremental approach was necessary to deal with the complexity entailed in a comparison in which entities of low-level abstraction are involved.

The results from the matching were summarized in Table 1.

**Harmonize and Integrate**

To obtain an agreed basis of generic management system processes multiple process reference models need to be harmonized. To harmonize multiple process reference models a systematic stepwise approach presented by Baldassarre [16] was used as this is intended for the harmonization of models. Also the practical method for the integration of multiple management systems standard requirements into one overall integrated management system, presented in [2, p. 49, 66], was considered. For the scientific analysis, an adaptation on the Models and Standards Similarity Study method by J. A. Calvo-Manzano et al. [18] was used. The method was as follows:

1. **Select the models and standards to be analyzed**
2. **Choose the reference model** – as reference model ISO/IEC Directives, Part 1 Consolidated ISO Supplement - Procedure for the technical work - Procedures specific to ISO - Annex SL Harmonized approach for management system standards [1] is chosen.
3. **Select the process**
4. **Establish a coherent level of detail** – as all analyzed standards are international standards and are applicable to all organizations independent of their size, objectives, business model, location et cetera. The contained information about management system processes are generic requirements and only their application is specific. Therefore, a similar level of detail is chosen to analyze the standards.
5. **Create a correspondence template** – Instead of a detailed correspondence template a process profile template was created.
6. **Identify the similarity among models** – The process templates were completed with information obtained from the standards.
7. **Show obtained results**

The harmonization strategy of Baldassarre [16] is based on the process and the framework for supporting multi-model harmonization of [18]. A theoretical comparison process is used as the harmonization process, because mapping is one of the most widely used strategies for the harmonization of models [16]. The purpose of this process is to perform a step-by-step comparison and a mapping of different models, aiming to guarantee the reliability and robustness of obtained results. For the theoretical comparison [1] was considered as a starting model, as it is considered as the blueprint for every ISO management system standard.

## 4   Generic Process Reference Model for Management Systems

Table 1 contains a matrix of analyzed standards and the identified possible generic management system processes. This matrix shows which cross-domain processes are described in the established management system standards and to what extend they are related.

Processes will be differentiated in governance/management, core, and supporting processes according to [19] as core elements of every management system.

**Table 1.** Matrix of analyzed standards and contained cross domain management system processes

| Process category | ISO Annex SL/IUMSS-process | ISMS – process (relationship grade) | IPMS – process (relationship grade) |
|---|---|---|---|
| Governance/Management process | Governance process for the management system [1, p. 17, 22], [2, p. 17, 39] | Information security governance process (P) | Information privacy governance process (P) |
| Core process | Policy management process [1, p. 18], [2, p. 39, 51] | Security policy management process (P) | Privacy policy management process (P) |
| Core process | Requirements management process [1, p. 17], [2, p. 13] | Requirements management process (P) | Requirements management process (P) |
| Core process | – | – | Process to ensure a lawfulness processing of PII[a] including PIA[b] (N) |
| Core process | – | – | Process to ensure the rights of the data subjects (N) |
| Core process | Risk assessment process [1, p. 18], [2, p. 39] | Information security risk assessment process (P) | Information privacy risk assessment process (P) |
| Core process | Risk treatment process [1, p. 18] | Information security risk treatment process (P) | Information privacy risk treatment process (P) |

*(continued)*

**Table 1.**  (*continued*)

| Process category | ISO Annex SL/IUMSS-process | ISMS – process (relationship grade) | IPMS – process (relationship grade) |
|---|---|---|---|
| Core process | – | Security implementation management process (W) | Privacy implementation management process (W) |
| Core process | Process to control outsourced processes [1, p. 21] | Process to control outsourced processes (P) | Process to control commissioned data processing (P) |
| Core process | Process to ensure competence and awareness [1, p. 19], [2, p. 39] | Process to assure necessary awareness and competence (P) | Process to assure necessary awareness and competence (P) |
| Core process | | Information security incident management process (W) | Information privacy incident management process (W) |
| Core process | Change management process [1, p. 21], [2, p. 10] | Information security change management process (P) | Information privacy change management process (P) |
| Core process | Internal audit process [1, p. 21, 22], [2, p. 39] | Internal audit process (P) | Internal audit process (P) |
| Core process | Performance evaluation process [1, p. 15, 16, 21], [2, p. 39] | Performance evaluation process (P) | Performance evaluation process (P) |
| Core process | Improvement process [1, p. 16, 23], [2, p. 27] | Information security improvement process (P) | Information privacy improvement process (P) |
| Support process | Process to control documented information [1, p. 20], [2, p. 39] | Process to control documented information (P) | Process to control documented information (P) |
| Support process | – | – | Process to document and maintain records of processing activities (N) |

(*continued*)

**Table 1.** *(continued)*

| Process category | ISO Annex SL/IUMSS-process | ISMS – process (relationship grade) | IPMS – process (relationship grade) |
|---|---|---|---|
| Support process | Resource management process [1, p. 19], [2, p. 39] | Resource management process (P) | Resource management process (P) |
| Support process | Communication process [1, p. 20], [2, p. 39] | Communication process (P) | Communication process (P) |
| Support process | – | Information security customer relationship management process (W) | Information privacy customer relationship management process (W) |

[a]PII – Personally Identifiable Information.
[b]PIA – Privacy Impact Assessment.

Table 1 shows, that all processes identified as potential generic management system processes within [1, 2] have a representation within the Information Security Management System and the Information Privacy Management System. Therefore, it is deemed that they are generic management system processes. Processes identified as non-related (N) are dismissed as they are management domain specific processes and not part of a generic process reference model.

In the following, processes not formerly identified within [1, 2] but present as processes within the Information Security Management System or the Information Privacy Management System and classified as (W) will be discussed:

- Implementation management process – It seems obvious, that in every management system measures or actions need to be implemented/done to treat/mitigate the identified risks. Consequently, within [1, p. 18] the requirement is given to plan actions to address risks and opportunities. Beside this, it is noteworthy, that no requirement was formulated to implement/perform the planned actions. Nevertheless, an implementation management process for actions to address risks is obviously necessary and therefore it will be included in the generic process model for management systems.
- Incident management process – A process to deal with incidents was also not specifically named within [1, 2] but it is deemed to be part of prevention and reduction of undesired effects [1, p. 18] and therefore included in the generic process model for management systems.
- Customer relationship management process – The active management of customer relationships combines aspects of external communication [1, p. 20], monitoring of requirements [1, p. 21] and stakeholder review [1, p. 22]. The process is also related to continually achieving the needs and expectations of interested parties [1, p. 17, 23].

Therefore, the process is also included in the generic process model for management systems.

As a result of the analysis and discussion above, the generic process reference model for management systems shown in Fig. 2 is proposed.

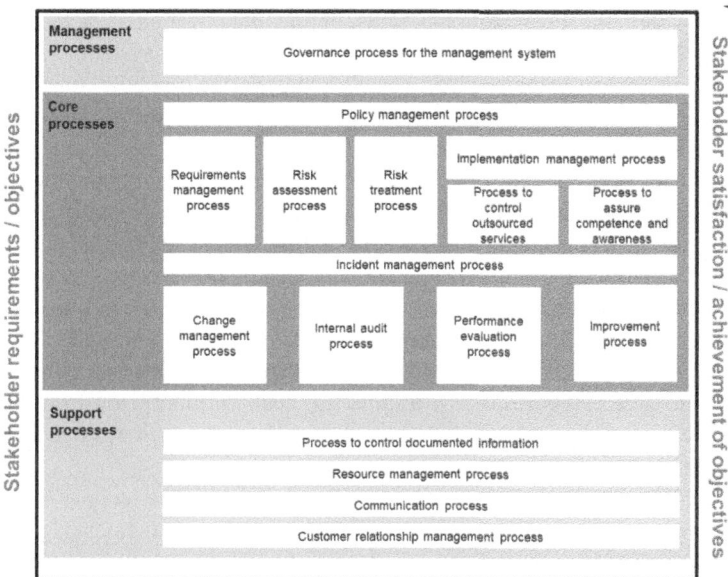

**Fig. 2.** Generic process reference model for management systems

By implementing a **governance process for the management system** an organization has the capability to align their management systems with the expectations, needs and objectives of the governing stakeholders.

The capability to manage the behavior and task execution of the employees in a risk-oriented way by having a defined set of policies, standards, procedures and guidelines within the management systems is addressed by the **policy management process**.

In every management system an appropriate understanding of framing conditions like the expectations, needs and objectives of interested parties is mandatory to achieve the objectives of the management system. This capability is developed within the **requirements management process**. In this process legal, statutory, regulatory and contractual requirements are identified, prioritized and provided for other processes of the management system like the risk assessment process, the internal audit process and the process to control outsourced processes.

Having the capability to identify, analyze and evaluate all relevant risks in the scope of the management system is achieved by implementing a **risk assessment process**. Documented, evaluated and prioritized risks including risk owners are outcomes of this process.

The capability to manage relevant risks within the scope of the management system by identifying and selecting risk treatment options, control objectives and controls is achieved by implementing a **risk treatment process**. Outcomes of this process are risk treatment plans including controls and control objectives, a control implementation plan and requests for changes for the change management process. Those are used as input for several other processes of the management system. Also, a documented acceptance of residual risks is an outcome of this process.

Having the capability to finally implement all selected controls of the risk treatment plans within the organizational units of the organization is achieved by an **implementation management process** with every management system.

If the organization is using services from third parties, the capability to manage risks introduced by using these third-party services will be achieved by a **process to control outsourced services** within each management system.

All personnel need to receive appropriate and necessary training and/or education within each management systems. The capability to achieve this is realized within the **process to assure necessary awareness and competence**. Outcome is an awareness, training and education program which is implemented by this process.

Even the best preparation and controls to prevent risks from occurring does not prevent incidents. The capability to manage occurring incidents is realized within the management systems by an **incident management process.** This process enables the organization to detect, report, assess, respond to, deal with and learn from incidents. Outcomes are identified and documented incidents. Those are used in several processes of the management system.

The capability of maintaining an acceptable level of risks in the scope of the management system while implementing changes within the management system is achieved by a **change management process**. Process outcomes are for example proposed and agreed on changes as well as results of changes (provided by and used in the risk assessment process).

The capability to independently assess the effectiveness and efficiency of the management system and the implemented controls is developed by implementing an **internal audit process**. This is differentiated from the **performance evaluation process** which is realizing the capability to continuously monitor, measure, analyze and evaluate the performance of the management system processes and of the implemented controls.

The **continual improvement process** is for developing the capability to ensure a continuous improvement of the management system in terms of efficiency and effectiveness as well as the adequacy of the management system and the controls.

Within the **process to control documented information** it is ensured that the organization has the capability to provide and give access to an appropriate documentation to prove the adequacy and operation of the management system.

Resources are needed to operate the management systems and to manage risks. The capability to identify, provide and monitor the usage of those resources is realized by the implementation of a **resource management process** in every management system. Outcomes of the process are for example determined resources to implement and operate selected controls as well as the management system processes including funding sources.

The capability to communicate with every stakeholder of the management system about the risks within the scope of the management system in an efficient, effective, planned and structured way is achieved within the **communication process** to stakeholders outside the management system.

While the governance process for the management system establishes an interface between the management system and its stakeholders, the **customer relationship management process** realizes the capability to manage the customer satisfaction at an operational level. This includes the capability to continuously demonstrate the added value of investments in the management system.

Synergy effects resulting from the integration of processes into an IMS should be identified and realized wherever possible ad suitable as all processes have the potential to be designed and implemented as integrated processes.

Detailed process profiles including input and outcome descriptions, process tasks and activities and process flowcharts are also results of the detailed mapping. They have not been included in this paper as it would disrupt the scale of this paper.

## 5   Evaluation

Evaluation was done by using the proposed generic process reference model for management systems to predict the processes for the management system domains of risk management as well as BCMS.

In a second step the standards again have been analyzed while using the already described methods for the identification of processes.

The following standards have been analyzed to identify processes of the risk management system:

- ISO 31000:2018 – Risk management – Guidelines [3]
- ISO/TR 31004:2013 – Risk management – Guidance for the implementation of ISO 31000 [20]
- ISO/IEC 31010:2019 – Risk management – Risk assessment techniques [21]
- ISO 31073:2022 – Risk management – Vocabulary [22]

The following standards have been analyzed to identify processes of the business continuity management system:

- ISO 22300:2021 – Security and resilience – Vocabulary [23]
- ISO 22301:2019 – Security and resilience – Business continuity management systems – Requirements [6]
- ISO 22313:2020 – Security and resilience – Business continuity management systems – Guidance [24]
- ISO/TS 22317:2021 – Societal security – Business continuity management systems – Guidelines for business impact analysis (BIA) [9]
- ISO/TS 22332 – Security and resilience – Business continuity management systems – Guidelines for developing business continuity plans and procedures [25]

The predicted processes were compared to processes mentioned in the relevant standards.

Every predicted process of the risk management system and the business continuity management system is named explicitly or with another term or indirectly in the relevant standards or a concept is included within the standards which leads to the implementation of the predicted process.

Because of this, the generic process reference model for management systems is deemed to be confirmed.

# 6  Conclusions and Future Work

As shown in the previous chapter, there is a generic process reference model for management systems, which the author of this article is proposing. The proposed generic process reference model for management systems was evaluated and confirmed by adopting it in the fields of risk management and business continuity management. It can be used as a blueprint or baseline structure for further necessary management system process models, which have not been developed yet.

The proposed generic process reference model for management systems can be utilized to integrate multiple management systems standards within one integrated overall management system of an organization. A vital step within the integration is to integrate the processes of the management systems, for which the proposed generic process reference model of management systems can be used. The proposed generic process reference model of management systems will also allow to integrate management systems for which a formal process model have not been developed yet. Nevertheless, future work should include the following:

- The proposed generic process reference model of management systems should be integrated within ISO Annex SL [1] and IUMSS [2].
- Missing processes of implementation management, incident management and customer relationship management should be added to ISO Annex SL [1] and IUMSS [2].
- The proposed generic process reference model should be tested within other management system domains to confirm or improvement the model.
- A full BCM process reference model should be determined including additional domain specific processes – for example like:

  - Process to develop BC plans and procedures
  - Process to exercise BC plans and procedures
  - Recovery process
  - Warning and communication process
  - Criticality analysis process

An additional framework validation via a large language model (LLM) [26] can provide further corroboration for the process reference model and conducted as follows:

- Set up a LLM model instance, for example [27]
- Train the LLM with process documentation from real world implementations
- Validate the LLM by checking its performance

- Use specific prompts to obtain answers about the relevance of specific process categories

**Disclosure of Interests.**  The author has no competing interests to declare that are relevant to the content of this article.

# References

1. International Organization for Standardisation and International Electrotechnical Commission: ISO/IEC Directives, Part 1 Consolidated ISO Supplement - Procedure for the technical work - Procedures specific to ISO - Annex SL Harmonized approach for management system standards, Geneva (2022)
2. International Organization for Standardisation and International Electrotechnical Commission: ISO Handbook - The Integrated Use of Management System Standards (IUMSS), Geneva (2018)
3. International Organization for Standardisation: ISO 31000:2018 - Risk Management – Guidelines, Geneva (2018)
4. International Organization for Standardisation and International Electrotechnical Commission: ISO/IEC 27001:2022 - Information security, cybersecurity and privacy protection - Information security management systems – Requirements, Geneva (2022)
5. International Organization for Standardisation and International Electrotechnical Commission: ISO/IEC 27701:2019 - Security techniques - Extension to ISO/IEC 27001 and ISO/IEC 27002 for privacy information management - Requirements and guidelines, Geneva (2019)
6. International Organization for Standardisation: ISO 22301:2019 - Security and resilience - Business continuity management systems – Requirements, Geneva (2019)
7. International Organization for Standardisation and International Electrotechnical Commission: ISO/IEC 27005:2022 - Information security, cybersecurity and privacy protection - Guidance on managing information security risks, Geneva (2022)
8. International Organization for Standardisation and International Electrotechnical Commission: ISO/IEC 29134:2023 - Security techniques - Guidelines for privacy impact assessment, Geneva (2023)
9. International Organization for Standardisation: ISO/TS 22317:2021 - Security and resilience - Business continuity management systems - Guidelines for business impact analysis (BIA), Geneva (2021)
10. Information Systems Audit and Control Association: COBIT 5 A Business Framework for the Governance and Management of Enterprise IT. Information Systems Audit and Control Association (2013)
11. International Organization for Standardisation and International Electrotechnical Commission: ISO/IEC 33004:2015 - Information technology - Process assessment - Requirements for process reference, process assessment and maturity models, Geneva (2015)
12. International Organization for Standardisation and International Electrotechnical Commission: ISO/IEC Directives, Part 1 Consolidated ISO Supplement - Procedure for the technical work - Procedures specific to ISO - Annex SL Harmonized approach for management system standards - Appendix 2, 2nd ed., Geneva (2023)
13. Haufe, K.: Maturity based approach for ISMS Governance. Universidad Carlos III de Madrid, Madrid (2017). https://e-archivo.uc3m.es/handle/10016/25128
14. Gentner, D.: Structure-mapping: a theoretical framework for analogy. Cogn. Sci. 7(2), 155–170 (1983)

15. Guo, W., Kraines, S.B.: Explicit scientific knowledge comparison based on semantic description matching. Proc. Am. Soc. Inf. Sci. Technol. **45**(1), 1–18 (2008)
16. Pardo, C., Pino, F.J., García, F., Piattini, M., Baldassarre, M.T.: A process for driving the harmonization of models. In: Proceedings of the 11th International Conference on Product Focused Software, pp. 51–54 (2010)
17. Haufe, K., Colomo-Palacios, R., Dzombeta, S., Brandis, K., Stantchev, V.: ISMS core processes: a study. Procedia Comput. Sci. **100**, 339–346 (2016)
18. Calvo-Manzano, J., Cueva, G., Muñoz, M.: Project Management Similarity Study: Experiment on Project Planning Practices Based on CMMI-Dev v1. 2. EuroSPI 2008-Proceedings, p. 11 (2008)
19. International Organization for Standardisation: ISO 9000:2015 - Quality management systems - Fundamentals and vocabulary, Geneva (2015)
20. International Organization for Standardisation: ISO/TR 31004:2013 - Risk Management - Guidance for the implementation of ISO 31000, Geneva (2013)
21. International Electrotechnical Commission: IEC 31010:2019 - Risk Management - Risk Assessment Techniques, Geneva (2019)
22. International Organization for Standardisation, ISO 31073:2022 - Risk Management – Vocabulary, Geneva (2022)
23. International Organization for Standardisation: ISO 22300:2021 - Security and resilience – Vocabulary, Geneva (2021)
24. International Organization for Standardisation: ISO 22313:2020 - Security and resilience - Business continuity management systems – Guidance, Geneva (2020)
25. International Organization for Standardisation: ISO/TS 22332:2021 - Security and resilience - Business continuity management systems - Guidelines for developing business continuity plans and procedures, Geneva (2021)
26. Chang, Y., et al.: A survey on evaluation of large language models. ACM Trans. Intell. Syst. Technol. (2023)
27. Touvron, H., et al.: Llama: Open and efficient foundation language models. arXiv preprint arXiv:2302.13971 (2023)

# Protecting the Right to Private and Family Life Under the European Artificial Intelligence Act: Is a Risk Based Approach Enough?

Juliusz Mroziński[(✉)] [iD]

University of Wrocław, Uniwersytecki Pl. 1, 50137 Wrocław, Poland
`juliusz.mrozinski@uwr.edu.pl`

**Abstract.** The research discusses the European Artificial Intelligence Act ('AIA') as a groundbreaking legal framework aimed at standardizing risk management associated with artificial intelligence technologies. It explores the act's implications for protecting fundamental rights, with a focus on the right to private and family life, as guaranteed by the European Convention on Human Rights ('Convention' or 'ECHR') and the EU Charter of Fundamental Rights ('Charter'). The paper critically evaluates the risk-based approach employed by the AIA, particularly its provisions for high-risk AI systems, and their capacity to address potential intrusions into personal privacy and autonomy. It also investigates judicial protection mechanisms under the AIA, highlighting jurisdictional overlaps between the Court of Justice of the European Union ('CJEU') and the European Court of Human Rights ('ECtHR'). The analysis raises concerns about the adequacy of safeguards for specific vulnerable groups, such as minors, and critiques the privatization of certain oversight functions. The study concludes with recommendations for enhancing the regulation's effectiveness in preserving individual rights against AI-induced risks.

**Keywords:** Right to Privacy and Family Life · European AI Act · Risk Management System · Risk Based Approach · Moral and Physical Integrity

## 1 Introduction

The 9th of December 2023 was marked by an initial settlement between the European Parliament and the Council of the EU on a general AI usage regulation. On the 13th of March 2024 the final text of the act was adopted [12, 19] by the European Parliament and, eventually, on the 21st of May the Council approved it. Having been published[1], finally, on the 12th of July 2024, the legislation become not only legally binding for all entities within the EU, but shall be directly applicable by courts and executable by

---

[1] OJ L, 2024/1689, 12.7.2024, ELI: http://data.europa.eu/eli/reg/2024/1689/oj.

F. Bieker et al. (Eds.): Privacy and Identity 2024, IFIP AICT 705, pp. 147–165, 2025.
https://doi.org/10.1007/978-3-031-91054-8_8

proper enforcement bodies[2]. The so called 'European Artificial Intelligence Act' (AIA) [55] may be recognized as the first, vanguard attempt to standardize – in a legal way – the risks necessarily connected with commercial and non-commercial exploitation of artificial intelligence. It marks the most feasible trends in the usage of AI and reflects certain threats induced by it, *inter alia* in the field of fundamental rights guaranteed by the European Convention on Human Rights [10] as well as the Charter of Fundamental Rights of the European Union [8]. Some similarities – with respect to the focus on risk – can be noted in the context of corresponding legislative attitude of the Intergovernmental Panel on Climate Change [48]. Not by chance is this feature also perceived as a main point of regulatory gravity, providing the governmental and non-governmental supervision over the AI, establishing mode in which specific risks caused by algorithms are to be managed. Among many questions arising in the context of the legislation probably the most ponderable from the perspective of a natural person regards its impact for sustaining the effective protection of private and family life.

The risk based approach on which the key provisions of the AIA are based, attempts to optimise the degree of supranational protection of fundamental rights, making it proportionate to the potential for the development of artificial intelligence in the EU internal market [59]. It is reflected in the obligations imposed by the AIA to shape risk management systems accordingly. The aim of this work is to analyse the adequacy and sufficiency of the risk management procedure, as it is designed in final version of the European AI Act, for safeguarding fundamental rights stated by the Article 8 of the European Convention on Human Rights and Article 7 of the Charter of Fundamental Rights of the EU. Specifically, the text aims to address the following research questions:

1. Which sphere of the right to protect individual's private and family life could be particularly endangered by *'high-risk AI systems'*?
2. To what extent can the provisions of the AIA be executable for supranational institutions – specifically the CJEU and the ECtHR – on behalf of the individual, given the potentially competing nature of their jurisdiction in the field of fundamental rights?

Within the Introduction below, I aim to present a general assessment of a risk management procedure lain down in AIA provisions. In the following sections I am referring the scope of controversy around the 'high risk' AI systems for fundamental rights as well as the extent to which they could be effectively protected under Article 9 AIA. The foregoing considerations are focused on a correlation between the efficient control of the risk generated by the AI and the protection of the right to private and family life. Final conclusions are set out in the Summary.

The field of study demands to apply various scientific approaches and methods. In case of legal acts in force the formal-dogmatic method (textual approach) offers relevant

---

[2] As states the Article 113 of the Regulation, Chapters I (*General Provisions*) and II (*Prohibited AI practices*) shall apply from 2 February 2025. Chapter III Sect. 4 (*Notifying authorities and notified bodies*), Chapter V (*General Purpose AI Models*), Chapter VII (*Governance*), Chapter XII (*Penalties*) and Article 78 (*Confidentiality*) shall apply from 2 August 2025, with the exception of Article 101 (*Fines for providers of general-purpose AI models*) which is to become applicable in the general term (August the $2^{nd}$ 2026). Article 6 (para 1) and the corresponding obligations in Regulation shall apply from 2 August 2027.

outcome, whereas theoretical analysis of fundamental rights under considerations and the features of the AI systems require to provide the critical review of literature and other reliable sources as well. Whenever it is reasonable, the reflections shall regard the relevant case law of the Court of Justice of the European Union, the European Court of Human Rights and the national jurisdiction bodies.

## 2  Risk Management Procedure in the AIA: Context and an Assessment

However market regulation is the main purpose of the AI regulation within the EU, "Ensuring a high level of protection of health, safety and fundamental rights" (AIA Recitals, para 1) was a fundamental assumption for the authors of regulation. With that in mind, AIA ensures that AI systems to be placed on the internal market must be safe and trustworthy [50]. It is a truism, hence, to state that they must guarantee a proper level of fundamental rights protection. Even though the Union aims for establishing the uniform legal guarantees in favour of natural persons, the quality of the protection varies among the member states and specific rights. The well recognized interest of the EU includes the equality between its citizens in the context of the protection against possible unlawful interference with private life in the upcoming digital era [20]. As the general human rights protection regime does not address current 'digital dilemmas' in a comprehensive way [58], it is apparent, considering the legislative attitude of the Union's Institutions, that through AIA the EU aims for establishing a detailed legal framework for the protection of individuals' data and privacy. That all could have been the reason for choosing a directly effective and applicable 'regulation' (instead of 'directive') as a method of legal intervention. Ever since algorithms have become a subject of legislative works, which includes not only the AIA but GDPR as well, the institutions of the European Union seem to have been mindful that only a pan-European unified set of legal solutions has a chance to have a real impact on the activities of multinational corporations doing business in the development of artificial intelligence. This realisation is reflected in the Introduction to the White Paper on Artificial Intelligence, explicitly referring to the need to prevent fragmentation of legislation in this area [23]. Although nowadays – as O. Lynskey [39], for example, points out – data protection has grown into a self-contained area of Union's law[3], at its very core it exhibits a functional coupling with the right to protection of privacy. Hence, I have included in the paper a perspective on the scope of application of both rights.

Articles 8(1) and 9(1–10), along with Annex III of the AIA, establish stringent rules for risk management. While the primary focus of the regulation is on ensuring the quality of digital products (as outlined in Article 17 onward), the introductory provisions emphasize tools for algorithm control. An obligation to 'establish, implement, document and maintain' an effective risk management procedure applies only in case of systems imposing 'high risk'. The wording of Article 9 AIA is in this context quite explicit [59].

---

[3] In 2000, the right to the protection of personal data as the fundamental right received its own legal basis in the EU regime. Article 8 of the Charter, compared to the chronologically and substantively more relevant Article 7 affirming the right o the protection of privacy and family life, remains a highly detailed regulation.

A definitional approach to the latter, however, gives rise to multiple doubts reported in literature [42]. Keeping in mind the specific qualities of a 'high risk' systems enlisted in the Annex III AIA, it would not be appropriate to omit the suggestion contained within Article 6 para 3 AIA (*a contrario*): the system to be utilized in the scope described in para 3 (a–d), which does not 'pose a significant risk of harm to the health, safety or fundamental rights of natural persons, including by not materially influencing the outcome of decision making' shall not be qualified as a 'high risk' one. Hence, the purpose of a protective criterium encrypted in precise and professional wording used in Annex III is to protect the most essential values, whereas the 'significance' could be assessed on the basis of 'the severity of the possible harm and its probability of occurrence' (Recital 52) [48]. While exploring the idea of managing the risk, multiple works refer to International Organization for Standardization (ISO) norms [42, 59]. The idea behind a legal obligation to control the risk is determined – just as T. Mahler points out – by the need to provide a solution 'suitable for achieving proportionality and avoiding regulatory overreach'. For this reason, the risk management system should include means for identification (describing), analysis (estimating) and evaluation (assessment) of the risk understood as the probability and severity of a harm in the context of objective and subjective 'uncertainty of an object' [42]. Investigating the phenomenon of the risk itself, C. Novelli, F. Casolari, A. Rotolo, M. Taddeo and L. Floridi suggest to distinguish between an overall risk and an ancillary risk, whereas the latter could be a result of a process of regulation alone [48]. The same authors claim for employing the general proportionality test (verifying the suitability of measures, necessity of intervention as well as proportionality *sensu stricto*) while evaluating the risk and encourage the regulatory approach complying with the determinants of the risk: specific hazards, vulnerabilities of actors, likelihood of exposure and a possible response to the danger [48]. A similar view is shared by the J. Schuett, who stresses that the Article 9 (para 6 specifically) AIA 'is essentially a restatement of the principle of proportionality' [59]. Given the important role that the principle of proportionality, which has grown to become a general principle of EU law, has played in the jurisprudence of the Court of Justice of the European Union to date [23], it can be assumed that the three-stage proportionality test developed in Case 19/61 Mannesman [31] and progressively developed in the judgments (notably C-11/70 Internationale Handelsgesellschaft [32] and C-120/78 Rewe-Zentral AG [33]) will also apply in cases arising under the AIA [3].

The management of the risks generated by high-risk AI, under the provisions of the AIA, is, on the one hand, an obligation incumbent on providers ('implementation') and, on the other hand, has an impact on the process by which deployers use the AI system ('training' – where appropriate, certain aspects of assessment). The early stage of the AIA makes it possible to formulate only a general, *a priori* evaluation of the AI risk management system. An undoubted advantage of the relatively restrictive requirements outlined by the EU legislator is their diversification throughout the process of introducing an AI system to the market and its subsequent practical use. The opinion that such a legal framework will make it possible, first and foremost, to prevent risks before they actually arise, as well as to react dynamically to threats posed by systems already legally marketed in the EU, seems justified.

Keeping in mind the experience of nearly ten years of practical application of the GDPR provisions, already at this preliminary stage of implementation of the AIA, one may have doubts about the degree of proportionality of the protection it offers to minors. The literature systematically notes 'the gap between the recognition given to children's privacy at the declaratory level and the failure to recognize and protect children's privacy interest in practice' [1, 7]. Here, apart from general references to acts of general international law, in particular the United Nations Convention on the Rights of the Child [11], as well as documents of a non-normative nature (specifically General comment No. 25 on children's rights in relation to the digital environment [25]) made in recitals, the AIA does not make minors specifically the subject of protective regulations. People under the age of 18 (according to current research [27, 56]) are the group most vulnerable to the negative effects of the commercial use of artificial intelligence systems. It is young people, moreover, who remain the most deeply immersed in the digital world. The failure to consider the conclusions accompanying the proportionality assessment of the GDPR regulation in this regard puts the AIA in a negative light.

## 3   AI and Its Interference with the Right to Private and Family Life

Among the set of fundamental rights recognized by the common European legal framework for their protection the right to private and family life is appointed as the one which has been significantly affected by the developments of a digital revolution [16]. W. DeVries puts it clearly: 'Privacy law has traditionally developed in tandem with technology reshaping itself to meet the privacy threats embodied in new technology. The information revolution, however, is occurring so fast and affects so many areas of privacy law that the old, adaptive process is failing to address digital privacy problems.'[16].

The following are most commonly distinguished [35, 47] as the branches of the right enshrined by the Article 8 of the Convention for the Protection of Human Rights and Fundamental Freedoms:

1. right to protect private life,
2. right to protect family life,
3. right to protect home,
4. right to respect uninterrupted correspondence.

Considering the extensive ECtHR case law on Article 8 of the ECHR, 'private life' is arguably the broadest and most ambiguous aspect of the Convention [35]. The sphere of data protection, meanwhile, enjoys exceptional attention under already binding, tried and tested legislation. That regime has already been well described in literature [14, 22, 37, 39, 64], as well as in judiciary. Recital 10 of the AIA contains an explicit reference to particular legislation concerning data and privacy protection under the EU law. Specific regulations (EU 2016/679 [53], EU 2018/1725 [54]) and directives (EU 2016/680 [17], 2002/58/EC [18]) do not replace obligations established by the provisions of AIA but rather construe a parallel regime aimed for safeguarding the individuals' rights to privacy and data protection vis-a-vis algorithms and their applications. Hence, I believe that it would be more appropriate to introduce first some aspects of strictly understood private life and other rights stemming from the Article 8 ECHR, precisely – following the systematization presented by the ECtHR Registry [29] – physical, psychological or moral integrity, identity and autonomy, family life, home and correspondence.

According to U. Kilkelly, 'private live' *sensu largo* includes relationships and social activities (also in some business context) of an entity, collection and access of their personal data, the determination of legal ties, physical and moral integrity, whereas the 'family life' falls generally under its scope. Simultaneously, according to the extensive interpretation presented in multiple judgments rendered in Strasbourg [2, 9, 26, 29, 44, 46, 66], the right to protect home covers 'all living places' provided that the entity expresses the 'existence of sufficient and continuous links with a specific place'. A substance of the right to respect for uninterrupted correspondence, since the field of communication was marked with probably the most impressive development throughout last decades, got broadened in quite revolutionary manner. ECtHR decided on including within this sphere various 'uninterrupted and uncensored communications with others' instead relying only on written post service, as it was originally in fact [35] (Table 1).

Just a glance at the 'high[ly] risk[y]' features enlisted in the Annex III of the AIA creates an impression that most of them could interfere directly into the protected scope of physical, psychological or moral integrity. While in the case of biometric systems the potentially intrusive nature is intuitively discernible, in case of systems supporting the administration of critical infrastructure (Annex III, para 2) the field of particular exposure is undoubtedly education and vocational training. In the process of education, data that directly and unambiguously identify an individual, including information on the individual's 'physiological, genetic, mental, economic, cultural or social identity' (GDPR, Article 4(1)), are repeatedly processed. For such data, the General Data Protection Regulation (Article 9; Recitals, para 51) formulates a regime for 'special protection'. Analogous interference with an individual's information autonomy can be found in the case of systems applied in the field of employment, employee management and self-employment (Annex III, para 4) or law enforcement (para 5).

### 3.1 Moral and Physical Integrity

**Constitutional Issues.** An interesting aspect in this respect, which is worth taking into account when assessing the degree of potential interference of an artificial intelligence system in the physical, mental or – especially – moral integrity of an individual, is the right of parents to raise their child in accordance with their own convictions, as emphasised in the constitutions of the Member States of the European Union. The assumption, according to which parents are granted the right to ensure the moral and philosphical upbringing of their children correspondingly with choice, is clearly presented, for example, by the Constitution of the Republic of Slovenia of 23.12.1991 (Article 41 para 3)[4], Basic Law of Hungary of 25.04.2011 (Article 16 para 2)[5] or the Constitution of the Republic of Poland of 2.04.1997 (Article 48 para 1)[6]. Slightly less principled,

---

[4] Uradni list RS, št. 33/91-I z dne 28. 12. 1991 https://pisrs.si/pregledPredpisa?id=USTA1 [accessed 15.07.2024].

[5] Magyar Közlöny, 25.04.2011 No 43, p. 10656 https://njt.hu/jogszabaly/2011-4301-02-00#foot2 [accessed 15.07.2024].

[6] Dz. U. Nr 78, poz. 483 z późn. zm. https://isap.sejm.gov.pl/isap.nsf/DocDetails.xsp?id=WDU 19970780483 [accessed 15.07.2024].

**Table 1.** High-risk AI systems referred to in Article 6(2) AIA (Annex III).

| Area | Includes |
|---|---|
| Biometrics, in so far as their use is permitted under relevant Union or national law | 1. remote biometric identification systems (this shall not include AI systems intended to be used for biometric verification the sole purpose of which is to confirm that a specific natural person is the person he or she claims to be); <br> 2. AI systems intended to be used for biometric categorisation, according to sensitive or protected attributes or characteristics based on the inference of those attributes or characteristics; <br> 3. AI systems intended to be used for emotion recognition. |
| Critical infrastructure: AI systems intended to be used as safety components in the management and operation of critical digital infrastructure, road traffic, or in the supply of water, gas, heating or electricity | *No specification* |
| Education and vocational training | 1. AI systems intended to be used to determine access or admission or to assign natural persons to educational and vocational training institutions at all levels; <br> 2. AI systems intended to be used to evaluate learning outcomes, including when those outcomes are used to steer the learning process of natural persons in educational and vocational training institutions at all levels; <br> 3. AI systems intended to be used for the purpose of assessing the appropriate level of education that an individual will receive or will be able to access, in the context of or within educational and vocational training institutions at all levels; <br> 4. AI systems intended to be used for monitoring and detecting prohibited behaviour of students during tests in the context of or within educational and vocational training institutions at all levels. |

*(continued)*

**Table 1.** (*continued*)

| Area | Includes |
|---|---|
| Employment, workers' management and access to self-employment | 1. AI systems intended to be used for the recruitment or selection of natural persons, in particular to place targeted job advertisements, to analyse and filter job applications, and to evaluate candidates;<br>2. AI systems intended to be used to make decisions affecting terms of work-related relationships, the promotion or termination of work-related contractual relationships, to allocate tasks based on individual behaviour or personal traits or characteristics or to monitor and evaluate the performance and behaviour of persons in such relationships. |
| Access to and enjoyment of essential private services and essential public services and benefits | 1. AI systems intended to be used by public authorities or on behalf of public authorities to evaluate the eligibility of natural persons for essential public assistance benefits and services, including healthcare services, as well as to grant, reduce, revoke, or reclaim such benefits and services;<br>2. AI systems intended to be used to evaluate the creditworthiness of natural persons or establish their credit score, with the exception of AI systems used for the purpose of detecting financial fraud;<br>3. AI systems intended to be used for risk assessment and pricing in relation to natural persons in the case of life and health insurance;<br>4. AI systems intended to evaluate and classify emergency calls by natural persons or to be used to dispatch, or to establish priority in the dispatching of, emergency first response services, including by police, firefighters and medical aid, as well as of emergency healthcare patient triage systems |

(*continued*)

**Table 1.**  (*continued*)

| Area | Includes |
|---|---|
| Law enforcement, in so far as their use is permitted under relevant Union or national law | 1. (a) AI systems intended to be used by or on behalf of law enforcement authorities, or by Union institutions, bodies, offices or agencies in support of law enforcement authorities or on their behalf to assess the risk of a natural person becoming the victim of criminal offences;<br>2. AI systems intended to be used by or on behalf of law enforcement authorities or by Union institutions, bodies, offices or agencies in support of law enforcement authorities as polygraphs or similar tools;<br>3. AI systems intended to be used by or on behalf of law enforcement authorities, or by Union institutions, bodies, offices or agencies, in support of law enforcement authorities to evaluate the reliability of evidence in the course of the investigation or prosecution of criminal offences;<br>4. AI systems intended to be used by law enforcement authorities or on their behalf or by Union institutions,<br>bodies, offices or agencies in support of law enforcement authorities for assessing the risk of a natural person<br>offending or re-offending not solely on the basis of the profiling of natural persons as referred to in Article 3(4)<br>of Directive (EU) 2016/680, or to assess personality traits and characteristics or past criminal behaviour of natural persons or groups;<br>5. AI systems intended to be used by or on behalf of law enforcement authorities or by Union institutions, bodies, offices or agencies in support of law enforcement authorities for the profiling of natural persons as referred to in Article 3(4) of Directive (EU) 2016/680 in the course of the detection, investigation or prosecution of criminal offences. |

(*continued*)

**Table 1.** (*continued*)

| Area | Includes |
|---|---|
| Migration, asylum and border control management, in so far as their use is permitted under relevant Union or national law | 1. AI systems intended to be used by or on behalf of competent public authorities or by Union institutions, bodies, offices or agencies as polygraphs or similar tools;<br>2. AI systems intended to be used by or on behalf of competent public authorities or by Union institutions, bodies, offices or agencies to assess a risk, including a security risk, a risk of irregular migration, or a health risk, posed by a natural person who intends to enter or who has entered into the territory of a Member State;<br>3. AI systems intended to be used by or on behalf of competent public authorities or by Union institutions, bodies, offices or agencies to assist competent public authorities for the examination of applications for asylum, visa or residence permits and for associated complaints with regard to the eligibility of the natural persons applying for a status, including related assessments of the reliability of evidence;<br>4. AI systems intended to be used by or on behalf of competent public authorities, or by Union institutions, bodies, offices or agencies, in the context of migration, asylum or border control management, for the purpose of detecting, recognising or identifying natural persons, with the exception of the verification of travel documents. |

(*continued*)

**Table 1.** (*continued*)

| Area | Includes |
|---|---|
| Administration of justice and democratic processes | 1. AI systems intended to be used by a judicial authority or on their behalf to assist a judicial authority in researching and interpreting facts and the law and in applying the law to a concrete set of facts, or to be used in a similar way in alternative dispute resolution;<br>2. AI systems intended to be used for influencing the outcome of an election or referendum or the voting behaviour of natural persons in the exercise of their vote in elections or referenda (this does not include AI systems to the output of which natural persons are not directly exposed, such as tools used to organise, optimise or structure political campaigns from an administrative or logistical point of view). |

but equating the upbringing of children with an 'inherent right', is the wording given to the provisions of the Basic Law of the Federal Republic of Germany of 23.05.1949 (Article 6 para 2)[7]. It is further pointed out that an analogous belief of the legislator is reflected in Article 2 of the Protocol of 20.03.1952 to the ECHR [51]. It should be noted here that the AIA (Annex III, para 3 (b)) explicitly provides for the possibility of using – subject to the inclusion of a risk management system – 'AI systems intended to be used to evaluate learning outcomes, including when those outcomes are used to steer the learning process of natural persons in educational and vocational training institutions at all levels'. The aforementioned area of education and vocational training is at risk of potentially unauthorised interference with an individual's worldview autonomy, insofar as the machine learning mechanism shows a risk of perpetuating biases [34] and a tendency to reflect in the output the most frequently repeated patterns in the 'training' dataset [41]. AI training processes often rely on statistical data that fail to account for the nuanced context of social phenomena, the motivations behind behaviours, and the causal links between actions and their underlying circumstances. The issue of manual 'correction' of biases by a human supervisor of the system – as states recital 66 of the AIA – or moderating the training process raises separate questions, especially if one considers the fundamental differences in the understanding of, and degree of adherence to the principle of worldview impartiality of public authorities in different EU Member States [61]. A state of affairs in which control and coordination competences regarding the management of the risk of generating content that discriminates against persons identifying with religious or ethnic minorities are ceded to a private entity ('provider') seems

---

[7] BGBl. I S. 2478 https://www.gesetze-im-internet.de/gg/BJNR000010949.html [accessed 15.07.2024].

undesirable. Consideration should be given to the desirability of centralising (subjecting to external state control) the coordination of systems for managing the risks generated by artificial intelligence systems in areas of social coexistence involving, such as education, the individual's moral system. The situation of parents wishing to raise their child in accordance with the ethical system they have adopted deserves special attention. Certainly, a set of moral norms that can be reconstructed on the basis of all the activities of public authorities is not perfect, but it does guarantee a minimum degree of transparency and social control over the risk management system, which is not guaranteed by leaving this competence to a private entity. At the same time, a 'national competent authority' or even the European Commission AI Office can hardly be expected to have the resources to mitigate the controversies that arise in similar situations.

**Automatic Processing and Safeguarding Measures.** Analogous comments can be made with regard to software whose task is to deal with 'migration, asylum and border control management' (Annex III para 7). This provision refers explicitly to software used as polygraphs, systems intended to be used to assess a risk ('including a security risk, a risk of irregular migration, or a health risk, posed by a natural person who intends to enter or who has entered into the territory of a Member State'), systems 'intended to assist competent public authorities for the examination of applications for asylum, visa or residence permits and for associated complaints with regard to the eligibility of the natural persons applying for a status, including related assessments of the reliability of evidence', as well as systems intended 'to be used by or on behalf of competent public authorities, or by Union institutions, bodies, offices or agencies, in the context of migration, asylum or border control management, for the purpose of detecting, recognising or identifying natural persons, with the exception of the verification of travel documents'. Notwithstanding the importance attached by the Member States to the effective control of migration processes, having had the experience of the migration crisis in the middle of the second decade of the 21st century [60], it should once again be noted that systems with the capacity to qualify human beings on the basis of statistical factual regularities (often detached from the social context), and thus seriously interfering in the sphere of self-identification and autonomy, should be subjected to the most transparent, socially verifiable and responsive supervision possible, which, despite the best intentions, is not automatically guaranteed by business entities. The dangers of automated processing – including mere storage – of biological information identifying an individual were noted by the ECtHR even before the era of rapid development of artificial intelligence systems [43, 45]. The ruling in Marper v. The United Kingdom is unprecedented in that the Court explicitly referred to the unpredictable nature that characterises the process of developing algorithms using such data (paras 71–73), holding that the non-transparent regulation of the duration of their storage by a State bound by the Convention contravenes Article 8. Against the background of the analogous facts of Gaughran v. The United Kingdom [24], the ECtHR found a violation of the right to private and family life twelve years after resolving Marper's case.

# 4   AIA: In Search for an Effective Legal Remedy

In the post-war history of the industrial age, the driving force behind the formation, development and proliferation of fundamental rights was the strong involvement of the judiciary. Courts made it possible to materialise the momentous provisions of modern constitutions or the Convention for the Protection of Human Rights and Fundamental Freedoms [63]. With the advent of the latest technological revolution, a clear manifestation of which is the development of artificial intelligence systems – similarly as was the case in the middle of the twentieth century – the role that the judiciary can play in the process of guaranteeing the subjective position of human beings has only grown in importance. Just as the access to an effective legal remedy has grown to the rank of independent fundamental right [36], the future commitment of bodies established to provide legal protection to individuals subject to European Union law is crucial. It is clear that the provisions of the AIA will be the subject of interpretative activity by the CJEU or the courts (including common, administrative, constitutional courts) of Member States. It should be assumed that the breadth of the subject matter regulated under the AIA, as well as the still incompletely understood scope of risks caused by the use of AI systems, may result in the actions of the states applying the provisions of the AI Act being covered[8] by the ECtHR jurisdiction as well.

The right to private and family life is expressly recognised by both: the Charter (Art. 7) and the Convention (Art. 8), whereas the meaning of the ECHR in terms of its interpretation has so far been significantly more notable[9]. In the field of fundamental rights the Union's *acquis* – even though it is quite impressive – remains not self-reliant, as it has been superstructured over precedent national and international instruments. Considering here the lack of real prospects – despite the pompous announcements [28] – for the accession of the European Union to the ECHR, I take the view that the jurisdiction of the ECtHR is complementary to the powers exercised by the CJEU, although only the latter has the competence to verify the validity and to interpret applicable EU law. The jurisdictional spheres of these two bodies overlap[10]. The ECtHR bears power to rule on

---

[8] AIA contains several provisions according to which the Member States are encumbered with expressive obligations – just to mention a necessity to designate or establish a notifying authority providing the conformity assessment (under Art. 28 para 1) or a requirement to take the necessary 'corrective measures' accordingly with Commission's instructions (Art. 37 para 4). Failure to perform the Member State's duties under AIA, which results in an infringement of any ECHR provisions is quite likely to cause a litigation before the ECtHR.

[9] It is the provisions of the Convention – in parallel with the constitutional traditions of the Member States – that constitute the source of the interpretative references made in the process of understanding the fundamental rights contained in the Charter. The CJEU – although (likely because of its self-esteem) it does not do so in all circumstances – when ruling on the basis of the Charter, refers explicitly to the established case law of the ECtHR, including the concepts, theories and tests developed in its judgments [15]. Finally, in Article 52(3) the Charter itself recognizes a minimal scope of its rights as corresponding to Convention for the Protection of Human Rights and Fundamental Freedoms. As a result a proper interpretation of AIA's nomenclature demands not only a regard to ECtHR doctrinal achievements, but to the ECHR itself.

[10] Neither of those international courts would, however, deal with the case which had already been subject to the other one's resolution. As noted by F. Ippolito and S. Velluti, 'So far, the

cases with a wider objective scope insofar as there are significantly more states ratifying the ECHR, thus committing to respect the right to privacy and family life guaranteed by its Article 8, than there are Member States of the European Union[11]. It is conceivable that the provisions of the AIA could have, as intended (Article 2 para 1 (a)), an extraterritorial effect, resulting in a violation of the right guaranteed by Article 8 of the ECHR by a non-European Union Member State which is nevertheless a Member State of the Council of Europe and bound by the provisions of the Convention. In such a situation, the ECtHR will of course have exclusive competence to hear the case. The ECtHR, when confronted with an allegation that a State has violated Article 8 of the Convention as a result of a State-supervised or unsupervised use of an artificial intelligence system, may take into account, as the legal context, a European Union law applicable to Member States (as, for example, it did in S.A. Dangeville v. France [57]) and the general standard of protection binding on the State arising therefrom. In such a setting, the directly applicable (as a Regulation) AIA can provide the Strasbourg Court with a benchmark for reviewing the compatibility of actions taken by the State with its obligations under the ECHR. The current state of knowledge does not allow one to predict with certainty the exact scope of application of artificial intelligence systems. If one were to take into account the multitude of areas in which such systems are still being applied today, one would assume that most likely all areas of fundamental rights protected under the ECHR and its protocols show vulnerability to the occurrence of significant violations related to human use of AI. Although so far the ECtHR has not been directly confronted with the problem of such violations, I take the view that it is only a matter of time.

Taking the perspective of the Court of Justice of the European Union, on the other hand, it must be stated that the scope of its competence to verify the degree of respect for fundamental rights by Member States in the direct application of the provisions of the AIA is – compared (*ratione loci*) to the ECtHR – limited. The question of whether the CJEU is bound by the provisions of the Rome Convention and the scope of the direct application of its provisions in proceedings before the Court of Justice is still controversial [13]; moreover, in the legal regime of the European Union, there is a special regulation in the form of the Charter of Fundamental Rights, which is, after all, on a par in its legal force with the Treaties, and which, by virtue of its Article 7, establishes an analogous obligation towards the Member States with regard to respect for the privacy and family life of individuals. There is no doubt that the provisions of the Charter must be respected in the implementation of the AIA by the States, since the

---

Luxembourg and Strasbourg Courts have resolved their collisions and conflicts in an informal setting of cross-fertilisation and mutual acknowledgment [...]. This arrangement has been defined as a kind of < common supranational diplomacy >' [30].

[11] Indeed, due to the specific constitutional position of the ECtHR – its roots in the international rather than the supranational order – the possibilities to actually enforce the decisions of the Strasbourg court are limited. To the extent that the effectiveness of the CJEU's jurisprudence is based on the threat of imposing a substantially severe financial sanction on a state that evades its treaty obligations (Art. 260 para. 2 TFEU), the judgments of the European Court of Human Rights rather assume validity through the traditional authority of the Council of Europe and the European Convention on Human Rights. It is the ECHR that remains, after all, the document encased in the most extensive jurisprudence of international courts, including that of the Luxembourg-based Court itself [62].

implementation of a directly effective regulatory act of the Union may undoubtedly lead to a situation of 'application of Union law' within the meaning of Article 51 para 1 of the Charter. In any case – also pursuant to Article 51 para 1 – the rights guaranteed by the Charter must be respected by the institutions, bodies, organs and organisational units of the European Union. At the same time, the jurisdictional competence of the CJEU with regard to the application of the provisions of the AIA will be – compared to the ECtHR – broader in subject matter due to its coverage of the entire legal order of the European Union. Given that the standards of the AIA do not apply 'outside the scope of Union law', *a contrario* it can be concluded that, within the areas of the regulatory competence of the Union, the AIA will be applied by the CJEU in order to ensure the legal framework for the functioning of the single internal market of the EU, pursuant to recital 1 of the AIA (in order 'to improve the functioning of the internal market').

The internationalization of systems for protecting fundamental rights, a key development in 20th-century legal science, reflects the globalizing nature of society. In a more integrated Europe, remaining a part of the 'global village,' international courts like the ECtHR and supranational courts like the CJEU are likely to play a greater role in shaping 'e-jurisprudence.' National courts, including constitutional ones, are increasingly compelled to react – either by conforming to or confronting – trends driven by the international legal and social context, despite being rooted in their limited territorial frameworks. It is at least worth mentioning at this point that since at least the 1970s, the constitutional courts of the individual Member States, with the German Federal Constitutional Court at the forefront [4–6], have authoritatively recognised their own jurisdiction to review the standard of respect for fundamental rights within the EU legal regime [52]. Even today, although based on fundamentally different grounds than the need to respect fundamental rights, this trend is still discernible in the jurisprudence of the constitutional courts of European countries. On the other hand, the case of the Right to Be Forgotten I (German Federal Constitutional Court as well [49]), according to which also the provisions of national constitutional acts are to be interpreted in the light of EU law (paras 46, 60), makes it possible to see supranational regulations as a leading (especially for the future) factor in the development of a system for the protection of individual rights. With these circumstances in mind, it is safe to assume that in the undoubtedly attention-grabbing litigations, which have an artificial intelligence in their background, national judicial authorities will also try to make their mark.

## 5   Conclusion

The stages of the risk management process must consider the unique aspects of protecting individuals' rights to privacy and family life. The lack of inclusion in the final regulation of adequate ways to supervise the process of minimising the risks caused by the systems used in the field of education and vocational training is of concern. As I point out, artificial intelligence systems of this kind pose a threat of serious interference in the sphere of human moral and ethical autonomy and parental rights guaranteed under the constitutions of some Member States. In the strict sense of the right to private life, which includes the sphere of physical, psychological or moral integrity, risk management should be subject to subsidiary supervision by public authorities (specialized bodies, not just 'market surveillance authorities') with a view to full transparency in the implementation of procedures, as provided for in Article 9 of the AIA. Achieving the desired standard of effectiveness of the risk management process in a situation where the only responsible party is the provider appears to be highly difficult.

The EU context for the application of the AIA provisions determines the broad subject matter jurisdiction of the CJEU over legal disputes under the AIA. Nevertheless, it is to be expected that the provisions of the AIA will also find subsidiary application, in the role of a 'state-recognised standard' in cases before the ECtHR – and, as indicated, not necessarily involving only EU Member States directly bound by the provisions of the AIA.

# References

1. Blecher-Prigat, A.: Lost between data and family? Shortcomings of current understandings of the law. In: Families and New Media, p. 259 (2023)
2. Buckley v. the United Kingdom (20348/92) Judgment of 25.9.1996
3. Burda, J.: The principle of proportionality in EU law. Masaryk University, Faculty of Law (2018)
4. BVerfG, 2 BvL 1/97 of 06 July 2000 (Bananas)
5. BVerfGE 37, 271 (Solange I)
6. BVerfGE 73, 339 (Solange II)
7. Cantero Gamito, M.: Do too many cooks spoil the broth? How EU law underenforcement allows TikTok's violations of minors' rights. J. Consum. Policy **46**(3), 281–305 (2023)
8. Charter of Fundamental Rights of the European Union (OJ C 326, 26.10.2012)
9. Chiragov and Others v. Armenia [GC] (13216/05) Judgment of 16.6.2015
10. Convention for the Protection of Human Rights and Fundamental Freedoms, Rome, 4.XI (1950) https://www.echr.coe.int/documents/d/echr/convention_eng. Accessed 15 July 2024
11. Convention on the Rights of the Child adopted and opened for signature, ratification and accession by General Assembly resolution 44/25 of 20 November 1989. https://www.ohchr.org/sites/default/files/crc.pdf. Accessed 27 Nov 2024
12. Corrigendum to the position of the European Parliament adopted at first reading on 13 March 2024 with a view to the adoption of Regulation of the European Parliament and of the Council laying down harmonised rules on artificial intelligence and amending Regulations (EC) No 300/2008, (EU) No 167/2013, (EU) No 168/2013, (EU) 2018/858, (EU) 2018/1139 and (EU) 2019/2144 and Directives 2014/90/EU, (EU) 2016/797 and (EU) 2020/1828 (Artificial Intelligence Act) P9_TA(2024)0138 (COM(2021)0206 – C9-0146/2021 – 2021/0106(COD))
13. Craig, P.: EU accession to the ECHR: competence, procedure and substance. Fordham Int. Law J. **36**, 1114–1150 (2013)
14. Custers, B., et al.: EU Personal Data Protection in Policy and Practice. TMC Asser Press (2019)
15. De Búrca, G.: After the EU charter of fundamental rights: the court of justice as a human rights adjudicator? Maastricht J. Eur. Comp. Law **20**(2), 168–184 (2013)
16. DeVries, W.: Protecting privacy in the digital age. Berkeley Technol. Law J. **18** (2003)
17. Directive (EU) 2016/680 of the European Parliament and of the Council of 27 April 2016 on the protection of natural persons with regard to the processing of personal data by competent authorities for the purposes of the prevention, investigation, detection or prosecution of criminal offences or the execution of criminal penalties, and on the free movement of such data, and repealing Council Framework Decision 2008/977/JHA (OJ L 119, 4.5.2016)

18. Directive 2002/58/EC of the European Parliament and of the Council of 12 July 2002 concerning the processing of personal data and the protection of privacy in the electronic communications sector (Directive on privacy and electronic communications) (OJ L 201, 31.7.2002)

19. European Parliament legislative resolution of 13 March 2024 on the proposal for a regulation of the European Parliament and of the Council on laying down harmonised rules on Artificial Intelligence (Artificial Intelligence Act) and amending certain Union Legislative Acts (COM(2021)0206 – C9-0146/2021 – 2021/0106(COD))

20. Fabbrini, F.: Fundamental Rights in Europe. Oxford University Press, Oxford (2014)

21. Fraser, H., Bello y Villarino, J.-M.: Acceptable risks in Europe's proposed AI act: reasonableness and other principles for deciding how much risk management is enough. Eur. J. Risk Regul. **15**(2), 1–16 (2023)

22. Fuster, G.: The Emergence of Personal Data Protection as a Fundamental Right of the EU. Springer, Cham (2014). https://doi.org/10.1007/978-3-319-05023-2

23. Galetta, D.: The EU law principle of proportionality and judicial review: its origin, development, dissemination and the lessons to be learnt from the Court of Justice of the European Union. ECB Legal Conference, Publications Office of the European Union (2022)

24. Gaughran v. The United Kingdom (45245/15) Judgment of 13.02.2020

25. General comment No. 25 (2021) on children's rights in relation to the digital environment (CRC/C/GC/25). https://www.ohchr.org/en/documents/general-comments-and-rec ommendations/general-comment-no-25-2021-childrens-rights-relation. Accessed 27 Dec 2024

26. Ghailan and others v. Spain (36366/14) Judgment of 23.03.2021

27. Giannini, S.: Generative AI and the future of education. UNESCO (2023). https://www.laifit alia.it/wp-content/uploads/2024/01/385877eng.pdf. Accessed 27 Dec 2024

28. Gorjani, G., Muskaj, B.: Accession of the EU to the ECHR: a more developed fundamental rights law for the EU after the Lisbon treaty? Multidiscip. Rev. **7**, 2024150 (2024)

29. Guide on Article 8 of the European Convention on Human Rights: Right to respect for private and family life, home and correspondence. Council of Europe/European Court of Human Rights (2024). Accessed 9 Apr 2024

30. Ippolito, F., Velluti, S.: The relationship between the CJEU and the ECtHR: the case of asylum. In: Human Rights Law in Europe. Routledge (2014)

31. Judgment of the Court of 13 July 1962 – Mannesmann AG v High Authority of the European Coal and Steel Community - Case 19/61

32. Judgment of the Court of 17 December 1970 – Internationale Handelsgesellschaft mbH v Einfuhr- und Vorratsstelle für Getreide und Futtermittel (Case 11/70) ECLI:EU:C:1970:114

33. Judgment of the Court of 20 February 1979 – Rewe-Zentral AG v Bundesmonopolverwaltung für Branntwein (Case 120/78) ECLI:EU:C:1979:42

34. Keles, S.: Navigating in the moral landscape: analysing bias and discrimination in AI through philosophical inquiry. AI and Ethics, pp. 1–11 (2023)

35. Kilkelly, U.: The right to respect for private and family life. In: A Guide to the Implementation of Article 8. Human Rights Handbooks, vol. 1 (2003)

36. Kuijer, M.: Effective remedies as a fundamental right. Seminar on human rights and access to justice in the EU (2014)

37. Kuner, Ch., et al.: The EU General Data Protection Regulation: A Commentary. Oxford University Press, Oxford (2020)

38. Laux, J., Wachter, S., Mittelstadt. B.: Trustworthy artificial intelligence and the European Union AI act: on the conflation of trustworthiness and acceptability of risk. Regul. Gov. **1**(18), 3–32 (2024)

39. Lynskey, O.: The Foundations of EU Data Protection Law. Oxford University Press, Oxford (2015)

40. Madiega, T.: Artificial intelligence act. European parliament: European parliamentary research service (2023)
41. Mahesh, B.: Machine learning algorithms – a review. Int. J. Sci. Res. (IJSR) **9**(1), 381–386 (2020)
42. Mahler, T.: Between risk management and proportionality: the risk-based approach in the EU's artificial intelligence act proposal. Nordic Yearb. Law Inform., 245–267 (2022)
43. Marper v. The United Kingdom [GC] (30562/04; 30566/04) Judgment of 04.12.2008
44. McKay-Kopecka v. Poland (45320/99) Decision of 19.09.2006
45. Melinda, S.: Artificial intelligence: is the European court of human rights prepared? Acta Humana-Emberi Jogi Közlemények **11**(1), 93–110 (2023)
46. Menteş and Others v. Turkey [GC] (23186/94) Judgment of 28.11.1997
47. Miço, H.: The right to private and family life and the need for protection against the digital environment. Eur. J. Econ. Law Soc. Sci. **7**(2), 71–82 (2023)
48. Novelli, C., Casolari, F., Rotolo, A. et al.: Taking AI risks seriously: a new assessment model for the AI act. AI Soc. (2023)
49. Order of the Federal Constitutional Court (First Senate) of 6 November 2019 - 1 BvR 16/13 - (Right to be forgotten I)
50. Panigutti, C., Hamon, R., Hupont, I., et al.: The role of explainable AI in the context of the AI act. In: Proceedings of the 2023 ACM Conference on Fairness, Accountability, and Transparency, pp. 1139–1150 (2023). https://doi.org/10.1145/3593013.3594069
51. Protocol to the Convention for the Protection of Human Rights and Fundamental Freedoms, Paris, 20 March 1952. https://www.coe.int/en/web/echr-toolkit/protocole-1. Accessed 15 July 2024
52. Reestman, J., Besselink, L.: Sandwiched between Strasbourg and Karlsruhe: EU fundamental rights protection. Eur. Const. Law Rev. **12**, 213–222 (2016)
53. Regulation (EU) 2016/679 of the European Parliament and of the Council of 27 April 2016 on the protection of natural persons with regard to the processing of personal data and on the free movement of such data, and repealing Directive 95/46/EC (General Data Protection Regulation) (OJ L 119, 4.5.2016)
54. Regulation (EU) 2018/1725 of the European Parliament and of the Council of 23 October 2018 on the protection of natural persons with regard to the processing of personal data by the Union institutions, bodies, offices and agencies and on the free movement of such data, and repealing Regulation (EC) No 45/2001 and Decision No 1247/2002/EC (OJ L 295, 21.11.2018)
55. Regulation (EU) 2024/1689 of the European Parliament and of the Council of 13 June 2024 laying down harmonised rules on artificial intelligence and amending Regulations (EC) No 300/2008, (EU) No 167/2013, (EU) No 168/2013, (EU) 2018/858, (EU) 2018/1139 and (EU) 2019/2144 and Directives 2014/90/EU, (EU) 2016/797 and (EU) 2020/1828 (OJ L, 2024/1689, 12.7.2024, ELI. http://data.europa.eu/eli/reg/2024/1689/oj
56. Rosenberg, L.: Generative AI as a dangerous new form of media. In: Proceedings of the 17th International Multi-Conference on Society, Cybernetics and Informatics (IMSCI 2023) (2023). https://www.iiis.org/CDs2023/CD2023Summer/papers/HA408FU.pdf. Accessed 27 Nov 2024
57. S.A. Dangeville v. France (36677/97) Judgment of 16.4.2002
58. Salgado-Criado, J., Fernández-Aller, C.: Navigating through ethical dilemmas, human rights and digital governance. In: Research Handbook on Human Resource Management and Disruptive Technologies, pp. 51–73. Edward Elgar Publishing (2024)
59. Schuett, J.: Risk management in the artificial intelligence act. Eur. J. Risk Regul. **15**(2), 1–19 (2023)
60. Scipioni, M.: Failing forward in EU migration policy? EU integration after the 2015 asylum and migration crisis. J. Eur. Publ. Policy **25**(9), 1357–1375 (2018)

61. Sternberg, C.: Ideologies and imaginaries of legitimacy from the 1950S to today: trajectories of EU-official discourses read against Rosanvallon's democratic legitimacy. In: Conference EU Constitutional Imagination: Between Ideology and Utopia (2021)

62. Tinière, R.: The use of ECtHR case law by the CJEU: instrumentalisation or quest for autonomy and legitimacy? Eur. Pap. A J. Law Integr. **1**, 323–330 (2023)

63. Usiemure, Ch., Igwilo, R.: The judiciary and fundamental human rights. Rajpath J. Econ. Polit. Sci. Educ. Humanit. **1**(1), 48–60 (2024)

64. Voigt, P., Von dem Bussche, A.: The EU General Data Protection Regulation (GDPR). A Practical Guide, 1st edn. Springer, Cham (2017). https://doi.org/10.1007/978-3-319-57959-7

65. White Paper on Artificial Intelligence – A European approach to excellence and trust. European Commission, Brussels, 19.2.2020 COM(2020) 65 final (2020)

66. Winterstein and Others v. France (27013/07) Judgment of 17.10.2013

67. Zakharov v. Russia [GC] 47143/06 Judgment of 04.12.2015

# Exploring Cultural Values and Online Privacy Concerns: A Model for Immigrant Consumers in Online Markets

Atiyeh Sadeghi[(✉)] [iD]

Goethe University Frankfurt, Theodor-W.-Adorno-Platz 4, 60323 Frankfurt am Main, Germany
atiyeh.sadeghi@m-chair.de

**Abstract.** In e-commerce, companies collect customer data to identify customer needs, often using online tools such as cookies, registration forms, and other tracking tools. This approach serves as a double-edged sword: on one side, it enables companies to tailor their products to specific customer needs, enhancing customer satisfaction and driving demand; on the other side, it raises privacy concerns, as individuals may feel their personal information is being compromised. These challenges become even more complex when considering customers with diverse cultural values, varying cultural values significantly influence privacy concerns. Objective of this study is to suggest a model on the impact of cultural values on the formation of Online Privacy Concerns. In order to this, Information Boundary Theory (IBT) as well as Hofstede's cultural values dimension considered as a base model and adapted with immigrant context.

**Keywords:** Online Privacy Concern · cultural values · immigrant

## 1 Introduction

Within the domain of e-commerce, organizations frequently accumulate customer information through different means such as registration, order forms, surveys, cookies, and tracking software to extract customer preferences and needs. This approach gives companies the ability to customize their products and services to fit specific customer needs, which increases consumer satisfaction. The collection and utilization of customer data also raise privacy concerns, as people may feel their privacy is compromised due to unauthorized use of their individual information. In the information age, where vast amounts of data can be rapidly collected, stored and used by multiple parties, these privacy concerns have become increasingly important. The reaction of consumers to perceived breaches of privacy may perceive such practices as intrusive and may react negatively, thus creating a significant barrier to engaging in e-commerce activities [15].

I assumed that the complexity of this issue in online market becomes more pronounced when considering consumers with diverse cultural backgrounds. Different cultures hold varying perspectives on fair information practices, privacy, and trust in internet corporations. Therefore, it's crucial to delve deeper into the relationship between

F. Bieker et al. (Eds.): Privacy and Identity 2024, IFIP AICT 705, pp. 166–175, 2025.
https://doi.org/10.1007/978-3-031-91054-8_9

Online Privacy Concerns and cultural values, particularly considering the immigrant populations.

I assumed that this matter holds immense significance from several perspectives and it shows that this matter holds significance from several perspectives, and therefore deserves to be discussed with an interdisciplinary approach. Firstly, it's crucial for market management, particularly with the expanding immigrant population in European societies. Marketers are increasingly recognizing the potential of this demographic group, understanding their behaviours as a growing segment in European societies is paramount to effectively reaching them. This can also help companies target global markets more effectively. Secondly, it is vital for immigrant researchers as it enables them to address immigrant privacy concerns as a part of the integration process. Acknowledging and respecting these concerns fosters a conducive environment for immigrants to thrive in their new home. Lastly, it's indispensable for privacy researchers as it empowers them to enhance their social knowledge of immigrant communities and their privacy concerns. By gaining insights into these unique challenges, privacy professionals can better tailor their approaches to safeguarding privacy rights within diverse populations.

While existing studies have examined privacy concerns and cultural values as cross-cultural studies, this research specifically targets privacy issues within immigrant communities. In this study, the objective is to suggest a model on the influence of cultural values on shaping Online Privacy Concerns, focusing on immigrant populations. To elaborate our suggested model, Information Boundary Theory (IBT) as well as Hofstede's cultural values dimension is used as a based model and adapted with the immigrant context. The relevance of variables in IBT and Hofstede Models within the immigrant context is evaluated, determining which ones hold greater importance and which ones may be less significant in this suggested model.

In this paper, Sect. 2: Theoretical framework introduces the two models on which the research is based, the IBT and Hofstede's model. Then Sect. 3 Suggested Research Model outlines the suggested model, which I assume could examine the influence of cultural values on shaping Online Privacy Concerns on immigrant populations. Finally, the paper is concluded by a summary of the findings.

## 2 Theoretical Framework

### 2.1 Information Boundary Theory (IBT)

Information Boundary Theory (IBT) is a comprehensive paradigm for understanding the social dynamics of information disclosure, with a focus on how people regulate their personal informational spaces. These spaces are defined by borders, which can be either physical or virtual. According to IBT, these boundaries are dynamic and can be experienced as being violated when external entities try to infiltrate them [19]. Information Boundary Theory originated from research into organizational use of monitoring and surveillance technologies, integrating multiple theoretical frameworks. It synthesizes Communication Boundary Management Theory [14], Justice Theory [1, 2] and the Expectancy-Valence Framework for Privacy Protection [17]. At the heart of IBT is the concept of boundary regulation, which includes the dynamic process of "boundary opening" and "boundary closure." [16]. These processes are guided by psychological mechanisms that take into account the nature of connections, the intended use of disclosed information, and the perceived benefits of sharing information [13]. This regulation is very idiosyncratic and context-dependent, reflecting a person's constant evaluation of acceptable and undesirable disclosure situations. Individuals use a personal calculus to negotiate their limits, balancing the risks and advantages of sharing information. This calculation is influenced by elements such as confidence in the recipient, information sensitivity, and perceived control over the information once communicated [16]. The results of this calculation indicate whether the boundary is open, permitting information disclosure, or closed, preventing it.

IBT emphasizes the social aspects of information disclosure, highlighting how interpersonal dynamics and social contexts influence boundary regulation. Social factors such as trust, reciprocity, and social norms play significant roles in how individuals decide to share or withhold information. Breaches in these informational boundaries can lead to feelings of intrusion, particularly in digital and online environments where social interactions are mediated through technology [12]. This perspective underscores the importance of social cues and relational factors in shaping privacy behaviours.

IBT has been used in privacy studies, particularly among IT-intensive organizations. The theory offers a perspective through which to examine how people control their privacy in digital surroundings. For example, in the context of e-commerce, consumers evaluate requests for personal information by weighing the risks of disclosure against their control over the information. This assessment affects their privacy concerns and willingness to provide information [19]. Stanton and Stam's [16] research demonstrate the use of IBT to understand employee privacy within organizations. Employees set boundaries around their personal information and weigh organizational requests for information disclosure against the perceived dangers and advantages. Recognizing these personal limits and resolving employees' privacy concerns are essential components of effective privacy management within organizations.

The research model in Fig. 1 depicts the links between numerous components and their impact on privacy concerns (PCON). Privacy antecedents include privacy awareness and social norms, and institutional privacy assurance, and the mediating elements of privacy risk, disposition to value privacy, perception of intrusion, and privacy control. The IBT framework illustrates the intricate process of how various factors influence privacy concerns. It starts with the recognition that privacy awareness and social norms shape individuals' disposition to value their privacy. Privacy social norms pertain to the societal standards and expectations regarding privacy.

According to IBT, individuals create informational boundaries—physical or virtual. Attempts to breach these boundaries can feel intrusive, depending on personal and situational factors. Disclosure decisions are governed by "boundary opening" and "boundary closure" rules. These rules are context-specific, evolving from individuals' assessments of when disclosure is appropriate based on their relationship with the recipient, whether an individual or an institution. So, as shown in the IBT model, the effective variable includes individual factors such as privacy awareness, societal like social norms as well

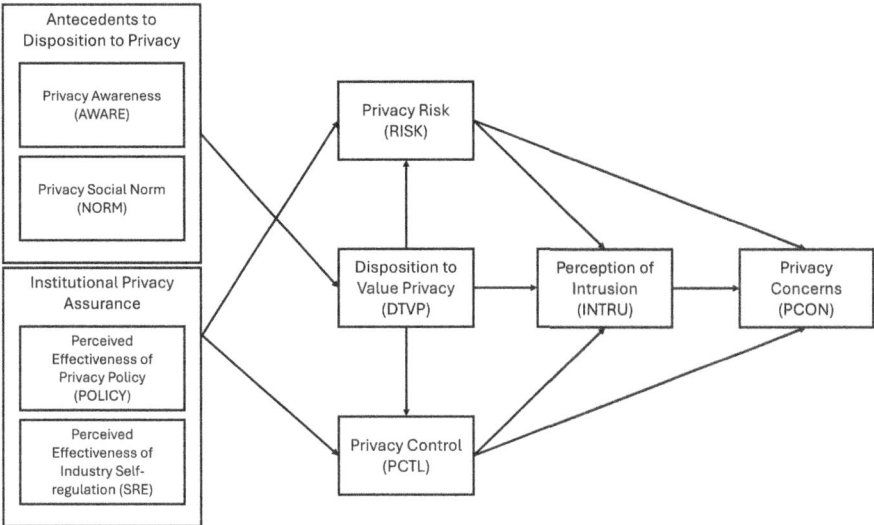

**Fig. 1.** IBT model [19]

as the institutional ones. In this model while the factors on the left are stable over a long period of time, those on the right are much shorter-term and more changeable.

The cultural traits of the social group that a person belongs to have long been linked to patterns and forms of privacy [3]. These norms influence individuals' attitudes toward privacy and their behaviours related to information disclosure. The model suggests that strong privacy social norms (NORM) enhance the disposition to value privacy (DTVP). When societal norms emphasize the importance of privacy, individuals are more likely to value and protect their personal information.

According to the IBT model, increased privacy awareness (AWARE) can influence the disposition to value privacy (DTVP), as well as affect privacy risk (RISK) and privacy control (PCTL). This disposition impacts how people perceive privacy risks, control, and intrusions. When individuals value their privacy highly, they tend to see greater risks and intrusions, yet feel less in control. A higher disposition to value privacy leads to heightened sensitivity to privacy risks and privacy control. Perceived privacy risk increases the sense of intrusion and overall privacy concerns. Conversely, perceived control over privacy reduces these concerns and the feeling of intrusion. Effective privacy policies and industry self-regulation can enhance this sense of control and mitigate perceived risks. When people feel their privacy boundaries are breached, their concerns escalate, underscoring the importance of maintaining effective privacy controls and awareness to manage these perceptions [19].

## 2.2  Hofstede Cultural Dimension

Hofstede identified several cultural dimensions [5] which include individualism-collectivism (IND), power distance (PDI), uncertainty avoidance (UAI), masculinity-femininity (MAS) and long-term orientation (LTO) (Fig. 2).

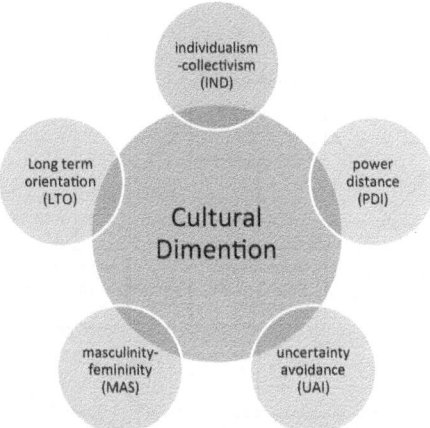

**Fig. 2.** Hofstede cultural dimension

Research by Dinev et al. [4] shows that cultural differences significantly influence privacy concerns and, subsequently, online behaviours: for instance, consumers in cultures with high uncertainty avoidance and individualism tend to have higher privacy concerns, which negatively impact their e-commerce adoption rates. The individualism-collectivism spectrum explores how individuals are integrated into their primary social groups. Hofstede shown that cultural individualism is the primary cause of the variations in information privacy concerns between cultures [5, 6].

Power distance pertains to how societies address the fundamental challenge of human inequality. It was also suggested that individuals who place a high value on power distance (PDI) will have lower privacy concerns, as the hierarchical nature of organizational structures emphasizes authority and control, making restricted knowledge exchange more acceptable [9]. Uncertainty avoidance (UAI) reflects how stressed a society becomes when dealing with an unpredictable future. Individuals who place a high value on uncertainty are more likely to be cautious about sharing personal information due to fears of potential misuse and unknown consequences. This caution can lead to higher privacy concerns [9], affecting their willingness to engage with e-commerce platforms.

The contrast between masculinity and femininity involves the emotional roles traditionally assigned to men and women. Individuals who prioritize the cultural value of masculinity (MAS), due to their strong emphasis on achievement, will "understand the need to forego a certain amount of privacy" [9] and consequently show reduced concerns about privacy. Lastly, the concept of long-term versus short-term orientation deals with whether a society focuses its efforts on future goals or immediate concerns.

## 3   Suggested Research Model

As mentioned in the Introduction, most of the existing studies have examined privacy concerns and cultural values in the frame of cross-cultural research. However, this research specifically targets privacy issues within immigrant populations. This research puts forward a model on the influence of cultural values on shaping Online Privacy Concerns, focusing on immigrant populations. The model shown in Fig. 3 is based on the Information Boundary Theory (IBT), enriched with Hofstede's cultural dimensions, and adapted to the immigrant's context. Some variables have been excluded, because deemed irrelevant to our model, while original variables that hold significant relevance within the immigrant context were kept into the suggested model, as further explained below. The variables in a green box are sourced from the IBT model and the variables with a blue box are sourced from the Hofstede cultural dimension.

In this suggested model, I assumed that the model can begin with variables related to privacy disposition, including privacy awareness, cultural values, social trust and demographic characteristics. I used cultural values instead of social norms from the IBT model. This was done to align the IBT model with Hofstede's theory for cultural value variable. These dimensions provide a foundational understanding of how different cultural values affect privacy perceptions, which is an important aspect of the research, since it focuses on immigrant populations, which might display cultural values that might be different from those of other populations in the same country/market.

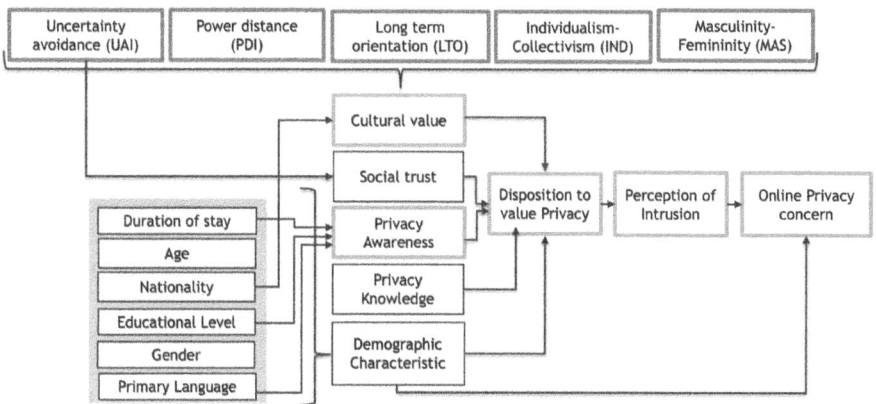

**Fig. 3.** Research Model

Furthermore, Privacy Awareness from the IBT model was kept in the suggested model, as cultural values also interact with privacy awareness to shape the disposition to value privacy. Privacy awareness refers to the extent to which individuals are informed about privacy issues and the implications of disclosing personal information. Individuals with high privacy awareness, will pay special attention to privacy issues, the potential implications of a loss of privacy due to inadvertent, malicious, or intentional leakage of personal information, and the establishment of privacy regulations. According to the IBT model, as people become more aware of privacy issues, they tend to value more on their privacy concerns [19].

This contributed to consolidate the assumption that this variable could be crucial in valuing privacy, particularly among immigrants, due to several reasons. First, I assumed that privacy awareness among immigrants varies due to the diverse cultural backgrounds they bring with them to home country also it could be possible that many immigrants may be unaware of the privacy regulations in their new country, primarily due to differences in legal frameworks and cultural norms regarding data protection. Furthermore, language barriers and unfamiliarity with local systems can further complicate their understanding of privacy policies and practices. I have assumed that, in addition to cultural values and privacy awareness, social trust can also interact with them to shape the disposition to value privacy particularly among immigrant. In addition to privacy awareness, privacy knowledge could also be essential in this suggested model.

Mayer et al. [10] defined trust as "the willingness of a party to be vulnerable to the actions of another party based on the expectation that the other will perform particular action important to the trustor, irrespective of the ability to monitor or control that other party". In the online context, Jarvenpaa et al. [7] defined trust as the belief or expectation that a customer may rely on a retailer's word or promise and believe that they won't take advantage of the consumer's vulnerability. This led to the assumption that as building trust is a long process, recent immigrants, particularly those who are unfamiliar with their host country's regulations, often experience lower levels of trust in foreign websites. Additionally, in cultures with high uncertainty avoidance, trust becomes even more essential. If immigrants trust the privacy practices of a platform, they are likely to feel more secure despite being in a new country and also more value on privacy concern.

I assume that demographic characteristics is also a significant variable to shape the value on privacy concern. In this suggested model, age, gender, education level, primary language, nationality as well as duration stay in the host country have been considered. Highlighting the influence of demographic characteristics on online privacy concerns, Kim et al. [8] explored the impact of socio-demographic factors and personality traits on individuals' online privacy concerns. Their findings indicate that women, individuals with higher education levels, and those with greater wealth are more likely to exhibit heightened concerns about online privacy.

Regarding the duration of stay, I believe that as immigrants spend more time in their host country, they become more familiar with privacy laws, adapt to local cultural norms surrounding data protection, and build trust in institutions, then I assumed that this could be a significant variable in shaping privacy concern. Language proficiency and exposure to local privacy issues also improve over time, allowing long-term immigrants to better understand and navigate online privacy risks. In contrast, short-term immigrants often struggle with unfamiliarity, language barriers, and lower trust, leading to heightened privacy concerns. Additionally, the assumption is made that education level, primary language and duration of stay in the host country significantly impact their privacy awareness, with long-term immigrants generally having greater knowledge and confidence in local privacy regulations compared to short-term immigrants.

The model is based on the assumption that privacy awareness, cultural values, demographic characteristics and social trust, shape an individual's disposition to value privacy. Disposition to value privacy represents an individual's inherent inclination to regard privacy as important and worth protecting. Immigrant with a strong disposition to value privacy are more likely to perceive higher levels of intrusion when their personal data is requested or shared. This increased sensitivity can lead to a heightened state of vigilance and a stronger reaction to any perceived privacy invasion.

Patil and Kobsa [11] define and assess personal disposition towards privacy as the extent to which people "value privacy" [11], and they discovered that it is a strong predictor of privacy concerns. Hence, disposition to respect privacy was defined as a person's readiness to defend their private space or the refusal of disclosing personal information to others in a variety of settings and contexts. This construct mediates the relationship between privacy awareness and cultural values and the perception of intrusion and Online Privacy Concerns. This disposition to value privacy affects their perception of intrusion, as individuals with a higher valuation of privacy are more sensitive to perceived threats and breaches. Perception of intrusion refers to the individual's feeling of having their privacy boundaries violated.

I assumed that this perception is critical in determining how individuals respond to privacy threats and their overall concern for privacy. Consequently, this heightened perception of intrusion feeds into the overall Online Privacy Concern. Online Privacy Concerns are the apprehensions individuals have regarding the potential misuse of their personal information. In this context, the term "Online Privacy Concerns" refers to concerns that an internet business may obtain personal information, thereby compromising the privacy. These concerns are the ultimate outcome of the model, influenced by all preceding constructs. Online Privacy Concerns are directly affected by the perception of intrusion.

Finally, my suggested model offers a comprehensive framework that bridges the gap between social aspect and Online Privacy Concerns. It acknowledges that privacy concerns are not just immediate reactions but are shaped by deeper individual characteristics and values.

# 4 Conclusion

This study delves into the intersection of cultural values and Online Privacy Concerns, with a particular focus on immigrant populations in Germany. I have suggested a comprehensive model that elucidates how cultural factors influence Online Privacy Concerns. The cultural disposition of people with different backgrounds influences their perceptions of Online Privacy Concern, impacting their willingness to engage with online market. Ultimately, this suggested model offers a nuanced framework that bridges the gap between social aspects and Online Privacy Concerns. By acknowledging the multifaceted nature of privacy concerns, this study contributes to the broader discourse on online privacy, particularly within diverse cultural contexts.

Most existing studies have explored privacy concerns and cultural values within the framework of cross-cultural research. However, this study focuses specifically on privacy issues among immigrant populations. It proposes a model illustrating the influence of cultural values on shaping online privacy concerns, tailored to the immigrant context. The model, is based on the Information Boundary Theory (IBT) as well as Holstead cultural dimension and has been adapted to address the unique dynamics of immigrants.

## 4.1 Reflection on Challenges and Further Research

The proposed approach aims at offering a novel contribution to the literature on online privacy concerns among immigrant consumers in online markets. Nevertheless, while designing this approach some of its limitations and potential weaknesses were also taken into consideration. One of the possible weakness and limitations is using cultural value frameworks, such as Hofstede's dimensions. Even though this model has been widely used, it has been critiqued for its oversimplification of complex cultural dynamics. Consequently, it is acknowledged that this model may not fully capture cultural identities of immigrants, especially in a digital context.

Another potential weakness could lie in the measurement of privacy concerns and cultural values. To address this issue more concretely, subsequent longitudinal studies could explore more effectively how cultural values shape online privacy concerns among immigrants which allows researcher to follows immigrants during the integration in the host country. Furthermore, it must be pointed out that further research considering interdisciplinary perspectives, including sociology, psychology, and legal studies, would be an important way to complement the proposed approach, to provide better understanding of this complex issue.

### 4.2 Empirical Outlook: Survey Design and Sampling Strategy

The empirical phase of this research will involve conducting a survey designed to test the proposed model in Germany. Germany is an excellent test-bed for this model, since it hosts 15.8 million immigrants, and it is the most preferred destination for immigrants and refugees, with 18.8% of the total population and a 6% rate increase from 2015 until 2020 [18]. Naturally, in developing the survey instrument I will ensure to maintain reliability and validity.

To measure cultural values, established scales such as Hofstede's cultural dimensions (e.g., Individualism-Collectivism, Uncertainty Avoidance) can be adapted and validated for the immigrant population. Based on the sampling strategy, the population of the survey will consist of first-generation immigrants with over 18 years residing in Germany, ensuring representation across diverse backgrounds to capture the variability in cultural values and online privacy concerns. Some nationalities will be selected, based on the populations present in Germany. Stratified random sampling could be used to ensure representation of key demographic subgroups, considering the duration of stay in Germany. To enhance participation and data quality, the survey will be distributed through multiple channels, including immigrant associations, social media platforms, and community organizations.

## References

1. Alder, G.S., Tompkins, P.K.: Electronic performance monitoring: an organizational justice and concertive control perspective. Manag. Commun. Q. 10(3), 259–288 (1997)
2. Alder, G.S.: Ethical issues in electronic performance monitoring: a consideration of deontological and teleological perspectives. J. Bus. Ethics 17(7), 729–743 (1998)
3. Altman, I.: Privacy regulation: culturally universal or culturally specific? J. Soc. Issues 33(3), 66–84 (1977)
4. Dinev, T., Bellotto, M., Hart, P., Russo, V., Serra, I., Colautti, C.: Privacy calculus model in e-commerce–a study of Italy and the United States. Eur. J. Inf. Syst. 15(4), 389–402 (2006)
5. Hofstede, G.: Culture's Consequences. Sage, Beverly Hills (1980)

6. Hofstede, G.: Culture's consequences: comparing values, behaviors, institutions, and organizations across nations. Int. Educ. Prof. (2001)
7. Jarvenpaa, S.L., Tractinsky, N., Vitale, M.: Consumer trust in an Internet store. Inf. Technol. Manag. 1(1), 45–71 (2000)
8. Kim, Y., Choi, B., Jung, Y.: Individual differences in online privacy concern. Asia Pac. J. Inf. Syst. 28(4), 274–289 (2018)
9. Lowry, P.B., Cao, J., Everard, A.: Privacy concerns versus desire for interpersonal awareness in driving the use of self-disclosure technologies: the case of instant messaging in two cultures. J. Manag. Inf. Syst. 27(4), 163–200 (2011)
10. Mayer, R.C.: An integrative model of organizational trust. Acad. Manag. Rev. (1995)
11. Patil, S., Kobsa, A.: Uncovering privacy attitudes and practices in instant messaging. In: Proceedings of the 2005 ACM International Conference on Supporting Group Work (2005)
12. Pavlou, P.A., Gefen, D.: Psychological contract violation in online marketplaces: antecedents, consequences, and moderating role. Inf. Syst. Res. 16(4), 372–399 (2005)
13. Petronio, S.: Boundaries of Privacy: Dialectics of Disclosure. State University of New York Press (2002)
14. Petronio, S.: Communication boundary management: a theoretical model of managing disclosure of private information between marital couples. Commun. Theory 1(4), 311–335 (1991)
15. Schwaig, K.S., et al.: A model of consumers' perceptions of the invasion of information privacy. Inf. Manag. 50(1), 1–12 (2013)
16. Stanton, J.M., Stam, K.R.: Information technology, privacy, and power within organizations: a view from boundary theory and social exchange perspectives. Surveill. Soc. 1(2), 152–190 (2003)
17. Stone, E.F., Stone, D.L.: Privacy in organizations: theoretical issues, research findings, and protection mechanisms. Res. Pers. Hum. Resour. Manag. 8(3), 349–411 (1990)
18. United Nations Department of Economic and Social Affairs. News and updates. United Nations (2020). https://www.un.org/development/desa/en/news/2020
19. Xu, H., et al.: Examining the formation of individual's privacy concerns: toward an integrative view (2008)

# Workshop: DAM – A Digital Adaptation Model to Jointly Shape a Post-AI World

Benjamin Burde[1]([✉]) and Anna Czeschik[2]

[1] esatus AG/IDunion, Rheinstraße 5, 63225 Langen, Germany
office.burde@posteo.de
[2] esatus AG, Rheinstraße 5, 63225 Langen, Germany
a.czeschik@esatus.com

**Abstract.** As a pre-stage before entering the post-digital age, society is currently faced with a strong and continuous evolution of digital technology. In a holistic view of living, learning, and working environments, we as a society need to understand current developments in a socio-technological way, with AI presumably being the technology influencing most areas of life. In the proposed workshop we present a Digital Adaptation Model (DAM) as framework and guideline for that understanding.

**Keywords:** Digital Transformation · Data · Culture

## 1 Introduction

Digitalization and digital transformation, focusing on the integration of digital technologies into business as well as societal operations, has emerged as a critical driver of innovation and societal change, and has been widely studied. Explanatory models and frameworks can provide conceptual tools to help organizations *and* individuals to better understand and navigate the complexity that digital transformation entails. The most effective of those models extend beyond the pure integration of technology, but incorporating aspects such as culture, data, governance, and societal impact as determine factors [1]. Beyond that, cultural adaptability represents not only an important parameter for businesses to remain competitive in the digital area, but also a crucial success factor for practical digital transformation of society in general [2].

In the following a short literature review of some of those models is provided:

A significant body of research emphasizes the importance of holistic models that integrate technology, data, and culture into the digitalization process. These frameworks underscore that focusing solely on technology often leads to incomplete transformations, as the full potential of digitalization is realized only when organizational culture and data strategies are aligned. The St. Gallen Management Model is one of the most prominent frameworks in business context. Developed by the University of St. Gallen [3], this model provides a perspective on managing organizations in the digital era. It integrates strategic, operational, and cultural aspects with technology and data flows, proposing a

F. Bieker et al. (Eds.): Privacy and Identity 2024, IFIP AICT 705, pp. 176–184, 2025.
https://doi.org/10.1007/978-3-031-91054-8_10

systems-thinking approach to digitalization. The framework emphasizes that technology must be embedded into the organization's processes and culture. The model stresses the importance of creating environments that support employee engagement, creativity, and a shared vision for digital transformation.

Westerman, Bonnet, and McAfee's *Leading Digital* framework [4] advocates for a digital transformation that incorporates both operational technology and data-driven decision-making, while also fostering an organizational culture open to change and innovation.

Another influential framework, the MIT Digital Transformation Framework, developed by Kane et al. (2015), emphasizes that successful digitalization requires a balance of technology implementation and cultural adaptation [5].

A prominent approach is rooted in the socio-technical systems theory, which emphasizes the interdependence of social and technical subsystems within organizations and society. Trist [6] and Mumford [7] advocate for a view where successful digital transformation is achieved by integrating technological advances with social needs and values. This approach highlights the importance of addressing cultural and human factors alongside technological innovation.

Bostrom [8] applies socio-technical systems theory to Management Information Systems (MIS), advocating for the simultaneous optimization of social and technical aspects. It provides a framework for understanding how cultural and human factors must adapt alongside technological advancements to ensure successful digital transformation.

In addition to organizational models, digital ecosystems (as described for instance by Adner [9]) take a broader view of digitalization by considering the relationships between businesses, governments, and societal institutions. They represent frameworks that reflect the interrelatedness of business, consumers, governments and society institutions and emphasize that technology adoption and data management must be aligned with cultural and societal values, ensuring that digital transformation benefits both the economy and society at large.

Chesbrough's work [10] on open innovation underscores the importance of collaborative and adaptive strategies in digital transformation. By leveraging external knowledge and fostering a culture of openness, it is stated that organizations can better integrate technological and data-driven innovations to respond to evolving market and societal needs.

The rise of digital inclusion models (Verdegem [11], van Dijk [12]) further stresses the need to consider equity in digital transformation. These frameworks call for strategies that close the digital divide, ensuring marginalized communities are not left behind in the digital age. Public-private partnerships and government interventions are proposed essential to facilitate digital literacy, access to technology, and societal participation in the digital economy.

Taken together, these models and frameworks provide a diverse library, guiding businesses and governments in navigating the technological, cultural, and societal challenges of the digital age, many of them in an adaptive way. They often offer a holistic lens, ensuring that technological advancements benefit both organizations and society.

With the Digital Adaptation Model (DAM) presented in our workshop and summarized in this paper, we are proposing a practical approach for adaptive digital transformation building on and expanding the academic and theoretical base introduced before.

For the purpose of our model, we defer between adaptation and integration as following:

An adaptive approach emphasizes flexibility, learning, and responsiveness to change. It is rooted in the idea that organizations, systems, or strategies must continuously evolve in response to external and internal dynamics. Adaptive approaches are often associated with dynamic capabilities and agile methodologies, and they are particularly useful in rapidly changing environments, such as those shaped by technological disruption. Key characteristics of adaptive approaches include: Flexibility and interaction, continuous learning, decentralization, building resilience, and organizations' s dynamic capabilities. On the other hand, integrative approaches focus on aligning and combining different components or systems to work together in a cohesive and harmonious manner. While adaptive approaches emphasize responsiveness to change, integrative approaches seek to create stable, unified structures. Key characteristics include: Alignment and cohesion, integral planning, stability and coordination, cross-functional collaboration and comprehensive change management.

With our proposed model we shift the focus from a rather business and corporate perspective to a broad transferability to society as a whole. As explained below, the acknowledgement of the existence of pre-industrial systems is a key characteristic of DAM, as well as the consideration of culture shifts and overarching trends like individual-centeredness, both factors not explicitly stressed and promoted by previous approaches.

## 2 Digital Adaptation Model (DAM)

The development of technology over the last few decades represents an innovation upheaval comparable to that of the printing press and the development of the steam engine [13]. In a holistic view of living, learning, and working environments, including the objective of sustainable development, we as society and individuals need to understand current developments. Further, there is an overarching, society-wide need for the acquisition of digital cultural skills, the application of digital practices and an understanding how these can be translated into existing systems. To gain and deepen such an understanding, it is paramount to first acknowledge that our (western) societies consist of pre-digital systems: Work, learning and organizational structures originate from a time when digitalization did not exist as a determinant. All systems are therefore faced with the same need to master the digital transformation.

The Digital Adaption Model (DAM) as framework and guideline for that understanding depicts digitalization and transformation as a complex phenomenon, which is not a parameter originally included in pre-digital systems [14]. Therefore, it requires translation into systems (adaptation). Adaptation and integration differ from each other as following: while an integrative approach focuses mainly on digital technology and techniques, the adaptive approach goes further and includes the comprehensive repercussions of digital transformation on society, culture and the environment. We also refer to this as the feedback effect, in which technology influences or changes analogue conditions and culture. The formal education sector serves as a good example for a system being shaken by modern AI technology while struggling with the integration of digital technologies without incorporating structural changes.

## 3  DAM Workshop: Understanding Digital Transformation

To briefly summarize the workshop structure: In our workshop, we started with exploring the problem space, e.g. the factors and constraints, potential variables and requirements that need to be considered to find a solution. This we introduced with a question ("What is AI?"). We then developed the model and presented three possible areas of application for the model: Communication, process analysis and strategy development. A practical example was given for the topic of process analysis.

At the end, we reflected on the initial question ("What is AI?") again using the DAM and thus opened a more in-depth discussion. Combined with the advice and review provided by fellow researchers, the conclusion was formed.

We aimed at putting the following benefit and takeaways for the workshop attendees into effect: (1) Understanding the logic of digitalization: main characteristics, socio-technological influence; (2) Foster a systemic thinking towards digital transformation and its societal challenges; (3) Providing participants with an exemplary scheme and tool-set to analyse given structures and barriers in digital transformation and strengthen digital participation; (4) Understanding the concatenation between ID-Management, AI and Data.

With the workshop we put our impact and explanation model up for interdisciplinary discussion. Based on the core theme of the conference we asked the not trivial question "What is AI?" and collected exemplary defining characteristics as the following:

- computing technique/research field/umbrella term
- machine capable of proceeding input and generating information
- embedded intelligence in a system
- statistics on steroids

The different answers and perspectives on the topic helped to emphasize the relevance of models that help us to gain and apply a basic understanding of the topic of digitalization and to facilitate digital transformation.

As a basis, it was shown that digital transformation in systems takes place through the integration of digital technologies. Using the example of the (formal) education sector, it was demonstrated that this approach disrupts the routines and comparability of knowledge transfer. For example, personalized learning settings, facilitated by technology, require adapted performance assessment. We refer to this as the cascade effect: if digital technology is used, further adjustments to the system become necessary. Digital transformation can therefore be described as a continuous process of synchronizing pre-digital systems with a changing society. One example of this is the issue of skills-based learning and hiring, to which formal education has to respond. These cascade effects occur in every pre-digital system.

**Developing an Approach: Technology + Data + Culture**

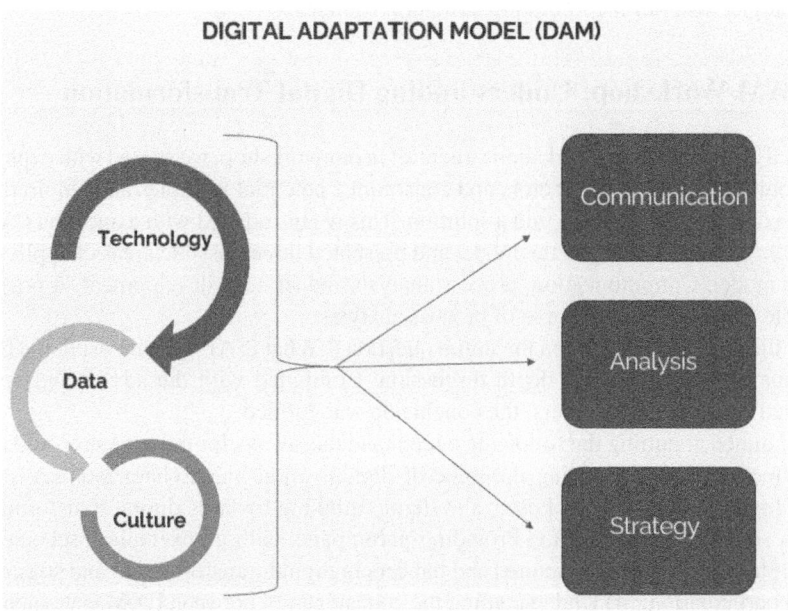

**Fig. 1.** Digital Adaption Model – Possible layers of application: Communication, Analysis, Strategy

If the integration of technology is an inadequate, albeit obvious, approach, what other approaches are available?

In order to grasp the concept of digitalization, the topic of social media was introduced. In contrast to many current topics, such as fake news or disinformation, which have existed in every era, social media represents a real novelty of digitization, with far-reaching effects for society and the focus on the individual. Social media has changed the culture of communication and has led to individuals and institutions being public 24/7 worldwide, without being so in the pre-digital sense. This also resonates with a statement from Prof Jose Such keynote ("Human-centered AI Security, Ethics and Privacy") lecture during the summer school, stating that we need to contextualise the concept of privacy.

Social media has three core aspects that help determine the understanding of digitalisation:

- Technology: Without it, we cannot participate.
- Data: These are exchanged as soon as we are online.
- Culture: Private and public space are becoming less distinct.

Technology, data and culture are the central concepts of digital adaptation. In this totality, digitalisation can be understood as a determinant of social change and thus, new approaches to action for pre-digital systems are emerging. Albeit the concept of culture is often received as blurred, when applying the model as mentioned, the definition of the concept sharpens and culture is attributed with the extent to which a system succeeds in adapting to the changing values of society and synchronising itself with these. This is also one reason for the increasing problems (cascade effects) faced by systems that only integrate digital technology.

When analysing existing transformation processes, the DAM model helps to examine the level of consideration in all three of the mentioned elements crucial in successful digitalization. For example, whether consideration is given to which data should be used after the implementation of technology to accelerate the further cultural development and adaptation of systems. This aspect is extremely relevant as there is currently a strong emphasis on 'data protection'. But what is the point of digitalisation without data evaluation and its far-reaching linking? Both are necessary steps in the digital transformation. This does not mean that the protection of personal data is obsolete. On the contrary. Nevertheless, the aforementioned facts must be acknowledged and solutions (e.g. anonymization) must be pursued.

This condensation point of the DAM model was the subject of lively and critical discussion in the workshop. The objective analysis of a potential sensitivity towards data exchange and data analysis requires further investigation and source research.

Even if the model appears to be multifaceted in its current state and the respective field testing still needs to be carried out, it can already be noted that the model has the potential to enable more transparency and exchange between individuals in the communication of digitalisation and in the processes of digital transformation. The threefold division (technology + data + culture) of our model makes it possible to differentiate between levels in order to put a subject area that is overwhelming in its diversity into a comprehensible framework.

## 4   Discussion

The following topics were addressed during the discussion of the model and its implementation:

**Technology**
While the model basically views technology as a tool and enabler, the question was raised, how the selection of hardware and software also influences the aspects of data and culture. In other words, what are the determining influences of the choice of technology, for example AI or - in the future - quantum computing, on the other aspects of the model? This indication appears to be of greater relevance, as to date the model aspects of data + culture have been given greater relevance in relation to the shaping of transformation processes. This was also the direction taken by suggestions that human-machine interaction should be added to the model as a further element, or that the state of research in this area should be taken into account.

**Learning and Personal Responsibility**
As part of the explaining the educational example, it was discussed in the workshop that technology promotes the area of personalised learning and is also associated with greater personal responsibility (keyword: intrinsic motivation to learn). This raised the question of the extent to which pupils are currently able to learn and solve tasks independently. Furthermore, how learning progress can be measured here if comparison with peer groups is less possible due to individual learning paths.

**Advice and Best Practice**
It was recommended that the approach of the DAM model be pursued further and that networking be incorporated more strongly into existing research. For example, taking into account the work of Peter-Paul Verbeek. Verbeek systematically analyses the influence of technology on human behaviour. In particular, this could help to better emphasise the importance of culture in our model. In general, it seems necessary to delve deeper into the aspects of technology and culture in the DAM model. This could help to make the model more applicable.

At the end of the workshop, we gave a thought-provoking outlook: If we can overcome silo-thinking in terms of sectors and fields, as in the fading current industrial culture, and reduce everything to data and information, will this development lead to anti-disciplinarity? Will data from all the currently separate areas be combined into one huge sea of data? In other words: Will digitalisation go from being a defining aspect of culture to the ultimate determinant of human culture?

## 5   Conclusion

The DAM model has wide-ranging possibilities and areas of application. The comparable models mentioned in the introduction focus on specific processes and structures of entities and companies and place these at the center. Their focus is to some degree on an optimization strategy (University of St. Gallen model). In this, the system should embed various aspects, and digitalization should flow into the culture of the company. A major focus is on building an adaptive and innovative organizational culture. With today's knowledge this could be summarized as the need to adapt governance structures in particular.

In addition to organizational models, digital ecosystems as described by Adner [15] take a broader view of digitalization by considering the relationships between entities and institutions. These frameworks reflect the interrelatedness of business, consumers, governments and society institutions and emphasize that technology adoption and data management must be aligned with cultural and societal values, ensuring that digital transformation benefits both the economy and society at large.

This is where DAM takes a different approach in its derivation and initially creates a universal model for understanding digitalization, i.e. its determining aspects, logics and also constraints on action. The latter lie, for example, in the need to *actively* use and evaluate data that can be generated through the use of technology. In other words, the DAM approach is based less on the question of the benefits of digitalization and more on the recognition that it represents a fixed and expanding determinant of overall social development.

A second distinguishing feature is that DAM can be used in any sector, as it does not place the entities themselves at the center of the considerations. This is based on the realization that the structures surrounding us are still of pre-digital origin and that digitalization is a determinant that is not inherent in their design. In the context of digital transformation, the focus is no longer on the specificity of an entity, as it was in the industrial era.

In the workshop, the DAM's understanding of digitalization was derived from the social media determinant. In other words, a determinant that did not yet exist in its current form and impact at the time of the development of comparable models such as those listed in the introduction. The model describes the cultural shift towards a focus on the individual as the starting point and a characteristic of digital transformation. We developed and demonstrated this using several examples (social media, personalized learning, self-management). The focus on the individual is a key cultural aspect of the digital transformation, i.e. the epochal shift from an industrial to a digitalized society, which has a deep impact on entities and their culture. Synchronizing with this development, i.e. with its effects in all sectors, is part of the task of entities to achieve digital transformation.

Although the DAM approach shows many parallels to other models, it is more flexible in its possible areas of application, such as communication, process analysis and strategy development. Individuals can use this approach on a daily basis in both professional and private contexts. At the same time, large entities can also use and apply this model. This universality of the DAM, which is equivalent to an understanding model of the determinant of digitalization, makes it challenging to clearly define starting points for its use. On the other hand, it is precisely this flexibility of the model that distinguishes it from others and thus possibly also lies closer to the topic of digitization itself, which eludes structuring and ordering approaches due to its complexity. This is also reflected in our consideration that, strictly speaking, the process of adapting to digitalization can only be a translation process, as pre-digital systems have been shaping our socio-economic systems for decades and this shaping also limits our perception of digitalization. It is also necessary to build on what already exists, i.e. to combine the old with the new. It therefore seems logical to name communication as the first implementation and action approach. Communication forms the basis. The different perceptions of what the term digitalization means complicate the process of digital transformation and lead to frictional losses. In order to make this cooperative and transparent within a group or entity, it makes sense to use the tripartite division of digitalization = technology + data + culture. This enables the participation of non-specialized individuals, as an easily adaptable structure is incorporated into the communication. This not only allows individuals to structure topics in a simple way, but also empowers them to communicate their individual perceptions and observations. This emphasis on exchange in the current collective upheaval into a new era is relevant due to the speed of change together with new values such as transparency and can be subsumed under the term agility. A comparable approach can be found in the aforementioned model from the University of St. Gallen. The model emphasizes the importance of creating environments that promote employee engagement, creativity and a shared vision for digital transformation.

Once this culture of discussion and orientation has been established, for example in the form of open and regular exchanges, the same tool can be used in a subsequent stage to communicate about the analysis of existing processes and, in a third stage, about strategies to be implemented. The topic of process analysis was also exemplified in the workshop. The prerequisite for this is the recognition of the need to include transparency as a value, as is also documented socio-culturally in the area of technology in the sense of open source and open data, for example.

Anti-disciplinarity and transparency are required to achieve digital transformation. Both aspects also form the antithesis to industrial and pre-digital value-based thinking, with its norms, specializations and hierarchies. In the age of the digitalized society, these (analogue) approaches and values are being questioned and redefined. This is where the target aspect of the DAM comes into play: the continuous synchronization with the change in values and culture of society as a whole, which in our understanding represents the core of digital transformation.

# References

1. World Economic Forum: Digital Culture: The Driving Force of Digital Transformation (2021). https://www.weforum.org/publications/digital-culture-the-driving-force-of-digital-transformation. Accessed 21 Nov 2024
2. Int. J. Sci. Res. Arch. **10**(0), 396–401 (2023)
3. St. Gallen Management Model: University of St. Gallen (n.d.). https://de.wikipedia.org/wiki/St._Galler_Management-Modell
4. Westerman, G., Calméjane, C., Bonnet, D., Ferraris, P., McAfee, A.: Leading Digital: Turning Technology into Business Transformation. Harvard Business Review Press (2014)
5. Kane, et al.: Strategy, not technology, drives digital transformation - becoming a digitally mature enterprise. MITSloan Manag. Rev. (2015). https://sloanreview.mit.edu/projects/strategy-drives-digital-transformation/. Accessed 24 Oct 13
6. Trist, E.: The evolution of socio-technical systems, occasional paper no. 2. Ontario quality of working life center (1981). ISBN: 0-7743-6286-3
7. Mumford, E.: Inf. Syst. J. **16**, 317–342 (2006)
8. Bostrom, R.P., Heinen, J.S.: MIS problems and failures: a socio-technical perspective. MIS Q. **1**(3), 17–32 (1977)
9. Adner, R.: Match your innovation strategy to your innovation ecosystem. Harv. Bus. Rev. **84**(4), 98–107 (2006)
10. Chesbrough, H.: Open Innovation: The New Imperative for Creating and Profiting from Technology. Harvard Business Review Press (2006)
11. Verdegem, P.: Social Media for digital and social inclusion: challenges for information society 2.0 research & policies. tripleC **9**(1), 28–38 (2011)
12. van Dijk, J.A.G.M.: Digital divide research, achievements and shortcomings. Poetics **34**(4–5), 221–235 (2006)
13. Many refer to this as the fifth innovation or Kondratieff cycle from a historical perspective, which therefore also represents a historical and cultural-technical understanding of digital transformation
14. Mergel, I., Edelmann, N., Haug, N.: Defining digital transformation: results from expert interviews. Gov. Inf. Q. **36**(4), 101385 (2019)
15. Adner, R.: Match your innovation strategy to your innovation ecosystem. Harv. Bus. Rev. **84**(4), 98–107 (2006)

# Author Index

The manufacturer's authorised representative in the EU is Springer
Nature Customer Service Centre GmbH, Europaplatz 3, 69115 Heidelberg,
Germany. If you have any concerns regarding our products, please
contact ProductSafety@springernature.com

Printed and bound by CPI Group (UK) Ltd, Croydon, CR0 4YY
28/04/2026
02098520-0001